Every owner of a physical copy of this edition of

The Deals of Warren Buffett
Volume 3

can download the eBook for free direct from us at Harriman House, in a DRM-free format that can be read on any eReader, tablet or smartphone.

Simply head to:

ebooks.harriman-house.com/register/dealsofwb3

to get your copy now.

The Deals of Warren Buffett
Volume 3

The Deals of Warren Buffett

Volume 3
Making America's
largest company

Glen Arnold

HARRIMAN HOUSE LTD
3 Viceroy Court
Bedford Road
Petersfield
Hampshire
GU32 3LJ
GREAT BRITAIN
Tel: +44 (0)1730 233870

Email: enquiries@harriman-house.com
Website: harriman.house

First published in 2021.
Copyright © Glen Arnold

The right of Glen Arnold to be identified as the Author has been asserted in accordance with the Copyright, Design and Patents Act 1988.

Hardback ISBN: 978-0-85719-649-1
eBook ISBN: 978-0-85719-650-7

British Library Cataloguing in Publication Data
A CIP catalogue record for this book can be obtained from the British Library.

All rights reserved; no part of this publication may be reproduced, stored in a retrieval system, or transmitted in any form or by any means, electronic, mechanical, photocopying, recording, or otherwise without the prior written permission of the Publisher. This book may not be lent, resold, hired out or otherwise disposed of by way of trade in any form of binding or cover other than that in which it is published without the prior written consent of the Publisher.

Whilst every effort has been made to ensure that information in this book is accurate, no liability can be accepted for any loss incurred in any way whatsoever by any person relying solely on the information contained herein.

No responsibility for loss occasioned to any person or corporate body acting or refraining to act as a result of reading material in this book can be accepted by the Publisher, by the Author, or by the employers of the Author.

Contents

About The Author	vii
Acknowledgements	ix
The Origins Of This Book Series	xi
Preface	xiii
Investment 1 – Wells Fargo	1
Investment 2 – USAir	57
Investment 3 – American Express	79
Investment 4 – The Shoe Group – H. H. Brown, Lowell, Dexter	106
Investment 5 – Helzberg Diamond Shops	124
Investment 6 – R.C. Willey	143
Investment 7 – FlightSafety International	166
Investment 8 – Dairy Queen	190
Investment 9 – NetJets	211
Investment 10 – General Re	234
A distance travelled	275
Notes	277
Index	295

Also By Glen Arnold

The Deals of Warren Buffett, Volume 1, The First $100m

The Deals of Warren Buffett, Volume 2, The Making of a Billionaire

The Financial Times Guide to Value Investing: How to become a disciplined investor

The Financial Times Handbook of Corporate Finance

The Financial Times Guide to Investing: The Definitive Companion to Investment and the Financial Markets

The Great Investors: Lessons on Investing from Master Traders

The Financial Times Guide to Banking

Modern Financial Markets & Institutions: A Practical Perspective

Corporate Financial Management

Essentials of Corporate Financial Management

The Financial Times Guide to Financial Markets

The Financial Times Guide to Bond and Money Markets

Get Started in Shares: Trading for the First Time Investor

About The Author

What works in investing?

That was the question Glen Arnold sought to answer in his tenure as professor of investing; drawing on academic insights, great investors' ideas and his own experiences to teach value investing techniques to students and to fund managers new and old.

Along the way, Glen authored the UK's bestselling investment book (*The Financial Times Guide to Investing*) and bestselling UK corporate finance textbook (*Corporate Financial Management*), alongside titles on value investing (*The Financial Times Guide to Value Investing*) and investment trailblazers (*The Great Investors*).

2013 saw Glen start a new chapter. Swapping his professorship for the real-world rigours of active fund management, Glen would test his ability to outperform the stock market by investing his own money using the lessons he'd learned during his academic career. In doing so, Glen would offer full public disclosure of his buy and sell decisions online in a newsletter to followers, sharing each success and struggle along his investment journey.

Glen's new fund management adventure saw him become a Berkshire Hathaway shareholder and attend many annual general meetings in Omaha.

Elsewhere in the audience – and unbeknown to Glen – was Tom Spain; another UK Buffett enthusiast building his own reputation for fund management by adopting Buffett and Munger's investment philosophies for his firm, Henry Spain. When several of their other investment choices overlapped, Glen and Tom found themselves attending the same annual general meetings, where they grilled directors with polite but penetrating questions that other shareholders rarely matched.

After eight years investing only his own money and that of his wife, Lesley, Glen was satisfied that he had proven his ability to outperform the stock market by applying the tested value investment techniques he'd taught for many years.

In 2021, Glen joined Henry Spain Investments to run an open fund focused on neglected, unloved and under-priced UK shares.

To find out more, go to henryspain.co.uk or glen-arnold-investments.co.uk.

Acknowledgements

This series of books would not have come about without a great deal of help from others. Firstly, I would like to thank Warren Buffett and Charlie Munger for their willingness to take time to help other investors by writing about and discussing publicly their philosophies and experiences in the adventure of investing. I'd also like to thank them for permitting the use of their material in this book, and for stewarding a portion of my savings held in Berkshire Hathaway shares.

Bill Child, who built R.C. Willey (the sixth investment in this book) into a billion-dollar furnishing retailer from a 600 sq. ft store, was very generous in offering to review the chapter written about his creation and its sale to Berkshire. He added some important material to give a richer picture. Thank you, Bill.

Many scholars have written about Berkshire Hathaway, Warren Buffett and Charlie Munger, not least Robert P. Miles, Carol J. Loomis, Adam J. Mead, Alice Schroeder, Roger Lowenstein, Robert G. Hagstrom, Lawrence A. Cunningham and Andrew Kilpatrick. I am grateful for their work, which creates a bedrock of well-researched and reliable sources of information.

Craig Pearce at Harriman House has been a more supportive and patient editor than I deserved (I was about a year late delivering the manuscript). He did a great job of editing the work and enthusing the rest of the team. Tracy Bundey, Charlotte Staley, Lucy Scott, Sally Tickner and Suzanne Tull at Harriman all played assiduous, creative and energetic roles to ensure the success of the book – thank you all.

The Origins Of This Book Series

It all began in 2013, when I took the decision to stop other activities to allow full concentration on stock market investing. This meant giving up a tenured professorship, ceasing teaching in the City of London and, ironically, pulling back sharply on writing books.

To create a record of the logical process in reaching a decision to select a share, I wrote blogs laying out my analysis on a simple website and made them free to all. It was galvanising to be forced to express clearly and publicly the reasoning behind allocating capital in a particular way. And besides, I needed a way to review, a few months down the line, the rationale for the investments made.

The blog became popular, and then the investment website ADVFN asked if I would transfer it to their newsletter page. I accepted, and one strand of my writing there became a series of articles about the rationale behind the investment deals of Warren Buffett (I didn't always have a potential investee company to analyse and I thought readers might be interested in Buffett's decision making, experiences and lessons). It is from those articles that this book has been created.

The 'Why?' question

You might think that Warren Buffett has been covered in dozens of published volumes and there is nothing new to say. But having read much of this literature myself, I was left unsatisfied. Other writers address what he invested in and how much he made from it. But I wanted to know why. What were the special characteristics of the companies Buffett chose that made them stand out? Was it in the balance sheet numbers, the profit history, the strategic positioning and/or the qualities of management? I wanted to know the detail. How did

Buffett go from step to step in rational investing, from having virtually no money to being very rich?

For each investment, this required fresh investigation, tapping many sources. The priority was to focus on the analysis of Buffett's selected companies, which meant very little time spent on his personal life, which has been thoroughly covered elsewhere.

I hope you enjoy reading how Warren Buffett turned Berkshire Hathaway into one of the greatest companies of all time.

Glen Arnold
Summer 2021

Preface

What this book covers

Warren Buffett was only just getting into his stride as he approached the normal retirement age. Already a billionaire, he just couldn't stop himself from 'tap-dancing' to work. He loved finding excellent companies at reasonable prices. Delving into what made a company tick was his idea of fun; he had the joy of seeing his analysis proved right time and again.

The analytical techniques he used are simple to explain as principles, such as find a good quality franchise run by competent and honest managers, and don't overpay. Stating these principles is one thing; applying them to companies is something else.

We so frequently find ourselves distracted by the less important firm characteristics, failing to put enough emphasis on absolute core elements.

By examining Buffett's decisions and the analytical logic he used, we can gain some inoculation against asking the wrong questions or not giving enough emphasis to the truly vital factors.

This book examines ten fascinating deals which helped propel Berkshire Hathaway from a company with a market capitalisation of $5bn to one of the world's giants, with its shares valued by Wall Street at well over $100bn. And all this was achieved in just ten years, between 1989 and 1998. Warren Buffett and his wife Susan retained a 34% equity interest in the company and by 1998 had a holding worth tens of billions of dollars.

As in earlier periods, these deals are comprised of an intriguing mixture of family-led enterprises, such as FlightSafety International and Helzberg, alongside giants such as Wells Fargo and American Express.

It has to be acknowledged that this remarkable performance occurred at a time of a stock market boom in the lead up to the dot-com bubble. But it's interesting to compare the performance of the booming market as a whole with that of Berkshire. Figure A shows that the S&P 500 rose over 300% over those ten years. Impressive, and more than enough to please the average investor if he or she had simply jumped in the market to ride it on its upward course.

Figure A: S&P 500 (January 1989–December 1998)

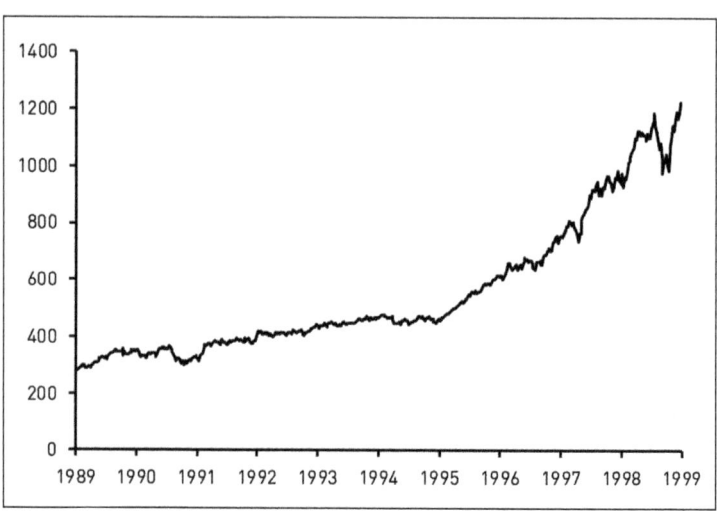

But Warren Buffett is not an average investor. His decisions, in partnership with Charlie Munger, caused the market value of Berkshire's shares to rise 14-fold, from $4,700 each to $68,000 in December 1998 (see Figure B). To put these numbers in context, when Buffett first bought into Berkshire Hathaway in 1962, he paid $7.50 per share.

Figure B: Berkshire Hathaway shares, USD (January 1989–December 1998)

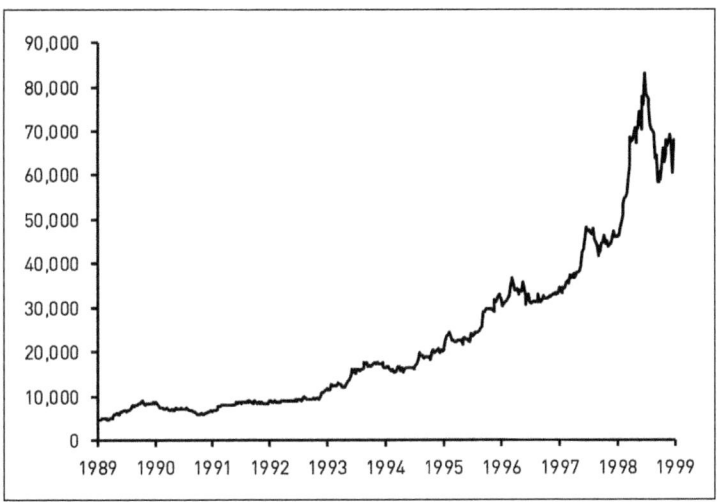

Those of us who aspire to invest in a Buffett-like manner, and who carry the hope of raising our game sufficiently to move some way towards his performance, are keen to know the secrets behind raising portfolio value 14-fold over a decade.

This book is designed to help by looking at the rationale behind Buffett's choices and the lessons he, and we, can gain from his logic and experience. Most of the deals covered in this book were great successes but there were also failures. Buffett freely admits that he made many mistakes during this period. What is important for him is that he learned from them. And so can we.

The deals

Berkshire's buying of a large holding in **Wells Fargo**, the first case study here, came in two phases. The first, bought between 1989 and 1996, worked out brilliantly, producing at least $14 for each dollar put in. Buffett went against the consensus by investing at a time of recession in California, where Wells Fargo lent to businesses and families. He analysed the fundamentals and saw a strong franchise and balance sheet; a company that could ride out near-term trouble. It seems that the

Wall Street crowd couldn't see these factors, or at least could not bring themselves to weight them more than their fear of customer defaults.

The second phase of investment, 25 times as large as the first, can be counted as a failure, from which we learn many things – notably, the centrality of a culture of business integrity for long-term profitability (Wells' managers badly damaged the firm's long-cherished reputation). Buffett committed $12.4bn to Wells shares during the period 2003–15. The return on the $12.4bn was not negative, but it barely managed to keep pace with inflation, let alone with the rapidly advancing S&P 500.

At one stage Buffett had to mark down the 1989 investment in **USAir** to only 25c on the dollar. For years he thought he had lost most of the money invested. Fed up, he came out with glum humour, saying things like it would have been better if Orville had failed to get off the ground at Kitty Hawk because the more the industry grew the worse the disaster for owners. He also says he now calls a 0800 number if he ever has the urge to buy into airlines and says, "'My name is Warren, I'm an air-aholic' and they talk me down."

The American airline industry had appalling economics, with overcapacity and cut-throat pricing. Through this case study we learn many things, the most important being that business growth tells us little about value. Profitless growth is always possible, and quite common. Buffett describes his work prior to investing as consisting of sloppy analysis inspired by hubris. In the end the investment was saved, but it was a close-run thing.

With the third investment we come, at last, to a clear winner. The $1.47bn spent buying **American Express** stock has increased over 20-fold so far. When Buffett was 33 in 1964, he observed the strength of the American Express business model by sitting in a diner and noting the regular use of its card. In the mind of customers, it was a quality brand providing a unique service. He made a fortune for his investment partners in the 1960s by investing after Wall Street downgraded the stock following the salad oil scandal (volume one, investment eight).

In the 1990s, Buffett again observed similar franchise qualities at a time when Mr Market viewed the company with suspicion. It had been wasting money on adventures outside of the core business of charge cards and travellers' cheques. Apart from buying investment banks, brokerages and a Swiss private bank, it purchased a conference centre and, even more bizarrely, an art gallery. It was also under competitive threat from Mastercard and Visa. Buffett saw that underneath the rubble the high-quality economic franchise was intact with extremely loyal card members and travellers. He could visualise where the company could be ten years later if it went through a refocusing exercise conducted by managers he could trust.

The **Shoe Group** was disappointing but educational. Within this case study we have what Buffett called his "most gruesome error". The shoe and boot manufacturers **H. H. Brown** and **Lowell**, bought in 1991 and 1992, had specialist niche markets where they could charge prices giving good returns on capital. These businesses cost Berkshire only $161m and $46m respectively and were doing well when, in 1993, Buffett committed to buying the mid-market shoe manufacturer and retailer **Dexter** for $433m. Worse, the payment was in the form of 25,203 Berkshire shares, amounting to 2.14% of the equity. Today, those shares are worth $10bn. The value of the Dexter business given in return was zero within a few years.

One of the lessons from this episode is that investors must pay great attention to industry competitive dynamics. Mid-market shoes manufactured in America were subject to intense competition from developing country producers who had much lower costs; it was a commoditised industry. Quick action was needed from Dexter's managers to move production to low-cost places, but they were slow.

Post-mortems to advance the quality of thinking are a key part of Buffett's investment journey. Painful though it was to rake over the coals of the Dexter disaster, Buffett continued to remind himself about the logic-path he took that led to such a poor purchase decision.

The fifth investment, **Helzberg Diamond Shops** in 1995, is useful for illustrating Buffett's valuation method. This family business had 143 jewellery stores. Buffett could see a record of steady sales growth, high productivity per store, good returns on capital employed, excellent managers and an owner who loved the business and cared deeply about what would happen to his people and customers.

Barnett Helzberg, Jr. was attracted to the Berkshire fold, like many other founders/entrepreneurs, because he trusted Buffett to continue with the team he had assembled, to reinforce its unique culture with its focus on doing right by the customer. He didn't want a financial butcher carving up his family's creation and selling it piecemeal; "I didn't want my associates spitting on my grave," he said.

Buffett did not interfere with the business once acquired by Berkshire. He didn't look to combined Borsheims with Helzberg even though they sold similar products. This was because he had promised autonomy to each set of leaders and he wanted to preserve their distinctive cultures. Also, he liked the nuanced strategic focus and *esprit de corp* of each organisation.

But there was one major change implemented, which is a theme at Berkshire: Buffett and Munger kept a tight rein on capital allocation. Basically, Buffett becomes the 'bank' for each company. Leaders may only draw money from the bank for expansion purposes if more than a dollar of value will be created from each one taken. In the case of Helzberg, far from expanding, the number of stores has actually fallen over the last 20 years. The bank has received much from Helzberg rather than the other way around.

Another common theme: Buffett bought without conducting formal due diligence. He says that the character of the people is far more important than conventional due diligence. He asks if they are people of integrity, honesty, competence and rationality.

R.C. Willey is another purchase where the owner was most concerned that both his team and unique company ethos would be preserved after acquisition. Before selling, Bill Child – who had built R.C. Willey from a 600 sq ft store at the side of a dirt track into a furnishing empire with $257m in sales – spoke with Irv Blumkin, who had sold a majority stake in Nebraska Furniture Mart to Berkshire 12 years before in 1983 (volume two, investment three). Blumkin said Buffett had kept every promise he made, including autonomy, preservation of culture and long-term focus.

Bill Child feels honoured to be one of Buffett's key executives, and even today, aged 89, he works to build on his legacy at R.C. Willey, despite it being 100% owned by Berkshire and despite his enormous wealth.

He is determined to make Buffett proud, something he has in common with many key Berkshire leaders.

So far, this investment has returned to Berkshire five times its purchase price. And that was achieved without breaking the Mormon rule of not opening stores on a Sunday – a day when, in most cities, a fifth of furniture sales occur. At first, Buffett would not allow expansion outside of areas with significant Mormon populations. But that changed after Child volunteered to pay for land and the cost of the build himself and sell the store to Berkshire only if it was successful in the first six months. Despite being closed on Sundays, the R.C. Willey value proposition is so strong that R.C. Willey stores outsell competitors, even in places like Las Vegas.

The seventh investment, **FlightSafety International** – costing $1.5bn in 1996 – was also a purchase from the innovator, Al Ueltschi, who, at 78, wanted his creation to go to a good home. Also note that this is yet another example of an entrepreneur selling to Berkshire a business that concentrated on one segment of one industry, where there was a continuous effort to improve the product or service, putting ever greater distance between themselves and less focused competitors.

Al Ueltschi fell out of a biplane in 1940 when a poor pilot carried out a manoeuvre. With only 150 feet to go the canopy opened so violently it ripped his underwear, which was further ripped by the briar patch he landed in. A lesson hard learned: the importance of a well-trained pilot who you could trust in all circumstances.

In 1951, Ueltschi took out a $15,000 mortgage on his home to set up the company that would become the world leader in simulator training. By 1996, it had 175 simulators for 50 different aircrafts and annually trained over 50,000 pilots and maintenance technicians.

So far, Berkshire has received over $4bn from its investment and FlightSafety continues to reliably generate cash due to its dominant market position. Despite being a capital-intensive business, it can charge enough to regularly produce returns on capital over 20%.

Dairy Queen has thousands of ice cream and fast hot-food stores. Warren Buffett had been a loyal customer since his boyhood – he even took a teenage date to an Omaha Dairy Queen. In 1996, the company was producing income after tax of $34m. Investing $587.8m, Buffett was paying a hefty price-to-earnings ratio of over 17. But he thought there was a lot of potential to grow profits and make high returns on capital with its excellent managers at the helm and its collection of local monopolies in many small American towns. There was a great deal of affection and nostalgia for the local DQ. The business had a "high share of mind".

Investment nine, **NetJets**, made losses in the 11 years following Berkshire's purchase in 1998 for $725m, becoming Buffett's "number one worry". Its costs were far out of line with revenues as it pushed hard for market dominance. Cash haemorrhaged, and it would have gone bust had it not been for Berkshire's backing.

NetJets offers fractional ownership of an aircraft for busy executives, celebrities, or just wealthy people. In return for buying, say, one-eighth of a share, you are entitled to 100 hours flying time per year and can book your aircraft or a substitute with only a few hours' notice. Richard Santulli invented the concept as a way of avoiding the cost of owning an executive jet outright or paying expensive fees to travel in charter jets.

When Buffett became interested, the company had annual sales of around $1bn and was determined to remain the biggest in the business by far. The plan was to have such a blanketing of planes that customers were assured one would always be available regardless of where they are or where they want to fly. Revenue doubled in the first two years under Berkshire's ownership.

But growth was expensive, and Berkshire borrowed over $1bn to support the drive to stay ahead of rivals. At first Buffett was all in favour of investing to create a deep and dangerous moat for rivals to try and cross. But as losses mounted, he veered more to restraining capacity growth and focusing on profits. This worked, and annual profits of over $200m have been achieved pretty consistently since 2010.

Whether the years of profit make up for the earlier years of losses is still a moot point, given the opportunity cost of the billions committed to NetJets. But at least we investors learn that in some cases, in some industries, achieving market superiority can be very expensive. Dominance does not always lead to good profits; this depends on strategic dynamics, volume of customers willing to pay up and the size of the potential market.

The **General Re** chapter is a long one because it doesn't only deal with this company but explains the economics of the insurance business, how to value property and casualty insurers, the development of Berkshire Hathaway Primary insurance from its roots in National Indemnity, and Ajit Jain's creation of Berkshire's Reinsurance business.

The performances of Berkshire's four insurance groups – GEICO, General Re, BH Primary and BH Reinsurance – are examined in terms of underwriting profitability and amount of money held in floats.

Before the $22bn purchase of General Re, Buffett had access to about $7bn of float money available to be invested until insurance claims were made. Its acquisition more than trebled Berkshire's float, allowing Buffett to invest in interesting equities on a vast scale.

But there was a dreadful cost, because General Re made losses on underwriting in the first five years of ownership accumulating to $7.9bn. After the 9/11 Twin Towers attack in New York it would have gone to the wall but for Berkshire's financial strength. Buffett thought he had made a terrible mistake as he discovered that managers had for years under-priced insurance contracts and made large losses on derivative deals.

Later however, with new managers focused on profitable business rather than growth in volume of premiums, General Re became a jewel, with both underwriting profits and billions of float for Buffett to invest.

Who this book is for

This book is for investors who want to learn – or be prompted to bring again to the front of the mind – the vital rules for successful investment, through a series of fascinating investment case studies.

How the book is structured

It is arranged in ten case studies. You can dip in and read about particular deals that take your interest if you wish, but I would encourage you to read chronologically to achieve an understanding of how Warren Buffett developed as an investor.

Investment 1

WELLS FARGO

Summary of the deal

Deal	Wells Fargo
Time	Phase 1: buying period 1989–1996. Phase 2: buying period 2003–2015.
Price paid	Phase 1: $498m, average $68.3 per share (after subsequent splits: $3.41) Phase 2: $12.4bn, average $24.8 per share
Quantity	Phase 1: 8%–14.5% of common stock. Phase 1 and 2 combined: 3.3%–9.9% of common stock
Sale price – adjusted for splits	Phase 1: $12 –$28 Phase 2: $23–$65
Profit	Phase 1: At least 14-fold Phase 2: So small that it barely kept pace with inflation
Berkshire Hathaway in 1989	Share price: $4,700–$8,825 Book value: $4,927m Per share book value: $4,296

At the heart of this story is fear; a dread of what is in the black box of a bank. Most of the time Mr Market is gloriously insouciant about what banks are doing with all those billions of dollars deposited by millions of families just so long as the bank reports rising quarterly earnings. He knows some of the money is lent out to people to buy houses and some goes to small businesses in the neighbourhood, but as for the rest of it, and how much risk is taken on, Mr Market is blissfully unaware.

Mr Market's logic is that if the big machine called a bank is producing good dividends, then the managers must have a firm grasp of risk, with sound diversification, thoroughly thought through lending decisions and stacks of collateral backing every loan. Certainly, the bank bosses always sound confident and competent, so that comforts him.

But then recession strikes. The market value of assets used as collateral plunge; indebted companies find orders drying up and they are no longer generating enough cash to meet their loan obligations. Mr Market is now scared. And when Mr Market is scared, he sells those nasty risky things called bank shares. And he can do it indiscriminately.

When recession lights up the corners of some black boxes the whole world can see the horror show. The managers have been lending to people who were on the edge even in the good times. Now that recession and redundancies are here, hundreds of thousands cannot service their mortgages. Bank underwriters were so desperate to lend to the 'companies of tomorrow' that they went easy on loan covenants, often not requiring sound collateral at all, or a trading history, or even proven cash-flow generation.

Oh, and then there is lending by way of purchasing financial instruments in the market, whether that be commercial paper, leveraged loans, high-yield bonds or some whizz-bang innovation in the derivative markets. Who knows what their true worth is – in recessions it's often zero.

Having looked into the dark recesses of some black boxes and been shocked to the core, Mr Market starts to fear that every bank is the same. An entire sector is sold off, share prices collapse.

In this moment of panic, in steps the true investor. That is, those people who ignore Mr Market's emotions and coolly assess the facts of each company. There will be no tarring with the same brush here.

Each company examined by a value investor is to be treated as though it was his/her own family business and thought is directed towards assessing its long-term viability, its potential to generate cash for shareholders decades into the future.

For that assessment, the value investor needs to make a judgement on the strategic position of the firm – does it have competitive advantages permitting high rates of return on capital employed?

Judgement is also required about the qualities of its managers – are they both competent and shareholder oriented?

And reassurance is needed about the bank's operational and financial stability both in the short and the long run – sure, it might have some temporary difficulties, but is there a reasonable prospect of lowering potential for financial distress in the medium term?

When recession struck in 1990, Warren Buffett and Charlie Munger were there to observe both Mr Market's panic regarding the banking sector and the strengths of Wells Fargo relative to other banks.

Here are some reasons for worry

I'm going to provide a very simplified version of what a bank is and how it is structured. It's not perfect but will serve to illustrate why Mr Market was correct to fear for the future of many banks in 1989–90.

Imagine you have two and half million dollars – I know, it's good to dream – and you decide to use that to start a bank. The corporation is registered with $2.5m shares of common stock as its equity capital. The magic of banks is that most of the money for lending comes not from shareholders but from other people. As a bank owner you can make profit by paying low/no interest on money attracted to cheque or deposit accounts, and then lend that money out to individuals or companies at higher rates.

Let's imagine that you establish 455 branches throughout California and a few other states. The money flows in at a great rate, and your branch managers get busy attracting families and firms to borrow from the bank. By the end of the year, you have drawn in $46.5m of deposits and lent out $49m.

On the $49m 'assets' the bank is, on average, earning such a high interest rate that for every dollar of loan each year it receives 5c more than what has to be paid in interest to attract that dollar as a deposit. That is, the 'net interest margin' is 5%.

If you were earning 5c only on each of your original $2.5m, that would amount to only $0.125m each year. But this is where the beauty of a bank's leverage comes in. You are not earning 5% of $2.5m, but 5% on $49m, i.e., $2.45m.

So, on your original capital of $2.5m you receive annually $2.45m, almost a 100% return per year. But we haven't yet taken into account the cost of 19,500 staff and maintaining all those buildings, etc. After doing that we find that the net income as a percentage of common stockholder equity is 24.49%, i.e., about $0.6m.

That's all fine in the good times when California is growing, house prices are rising and companies booming. But what if recession strikes and, say, 8% of the loans you have made turn sour – you are simply not going to be repaid on that 8%. That is a $3.9m hole blown in your accounts.

You now owe depositors $46.5m but your assets are only $49m − $3.9m = $45.1m. Rumours circulate about the soundness of your bank. Your customers can see what is happening to house prices in California and to businesses in their neighbourhood. The writing is on the wall. Your bank does not have enough money to pay back all those obligations in cheque/deposit accounts.

"I know," thinks a customer, "I'll get to the bank branch this afternoon and take my money out before other people realise just how bad it is." The bank holds some money in cash and liquid resources and so can repay the first few thousand customers who turn up wanting to withdraw. But most of the money is lent out on illiquid terms to build factories, offices, trading businesses, etc. These borrowers cannot, at the drop of a hat, return the money.

If the feeling that depositors may not be able to retrieve their funds unless they act very quickly grows, there will be a rush by millions to demand their money, i.e., a 'run on the bank'.

Obviously, the bank cannot satisfy them all – it has no choice but to close. This was happening (in approximate terms) in America in the early 1990s and there was much fear that Wells Fargo would be next.

The Wells Fargo case

The numbers in millions I used above are pretty much the real numbers, but you need to convert the millions to billions for Wells Fargo in 1990. It had lent out $49bn, and owed depositors and others $46.5bn. Common stockholders' equity was about $2.5bn. It had 455 branches, 19,500 staff and had made around 5% net interest margin in the late 1980s and in 1990. The return on common stockholders' equity was about 24%.

But it was vulnerable. Its lending included $14bn lent to commercial businesses and farmers; $4bn for real estate construction of offices, shopping centres, apartments, etc; $15bn for real estate mortgages (e.g., 70,000 Californian families); $9bn on consumer finance, e.g., credit cards; and another $1bn or so on other types of lending.

Imagine if you will – and many people did in 1990 – that many of the construction loans it had made were not going to be repaid because the developer could no longer make a profit by completing the building and chose bankruptcy instead, or that bad debt on credit cards rose as people were made redundant. You can see that it wouldn't take a large proportion of these borrowers to renege on their contracts for Wells Fargo's equity buffer to be used up.

Wells Fargo going down

In 1989, Wells Fargo shares had reached $87.40 as it reported fast growth in lending and exuded confidence about the future. But by the third quarter of 1990 it touched a low of $42.75 as troubles at many banks became apparent – the black boxes were exposed in all their ugliness.

Investors in Californian banks had recently witnessed the banking crisis over in Texas, resulting in 349 bank failures. The late 1970s/early 1980s boom in oil and gas prices and output had encouraged banks to lend to resource companies, real estate developers and families. Buildings went up everywhere, until, in 1987, it was apparent that supply far outstripped demand, e.g., in Dallas, Austin, Houston and San Antonio office vacancy rates were around 25–30%. The oil price had fallen but property developments had continued. Once the music stopped, unable to obtain cash, overstretched construction companies and developers couldn't repay loans.

There was also a boom in residential and commercial real estate markets in New England during the 1980s, fuelled by a strong regional economy. But the boom eventually led to over-building and irrational speculation in property assets. Late in the decade, boom turned to bust taking down dozens of banks.

The banking bears were out looking for the next banking-crisis geography, and California was a prime candidate. Between 1982 and July 1990 the 'Reagan boom' was particularly strong in California, with rapidly growing companies, real estate prices and lending. But in the late 1980s interest rates rose, and the Iraqi invasion of Kuwait lifted oil prices and decreased consumer confidence so much so that the USA entered recession.

California was particularly hard hit as the aerospace and defence sectors cut back sharply and commercial construction declined very quickly – they had overbuilt. Unemployment rose by over half a million and real estate values fell. Office vacancy rates were headed towards 18% in Los Angeles. There was massive shorting of the shares of Wells Fargo and other banks in 1990.

What Warren saw in 1990

Warren Buffett started building his holding in Wells Fargo in 1989, but it wasn't until October 1990 that the stake grew so large that he announced Berkshire Hathaway held 5m shares – almost 10% of its common stock – making it the largest shareholder.

What was it that made Buffett go against the crowd and spend $289m on a bank facing a recession in its home market?

A few months after the announcement, Buffett's letter in BH's 1990 annual report set out some of his thinking. Wells Fargo was "a superbly-managed, high-return banking operation". He then immediately highlights the dangers of investing in this sector. "The banking business is no favourite of ours. When assets are twenty times equity – a common ratio in this industry – mistakes that involve only a small portion of assets can destroy a major portion of equity. And mistakes have been the rule rather than the exception at many major banks."

He wrote this in the midst of a humdinger of a recession. But he laid the blame for these failures squarely at the door of bank managers who follow the "institutional imperative", mindlessly copying the behaviour of other bankers, even if that behaviour is foolish. In the *Financial Times Guide to Banking*, I warn readers not to think bank lending decisions as entirely rational. Many bankers seem to follow fashions as they come and go. They have a habit of rushing to one type of lending one year, say, house mortgages, which then become underpriced and banks become over-exposed there, and then, in another year, hurling themselves at another sector, say, warehouse builders or farmers. Buffett gloomily concluded that bankers, having "played follow-the-leader with lemming-like zeal; now they are experiencing a lemming-like fate".[1]

He noted that leverage of 20:1 had the effect of magnifying managerial strengths and weaknesses, with the implication that most banks in 1990 were beyond the pale and not to be touched, even if they appeared cheap. But Wells Fargo was different. It was different in a way that you'll not find on a spreadsheet or a database. The advantage lay in the fuzzy world of the qualities of people: "With Wells Fargo, we think we have obtained the best managers in the business, Carl Reichardt and Paul Hazen."[2]

In the banking sphere, these two were considered by Buffett to be as great as the combination of Tom Murphy and Dan Burke at Capital Cities/ABC in media. Three characteristics were possessed by both sets of partners:

- As a pair, they were stronger than the sum of the parts because each partner understood, trusted and admired the other.
- They were strict on costs – e.g., not having a larger staff than absolutely necessary – but they paid talented team members very well.
- They stayed within their respective circles of competence and let "their abilities, not their egos, determine what they attempt. (Thomas J. Watson, Sr. of IBM followed the same rule: 'I'm no genius', he said. 'I'm smart in spots – but I stay around those spots.')"[3]

Berkshire Hathaway purchased its 10% holding in Wells Fargo at a price about five times recent earnings after tax. Buffett pointed out, to perhaps sceptical recession-battered BH shareholders, that the bank had been earning more than 20% on equity, implying that with such fine managers it would again achieve such returns once the recession was over.

But he wanted to prepare BH shareholders for the possibility that good times might not prevail. He said ownership of a bank "was far from riskless" and went on to list the hits a Californian bank might have to take, including a major earthquake wreaking havoc on borrowers; a business recession or financial panic so severe it would imperil every highly-leveraged institution, no matter how intelligently run; and of course the risk that "West Coast real estate values will tumble because of overbuilding and deliver huge losses to banks that have financed the expansion. Because it is a leading real estate lender, Wells Fargo is thought to be particularly vulnerable."[4]

Buffett considered the likelihood of earthquake and an exceptionally severe recession or panic to be low. But the threat from tumbling real estate was much more likely. That led to the next question: how much of an impact would the anticipated downturn have on Wells Fargo's profits and balance sheet?

In his answer, Buffett pointed out that Wells Fargo produced well over $1bn pre-tax profits even after allowing $300m for loan losses. He reasoned that, even if one-tenth of all $48bn of the bank's loans were in trouble in 1991 with missed payments etc., as long as (after some forbearance on timing of payments and some nurturing of borrowers) no more than 30% of this was ultimately lost by the bank, it would roughly break even (30% of $4.8bn = $1.44bn in loan losses compared with income before loan losses of well over $1.3bn).

Buffett considered this scenario to be "a low-level possibility, not a likelihood". And even if there was a year as bad as that, it would not be distressing. "In fact, at Berkshire we would love to acquire businesses or invest in capital projects that produced no return for a year, but that could then be expected to earn 20% on growing equity."[5]

Should investors desire rising share prices or falling ones?

The decline in bank shares in 1990 neatly illustrates the attitude adopted by truly disciplined value investors – they celebrate when shares fall in price. With regard to Wells Fargo, Buffett wrote: "We welcomed the decline because it allowed us to pick up many more shares at the new, panic prices". Investors, that is, those who expect to continue buying investments throughout their lifetimes, should have the attitude of looking to buy when shares are cheap and therefore feel good when prices decline, "instead many illogically become euphoric when stock prices rise and unhappy when they fall."

Do you want food prices to rise?

Buffett points out that people are not irrational about pricing when it comes to food. They know that in their lifetime they will be buyers of food and so welcome falling prices and dislike rising prices. In his 1997 letter, Buffett is even more specific, focusing on his favourite food: hamburgers. "If you plan to eat hamburgers throughout your life and are not a cattle producer, should you wish for higher or lower prices for beef? Likewise, if you are going to buy a car from time to time but are not an auto manufacturer, should you prefer higher or lower car prices?"

Small portions of businesses, called shares, entitle you to a percentage of its income in future years, so you want to buy these rights on the cheap. "Many investors get this one wrong. Even though they are going to be net buyers of stocks for many years to come, they are elated when stock prices rise and depressed when they fall. In effect, they rejoice because prices have risen for the 'hamburgers' they will soon be buying.

This reaction makes no sense. Only those who will be sellers of equities in the near future should be happy at seeing stocks rise. Prospective purchasers should much prefer sinking prices ... So smile when you read a headline that says 'Investors lose as market falls.' Edit it in your mind to 'Disinvestors lose as market falls – but investors gain.' Though writers often forget this truism, there is a buyer for every seller and what hurts one necessarily helps the other. (As they say in golf matches: 'Every putt makes *someone* happy.')"[6]

Low prices are caused by pessimism. Sometimes fear influences share prices across the board, other times it is specific to a company or an industry. These moments are ideal for value investors; the moments of buying into sound companies with good long-term prospects at prices held down by undue pessimism. "It's optimism that is the enemy of the rational buyer."[7]

But don't be an indiscriminate contrarian

Most of the time a company is unpopular for very good reasons and Mr Market's pessimism is fully justified. Buying on a wave of pessimism would, in most cases, be unintelligent. "What's required is thinking rather than polling. Unfortunately, Bertrand Russell's observation about life in general applies with unusual force in the financial world: 'Most men would rather die than think. Many do.'"[8]

Was Warren correct to be greedy when others were fearful?

There are two parts to answering this question.

First, did the facts from the recent past support the idea that it was unlikely Wells Fargo would suffer significant losses in the Californian recession?

Second, does the evidence in the period after 1990 show a successful recovery after the dip?

How strong was Wells Fargo in the 1980s?

Carl Reichardt, having joined the company in 1970, became chairman and CEO of Wells Fargo in December 1982, so we'll trace its performance from then. Reichardt, ably assisted by vice chairman Paul Hazen, built a well-deserved reputation for controlling costs. Even once expenses were well under the norm for the banking industry he refused to relent.

A key measure in this area is non-interest expense, such as employment and property costs, as a percentage of total revenue. Revenue is net interest plus non-interest income such as fees for managing investments and bank account charges.

It is clear from a comparison of figure 1.1 and figure 1.2 that Wells Fargo ran a much tighter ship than the average US bank.[9] The average bank in the mid- to late-1980s tended to stay within the range of spending 66–69c on running costs of every dollar it received in revenue. At Wells Fargo Reichardt and Hazen managed to reduce the spend from over 70c per dollar of revenue in 1983 to a mere 53.6c in 1989.

Figure 1.1: US commercial banks' non-interest expense as a percentage of total revenue 1985–1997[10]

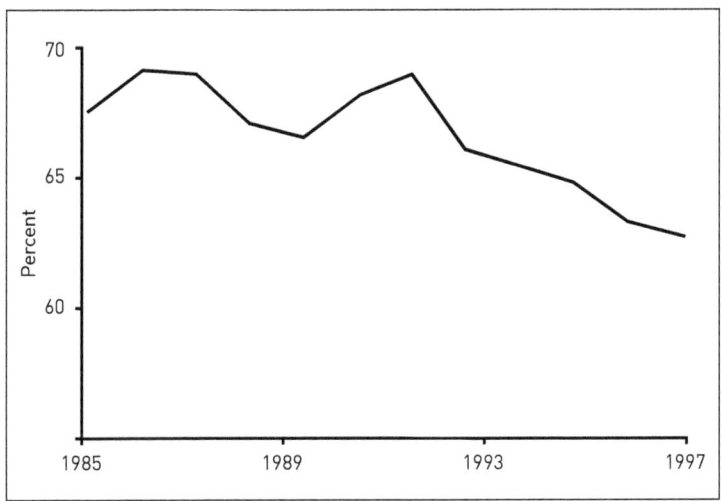

Figure 1.2: Wells Fargo non-interest expense as a percentage of total revenue (1983–1989)

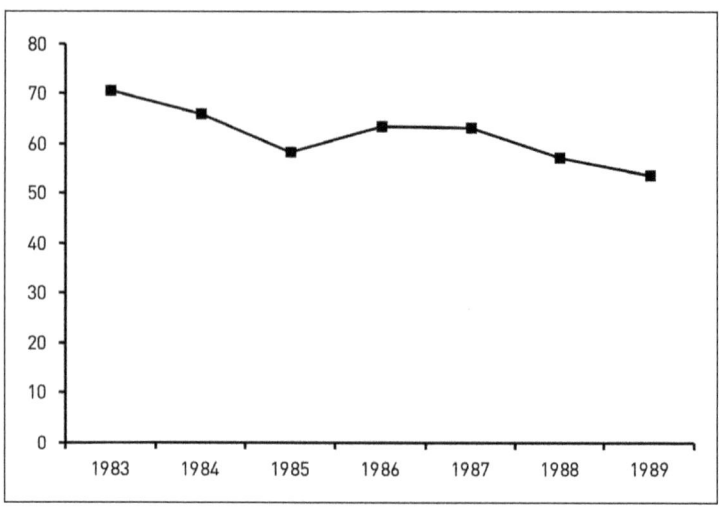

Source: Wells Fargo annual reports and accounts

When revenue is measured in billions, a percentage point saving can make a huge difference to profits. This is reflected in the return on common shareholders' equity and the return on asset numbers. Whereas the US banking sector as a whole achieved returns on equity (RoE) of roughly 10–11% in the period 1983–89 (excepting the bad year of 1987 – see figure 1.3), the Wells Fargo team generated between 12.51% and 14.81% returns for shareholders in the mid-1980s. They then raised their game dramatically in the last two years of the 1980s to achieve RoE's of 23.99% and 24.49% – far above the industry average (see figure 1.4).

A similar profitability superiority is shown in the returns on total assets (assets being all those loans and other rights held by Wells Fargo) in figure 1.5. Whereas the commercial banking sector made profits of around 0.6–0.7% as a percentage of assets in the 1980s, Wells Fargo lifted its RoA to 1.14% in 1988 and 1.26% in 1989.

Figure 1.3: US commercial banks' average return on equity and average return on assets 1970–1997[11]

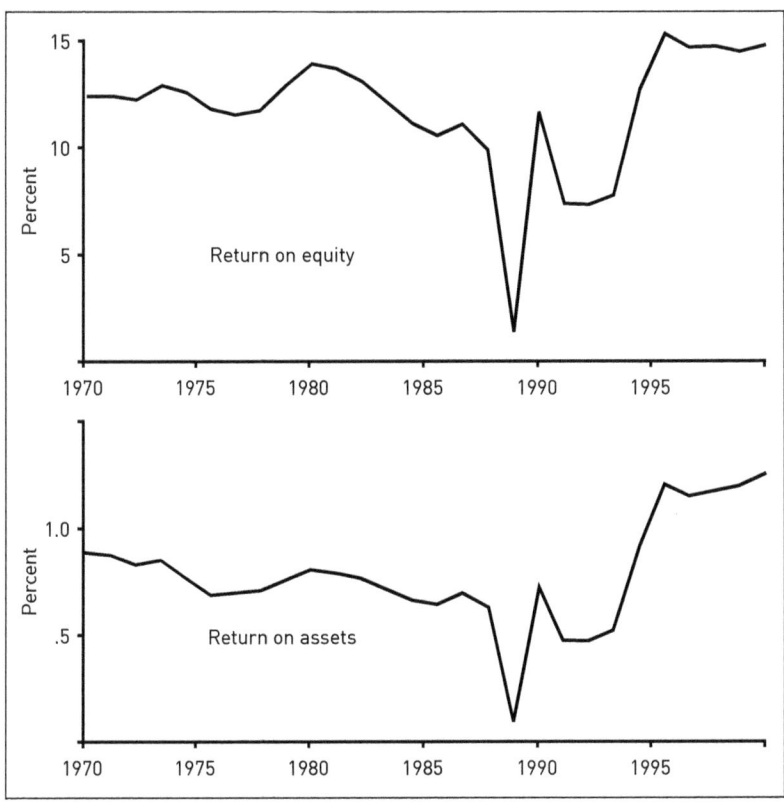

Figure 1.4: Wells Fargo return on equity % (1983-1989)

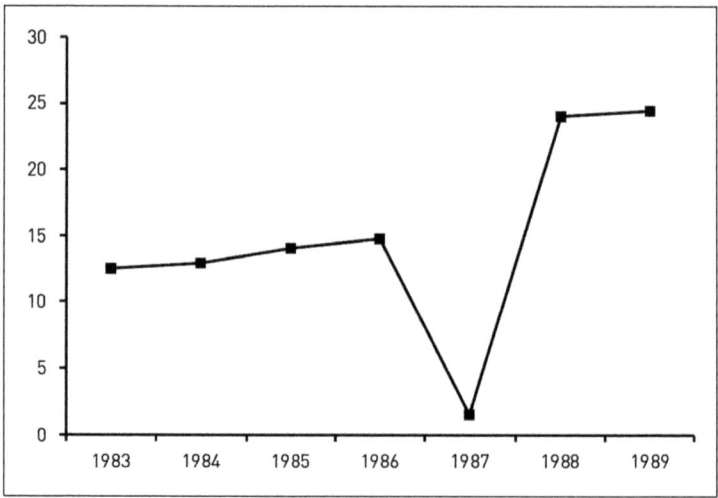

Source: Wells Fargo annual reports and accounts

Figure 1.5: Wells Fargo return on assets (on loans granted, etc.) % (1983-1989)

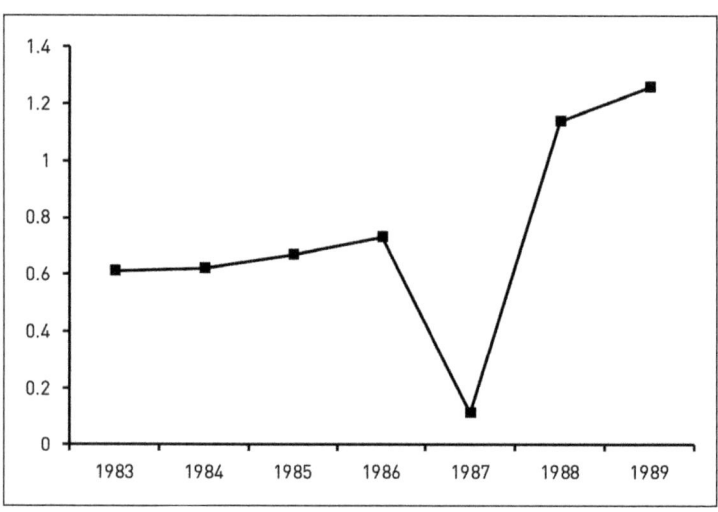

Source: Wells Fargo annual reports and accounts

A key measure of bank efficiency I've already mentioned is the size of the gap between the average interest rate it can charge borrowers and the rate it has to pay to attract deposits – the net interest margin.

For the commercial bank industry in the period 1983–89, the net interest margin was between 3.7% and 4% (see figure 1.6). Wells Fargo far exceeded these numbers, reaching a very rewarding 5.11% in 1989 (see figure 1.7).

Figure 1.6: US commercial banks' average net-interest margin* 1976–1997[12]

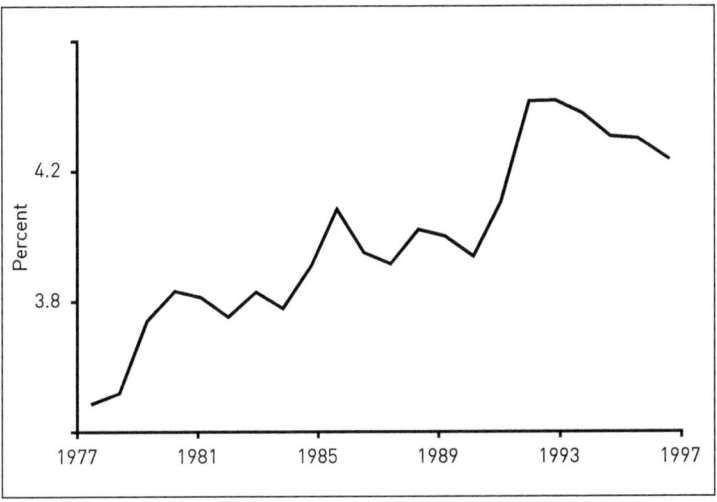

*Net interest margin is net interest income divided by interest-earning assets.

Figure 1.7: Wells Fargo net interest margin % (1983–1989)

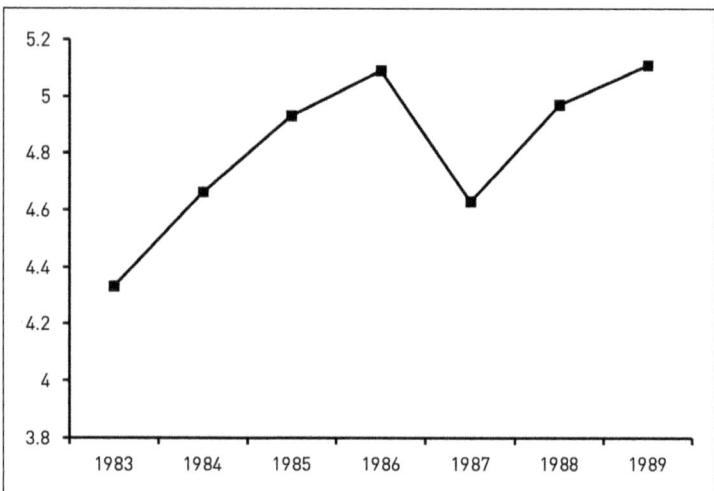

Source: Wells Fargo annual reports and accounts

It's all very well getting away with high interest margins, but what if the bank is achieving those exceptional margins by lending to high-risk borrowers – charging them more interest, yes, but exposing the bank to excessive risk? Such a policy could bring in money through interest charges which the bank then loses through defaults.

A measure of risk in lending decisions is the percentage of loans the bank anticipates will not be paid based on its experience in recent years – that is, its loss provision. This is shown for the average US commercial bank in figure 1.8 alongside the net charge-offs as a percentage of loans outstanding, which are different to provisions because they include expected recoveries on delinquent debt.

Figure 1.8: US commercial banks' average loss provisioning and net charge-offs as a percentage of loans 1980–1997[13]

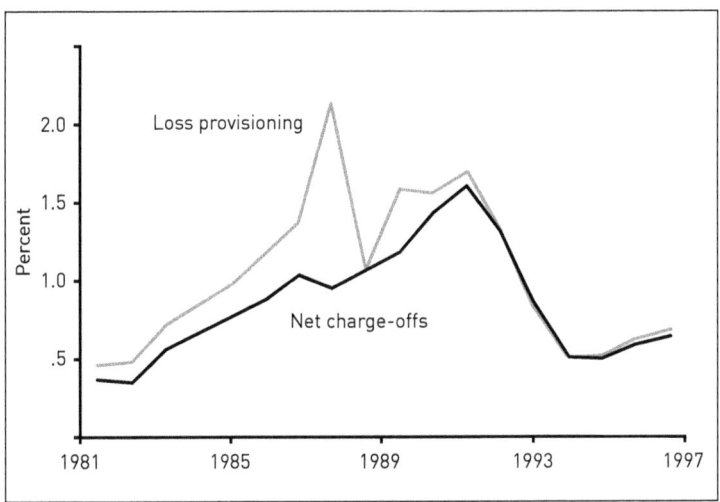

In the mid-1980s the typical commercial bank needed to provision for loan losses at a rate of around 0.7–1%. This rose to peak at over 2.1% in 1987, then fell back to around 1.5%. After allowing for recovery of money from defaulters, the net charge-off numbers did not reach such heights in the 1980s, staying below 1.1% of loans.

Over the 1983–89 period we find Wells Fargo allowing for loan losses at a similar rate to the industry (see figure 1.9) with the exception of 1987 where Wells Fargo, pressed by the banking regulator, allowed for a whopping 2.42% of debts to sour. But then, after allowing for recoveries from defaulters, the charge-off rate was only 0.73%.

Figure 1.9: Wells Fargo loss provisioning and net charge-offs as a percentage of loans (1983–1989)

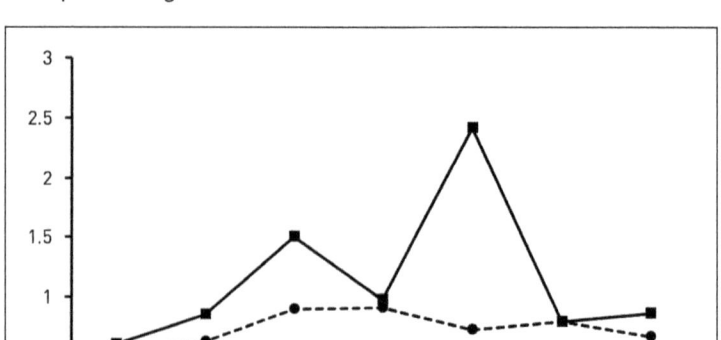

Source: Wells Fargo annual reports and accounts

So, there is no evidence here to support the theory that Wells Fargo's managers were taking on unusually high-risk lending. Indeed, the two leading executives were keenly aware of the need for caution in lending and preparedness for economic downturns, as this passage written by Reichardt and Hazen in Wells Fargo's 1989 annual report shows.

> "Some Californians will fondly remember the '80s as a period of vigorous growth, rising employment, soaring property values… and a mounting burden of personal debt.
>
> No one can foresee precisely how these legacies will affect the future of our economy. Nor can we visualise what new challenges the '90s will hold. All we know is that the decade is likely to be as full of challenges and surprises as the old one – and that we had best be prepared for them.
>
> At Wells Fargo… we have expended a good deal of effort in the past year preparing to deal with whatever changes in the economic and competitive environment the beginning of the new decade might bring.

Mainly, we have managed the mix in our loan portfolio along the lines that we believe will reduce the likelihood of unpleasant surprises, should the economy move into recession."

They astutely decreased lending to developing countries and shifted assets from commercial real estate to home mortgages which have a much lower rate of default in recessions. When lending to high-leverage companies, paying greater interest, they avoided taking large positions with one borrower.

As well as the operational efficiency data I've shown in the charts, Warren Buffett and Charlie Munger could look at the almost quadrupling of profits and earnings per share since Reichardt and Hazen started running things (see figures 1.10 and 1.11). For the shares bought in 1989 and 1990 Berkshire Hathaway paid an average of $57.89, which meant that the price-to-earnings ratio was merely 5.25 based on 1989's earnings, and dividend yield was 5.7%.

Figure 1.10: Wells Fargo profits after tax $m (1983–1989)

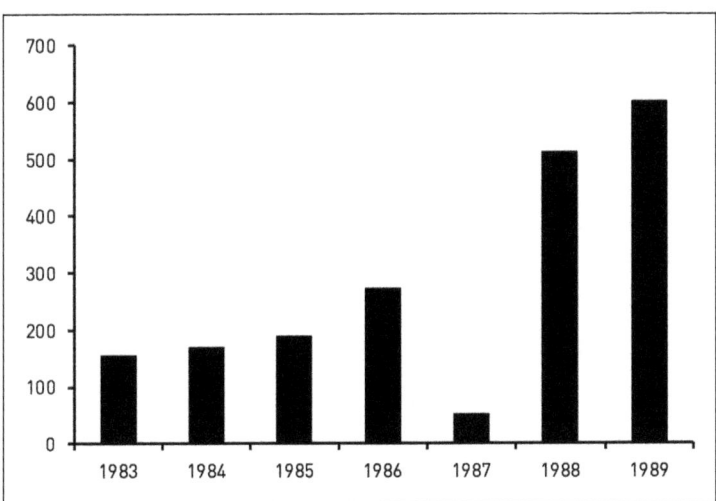

Source: Wells Fargo annual reports and accounts

Figure 1.11: Wells Fargo earnings per share and dividends per share 1983–89

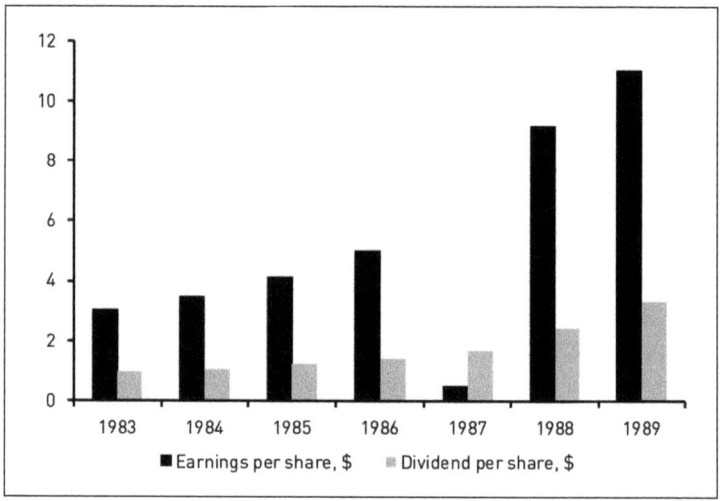

Source: Wells Fargo annual reports and accounts

The question for Buffett and Munger in 1990 was, given this profit history, what is Wells Fargo's earnings power? Is it over $600m – in which case a market capitalisation of less than $3bn means it is a bargain. Or was it merely a flash-in-the-pan good performer in the benign 1980s, but its vulnerabilities meant that the recession of the early 1990s would cause at best lower profits and at worst a complete failure?

The shorting of Wells Fargo

There were many doom-laden public declarations denouncing Buffett and Munger for making a terrible mistake. After all, Wells Fargo's balance sheet equity at $2.5bn was less than one-fifth of the $14bn it had lent to commercial businesses and farmers. And then there was another $4bn lent out for real estate construction. What if, say, a quarter of these borrowers could not pay back their debts? That's going to mean curtains for the venerable name of Wells Fargo, America's 11th largest bank.

A first crack? In June 1990, Moody's downgraded Wells Fargo's senior debt from A1 to Aa3 because of worries over California's worsening commercial real estate market and the bank's leveraged balance sheet.

At the time, America's most visible short sellers were the Feshbach brothers. Their organisation made money by borrowing from financial institutions shares in troubled companies so they could sell them, and later buy them back at a lower price. They announced that Wells Fargo's loan portfolio was in a worse state than the company let on. Tom Barton, a Dallas-based partner of the firm, said that if California real estate "craters off, it may not be over for the bank, but the situation would be dire."[14] He expected (hoped) Wells Fargo shares to fall to well below $20 (they were then trading at $50).

George M. Salem over at Prudential-Bache Securities' Wall Street office labelled Wells Fargo the most vulnerable of the Californian banks. He said: "Here's an analogy for Californians. Wells Fargo built a house for an earthquake of 6 on the financial-shock Richter scale, but we're going to have a 7 or 8 … [Wells Fargo's dividend] could deteriorate rapidly."[15]

Dean Witter's Richard X. Bove was equally negative. "The stock has gone to hell (because) Wells Fargo is a heavily loaned-up bank."[16] John Taylor wrote in *Forbes*: "Just 10% decline in the value of [its] loans would wipe out more than half of Wells Fargo's equity."[17] And veteran Californian property developer G. William Tischer estimated that "most of the offices built after 1984 are not worth the value of the loan."[18]

Carl Reichardt's response was calm and resolute: "If [the value of California real estate] plummets off the face of the Earth, that's going to create problems. Do I think that will happen? No."[19]

And clearly, Buffett and Munger did not agree with the naysayers. With our benefit of hindsight we can judge who was closer to the truth by looking at the profits and efficiency metrics over the following few years.

How did Wells Fargo perform through the recession?

The secret to running a successful bank is to lend at a good margin above the cost of obtaining those funds from depositors etc., while holding down operating costs and lowering losses inflicted by borrower default. It helps if there is plenty of non-interest income as well, such as fees from investment management. If all is going well on these fronts the bank will produce a high rate of return on equity capital.

The first key observation when looking at the period up to the big merger with First Interstate Bank in 1996 is that Wells' net interest margin was above 5% in every year, sometimes substantially above. It was 5.8% in 1995 and even in the recession year of 1992 it was 5.7%. This compares very well with the average US commercial bank, only achieving 4.2–4.3% net interest margin between 1990 and 1995.

So that's the first key element Buffett and Munger needed to see – plenty of money coming in the form of interest from lending out deposited cash. But what about the cost of running the banking operations needed to generate that interest, i.e., non-interest expenses?

These did jump by 18% in 1991 ($1.7bn to $2bn), but that was mostly due to the previous year's purchase of several Californian banks: the Great American Bank of San Diego (92 offices, $4.4bn in deposits), Citizens Holdings Bank (six offices, $207m in deposits), and four others that collectively brought in 28 offices and $1.5bn of deposits. Naturally, they brought with them day-to-day expenditure. Thereafter, expenses rose slowly, at about 2% per year until 1996.

To appreciate the impact of expenses on returns for shareholders we need to relate them to revenue, which is what you can see in figure 1.12. Revenue consists of net interest plus non-interest income (e.g., fees and commissions, service charges, trust and investment services, advisory services, etc.).

Figure 1.12: Wells Fargo non-interest expense as a percentage of total revenue (1990–1995)

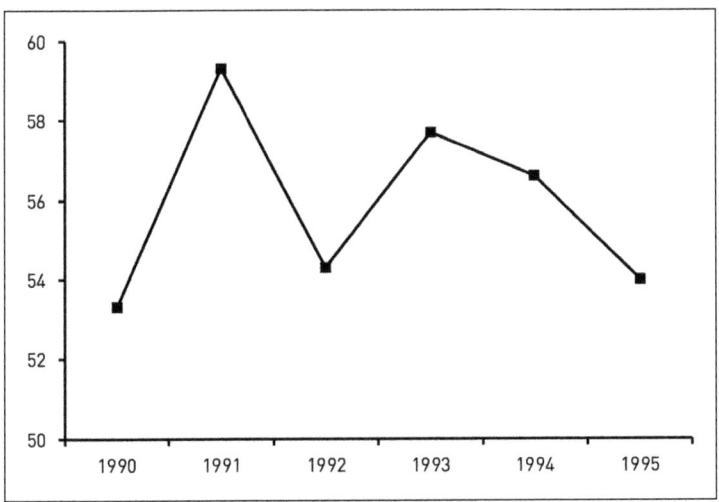

Source: Wells Fargo annual reports and accounts

Wells Fargo's expenses were kept below 60% of revenue before falling to 54% in 1995. The rest of the banking sector suffered a peak in non-interest expenses of around 69% and did not fall below 63% – see figure 1.1. Reichardt and Hazen's laser focus on costs paid off; Wells Fargo was one of the most efficient, if not the most efficient bank in America.

A large gap between revenue and expenses is good, but it is not sufficient to ensure high profits. We also need to know if a great deal of money was lost through loan write-offs and other defaults.

Loss provisions did indeed rise in the recession years. Whereas the directors set aside a mere $310m in 1990, they had to provision for $1,335m in 1991, $1,215m in 1992 and $550m in 1993. As a percentage of loans this was only 0.6% in 1990, but over 3% in 1991 and 1992.

Buffett was almost spot on with his loan provision estimate for a recession. In 1990 he had reasoned that even if one in every ten loans granted by Wells Fargo (totalling $48bn) entered a troubled period and, after some forbearance and restructuring, around one-third of these ultimately defaulted completely, the bank would roughly breakeven –

losses on defaults would amount to about $1.44bn and its income from net interest and non-interest sources (less running expenses) would amount to much the same.

We can see how it turned out in figure 1.13. After-tax profits did indeed plunge from $712m in 1990 to $21m in 1991 – the result of the billion dollar plus losses expected on troubled loans. But note that net interest income actually rose from $2.3bn to $2.5bn, and non-interest income stayed at $0.9bn. Both sources of income then rose steadily through to 1995, while loan loss provisions fell to a very small amount in the mid-1990s. Hence, the large rise in profits – topping $1bn – earnings per share and dividends.

As figure 1.14 shows, earnings per share rose to $20.37 for 1995. Berkshire had paid an average of $57.88 for these shares.

Figure 1.13: Wells Fargo after-tax profits $m (1990–1995)

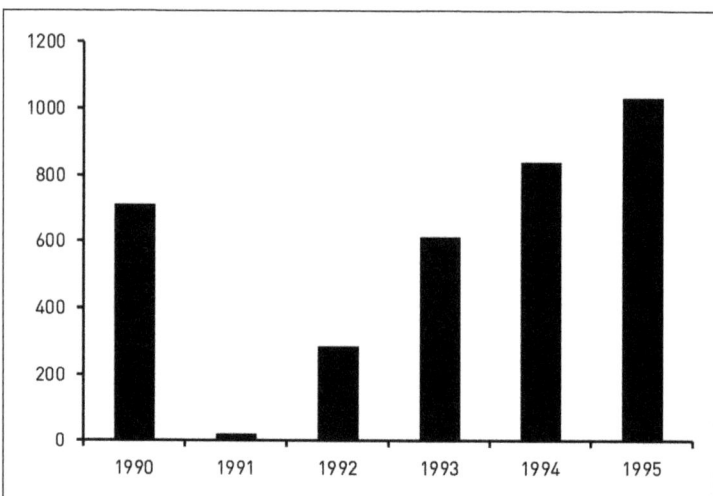

Source: Wells Fargo annual reports

Figure 1.14: Wells Fargo earnings per share and dividends per share $ (1990-1995)

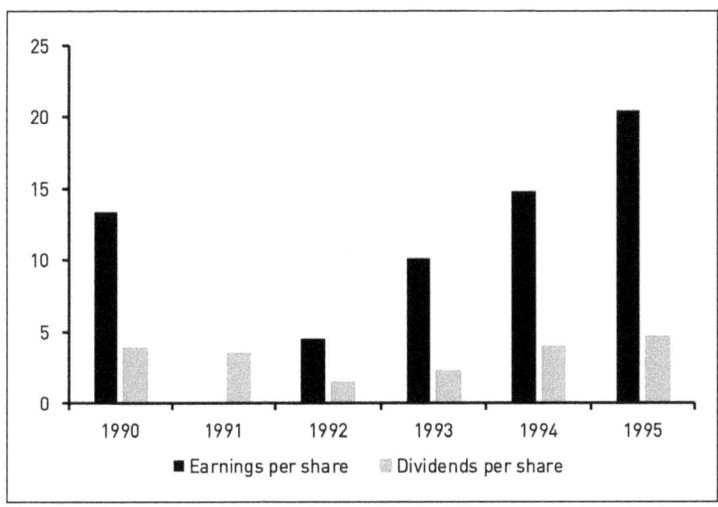

Source: Wells Fargo annual reports

By 1994, return on equity reached levels similar to that of the 1980s boom years at 22.4% – see figure 1.15. In 1995, an astonishing 29.7% return on common equity was achieved, far above the respectable 15% average for US commercial banks (shown in figure 1.3). In fact, Wells Fargo was the most profitable large US bank that year.

Figure 1.15: Wells Fargo return on equity % (1990–1995)

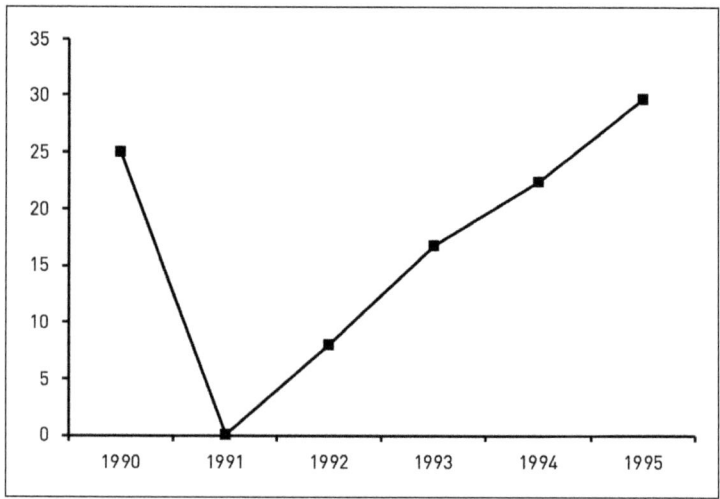

Source: Wells Fargo annual reports and accounts

Naturally the shares rose in response to the great numbers coming out of the bank – see figure 1.16. Within six years they quadrupled, touching $229 at one point in 1995.

Figure 1.16: Wells Fargo common stock price at year ends $ (1990–1995)

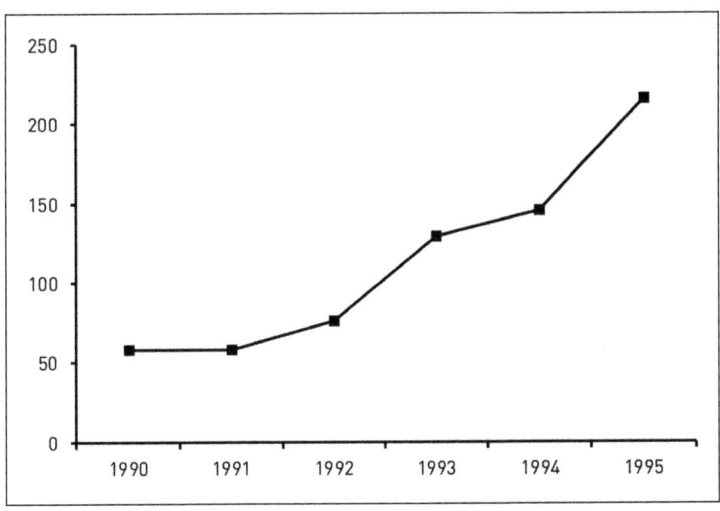

Source: Wells Fargo annual reports and accounts

Buffett and Munger had won their bet. The Feshbach brothers lost about $50m in 1991 on Wells Fargo because they were forced to repurchase shorted shares at high prices.[20]

Managing a bank: the basic principles

The business philosophy followed by Wells Fargo under the 12-year leadership of Reichardt gives us clues as to why it was able to easily withstand the 1990–93 Californian recession. The philosophy inculcated in every employee, from teller to senior executive, was set out in the 1994 annual report following Reichardt's stepping back from an executive role, aged 63.[21] The new chairman, Paul Hazen, and president, William Zuendt, were proud of the culture they had helped create under Reinhardt's leadership and so they prominently displayed the key principles which they said can be easily understood and applied by anyone working at Wells Fargo.

Run it like you own it

> "Our managers take responsibility for operating like owners of their business units. Owners know where every dollar is spent. They know the return they're earning on their capital. They set targets for the returns they expect from planned investments because they are using their own money. Their stake in the Company leads to disciplined decisions and solid accomplishments."[22]

They added that employee compensation was designed to encourage owner-like behaviour. For example, executive compensation was linked to company returns to shareholders. Senior executives were expected to hold a significant amount of the firm's shares, so they were rewarded alongside shareholders in the good times and shared in losses in the bad times. Furthermore, all employees were encouraged to hold shares through various employee stock purchase plans. Half took up the offer.

Know the numbers

> "Simply tracking revenues and expenses isn't enough. Managers must know the dynamics of their business – where they make money and where they lose it. They must test each potential deal or initiative for the risks involved against the rewards to be gained."[23]

Managers were held accountable for the extent to which they achieved above industry norms regarding return on the equity employed.

Know your customer

> "Knowing each of our wholesale customers and learning as much as possible about our retail customers are basic to our business … In our retail business, we do a great deal of behavioural analysis to know our customers."

This principle enhanced the ability to sell additional products. For example, customers' creditworthiness was assessed ahead of time so that when they asked for, or were prompted to consider, a consumer loan they were already pre-approved. Staff were encouraged to make a good loan offer when the customer next contacted the bank. They wanted to differentiate themselves from other financial service companies by providing superior customer service, always on the search for new products, often products customers hadn't even thought of getting from a bank. "Good products and delivery options attract new customers to Wells Fargo. Great service will keep them."

Develop good people

"We look for people who not only have the relevant knowledge and skills, who also understand the competitive environment, have a clear vision of how their job fits into the business, and then get the job done right."[24]

Managers were granted increased authority and autonomy if they proved worthy. This meant producing superior results for shareholders and customers. Entrepreneurial thinking and decentralised decision-making were considered important. "Over the years, our success in developing such managers has been measurable by the number who have gone on to run other financial companies."[25]

Control expenses

"Wells Fargo has become known for the efficiency of our operations. We know we can't control market forces or interest rates, but we can control operating expenses … It means constantly examining our businesses and exiting those that no longer make sense, then redeploying the funds to position us as the low-cost producer for the future.

We also know that we won't be able to rely solely on our low-cost structure to maintain the Company's historical returns to shareholders … We will have to grow customer revenues *and* remain one of the most efficient players in our industry."[26]

Charlie Munger told a story at Berkshire Hathaway's 1991 annual general meeting: A Wells Fargo manager wanted to buy a Christmas tree for the office. Reichardt said OK, but only with his own money. Munger said, "When we heard that, we bought more stock."[27]

The Reichardt legacy

Reichardt thought of himself as a businessman rather than a banker, who, like Buffett and Munger, saw the key measure of success as obtaining high rates of return on any equity capital employed in the business. He was not interested in growth for its own sake, but growth only where excellent return for shareholders was likely. He focused Wells Fargo's attention on California where the managers could operate within their circle of competence. He preached the need to concentrate on a few core businesses, to do the ordinary extraordinarily well and to bear down on costs at all times.

These principles were all well established at Wells Fargo before Berkshire was on the share register, so it must have warmed the hearts of Buffett and Munger when they heard Reichardt ramming home to staff these simple ideas and standards.

The team Reichardt and Hazen created earned the company the reputation as the most efficient bank in the country. But it was not a hunkered down and obsessive cost-cutting type of efficiency. Wells Fargo was also a highly innovative bank, quick on the uptake of the new, from ATMs to telephone banking.

> "One of Reichardt's legacies will be that he assembled a strong succession team." said Thomas Brown, an analyst at Donaldson, Lufkin & Jenrette Securities, "It's the greatest compliment to a CEO when you can say that the company is so well managed that it won't miss a heartbeat without him."[28]

Warren Buffett paid tribute in his 1994 letter, "Carl Reichardt ... encountered very tough industry conditions in recent years. But [his] skill as a manager allowed the business ... to emerge from [this] period with record earnings. [He] prepared well for departure and left [the] company in outstanding hands. We owe [him] our gratitude."

Berkshire Hathaway wants more of a good thing

Banking rules at first prohibited Berkshire Hathaway from acquiring more than 10% of Wells Fargo. But as those rules were relaxed Buffett was able to buy additional shares, reassured by the robust underlying performance numbers coming through and by the containment of loan losses as the recession progressed. He started to look at the economic recovery taking place in the rest of the country and knew that it wouldn't be long before California followed. Then profits would take off as loan losses almost disappeared, and buoyant consumers and businesses bought an ever-greater variety of services from Wells.

All told, in 1992 and 1993, BH bought another 1.8m shares at prices significantly higher than those bought in 1990, but still much less than what they were priced at by Mr Market only three or four years later – see table 1.1.

Table 1.1: Berkshire Hathaway's holdings of Wells Fargo shares, 1989–1995

	Number of shares	BH's percentage holding of Wells Fargo	Cost: that year's purchases and cumulative cost	Per share cost (those acquired that year)	Total market value – end of year
1989–90	Bought 5,000,000	Just under 10%	$289m	$57.9	$289m
1992	Bought another 1,358,418 shares. Total: 6,358,418	11.5%	Additional cost: $92m Total cost: $381m	$67.7	$486m
1993	Bought another 432,800 shares. Total: 6,791,218	12.2%	Additional cost: $43m Total cost: $424m	$98.7	$879m
1994	Wells Fargo re-purchase about one-tenth of its common stock. BH Total: 6,791,218	13.3%	Total cost: $424m		$985m
1995	Wells Fargo re-purchase about one-tenth of its common stock. BH Total: 6,791,218	14.5%	Total cost: $424m		$1,467m

Wells Fargo bought its own shares in 1994 and 1995 because "the company had been generating more capital than we can profitably employ in our business or in acquisitions that make economic sense to us."[29]

Assisted by Wells Fargo's programme of share buybacks (and BH not selling any shares) by the end of 1995 BH's holding grew to 14.5% of the equity. At this point, shares which had cost BH a total of $424m were priced by Wall Street at $1,467m.

Doubling the bank, then doubling again – all in two years

Wells Fargo was built on mergers. From its founding in 1852 until the mid-1990s it had acquired almost 500 companies. It usually obtained impressive operational synergies and was able to broaden and improve its service offer for customers.

The First Interstate takeover

In the early 1990s, Reichardt "openly lusted"[30] after Los Angeles-based First Interstate bank. An offer was made in February 1994 only for it to be rejected by First Interstate's directors. Reichardt carried on courting, but ruefully said: "It takes two to tango, and we're alone on the dance floor."[31]

Wells and First Interstate were similarly sized banks with comparable market capitalisations. Whereas Wells had about 974 offices, 19,000 staff and $51bn of assets, First Interstate had 1,150 offices, 26,000 staff and $58bn of assets. In California they both had a large rival to contend with, Bank of America, who had a 20% share of deposits. Wells Fargo was second with 11%, and First Interstate was third with 6%.

Combining the two companies offered Wells Fargo's managers the opportunity to repeat their highly efficient and innovative banking formula outside of California because First Interstate was already established in 13 western states, with 405 offices in California and 745 in other states.

But that very attraction also caught the attention of other large banks and in 1995, Banc One, NationsBank and Norwest were thought to be eyeing First Interstate. This meant that Wells would need to make its offer appealing. In summer 1995, Paul Hazen, now chairman, approached his opposite at First Interstate, William Siart, with the idea of a merger of equals. He hoped a friendly merger would appeal to the senior team and to their masters, FI's shareholders, allowing all to share in the spoils.

And Warren Buffett, aware of the pain, resentment and heightened risk associated with a hostile bid, favoured a mutually acceptable deal. He had been consulted on the negotiation. Indeed, he undertook a detailed analysis of First Interstate and concluded that the two banks were roughly of equal value as independent entities, but that there were gains to be had by uniting.

Siart was interested but wanted to delay a merger for several years so that the benefits of the investments his bank had recently made in new technology and marketing would be reflected in FI's share price.

As summer moved into fall, Wells' directors grew impatient and in October, while keeping Buffett informed, launched a takeover offer of 0.625 Wells shares for each FI share – valuing the target at $10.17bn. This was a rich price at 2.8 times book value (net asset value). Buffett follows a policy of trusting his key managers regarding the growth of their businesses, whether that growth be organic or through acquisition. So even though he is cautious of aggressive bids, he will not veto a proposition.

In general, when the market learns of a takeover offer the response is for the target shares to rise but the bidder's shares to fall. Analysts are fearful that the acquirer, in a fit of hubris and excitement, offered an excessive price.

But on the announcement of the Wells offer for First Interstate something remarkable happened: both shares rose, First Interstate's by 32% and Wells' by 7%. Despite the pricey offer, market opinion was that combining the banks would bring cost savings and increase customer service to such an extent that shareholders would gain improved future earnings from what would become America's eighth largest bank.

Wells' directors talked about achieving annual cost savings of approximately $800m within 18 months by cutting overlapping operations in California, sharing resources across state boundaries between Wells' offices and FI's branches in neighbouring states. They also pointed to the greater efficiency with which Wells "runs its franchise when compared to First Interstate"[32] and to a range of economies of scale.

The Tuesday night telephone call by Paul Hazen to William Siart explaining the unwelcome move caught him off guard. The next day, Siart issued a terse statement: "I am deeply disappointed that Wells Fargo would take this uninvited action." Nevertheless, he said the board of First Interstate would consider the bid "among other alternatives." Siart was hopeful that the price paid could be raised in a bidding war with Wells' rivals.

But that wasn't to be. Wells had pitched its offer at a level other banks could not match. "Wells has the most synergies, so it makes sense for them to pay up," said Denis Laplaige, president of the MacKay-Shields Financial Corporation, an investment manager holding 1.4m First Interstate shares. "Other banks may not have numbers that add up as well, but they may see this as their last opportunity to get into the California market, and it is."[33]

Major FI shareholders were keen for the directors to take this bird in the hand rather than wait for a better offer. Thus, an agreement was reached in January 1996, and the acquisition completed in April. Because it was an all-share exchange and Wells' share had risen, the final effective price paid was $11.3bn. Wells needed to offer so many new shares that the former FI shareholders ended up with 52% of the equity of the enlarged Wells.

Integration was implemented at speed. It was decided to convert all offices to Wells Fargo's system architecture, reduce staff by 8,900, change signage at over 1,000 FI locations and train FI's staff in Wells' procedures. And all this to be accomplished within one year.

Regulators required divestment of 61 Californian branches in places where Wells would have too much market power. The company was sub-scale in three states (Alaska, Montana and Wyoming) and so withdrew from these, leaving it with significant operations in ten states, including Texas.

Customers could benefit from interstate banking, such as being able to use a deposit account in many states; they had access to 4,300 ATMs; and FI customers could be introduced to 24-hour telephone banking and a better website.

It wasn't all smooth sailing, with some well-publicised failures in customer service. "Many random but significant telecommunications and system problems occurred in the initial months after the merger, creating major service issues and inconveniences for our retail and wholesale customers. Systems slow-downs, clogged telephone service centres, errors in customer accounts and long branch lines plagued our customers [and] placed an extra burden on employees."[34] Paul Hazen told *Business Week*[35] that the merger problems meant that 1996 was not a pleasant year for him.

Earnings per share fell from $20.37 in 1995 to $12.77 in 1997 as merger-related costs (premises, severance, etc.) of over $700m and disruption took a toll. Despite the hiccups, Wall Street approved of the long-term strategy and the shares rose from $229 in December 1995 to $339 by the end of 1997.

Buffett was far from idle during the integration period, exploiting a price dip to purchase another 500,200 shares in 1996, paying an average $147.90. They rose to $290 later in the year.

As the late 1990s bull market gathered pace, Buffett was able to sell 8.2% of BH's holding in 1997 at a price almost double that paid in the previous year – see table 1.2.

Table 1.2: Berkshire Hathaway's holdings of Wells Fargo shares, 1996–97

	Number of shares	BH's percentage holding of Wells Fargo	Cost: that year's purchases and cumulative cost	Per share cost (those acquired that year)	Total market value – end of year
1996	Bought another 500,200 shares. Total: 7,291,418	8.0% (Wells Fargo issued 52m shares to First Interstate Bank shareholders. Also repurchased about 8%)	Additional cost: $74m. Total cost: $498m.	$147.9	$1,967m
1997	BH sold 601,200 shares. Total: 6,690,218	7.8% (WF repurchase about 6% of stock)	Cash released: in the range $246 × 601,200 = $148m to $339 × 601,200 = $204m. Total cost of remaining WF shares: $413m	Sale price: in the range $246–339 per share	$2,271m

Norwest and Wells Fargo – stronger together

During the California gold rush, the two entrepreneurs Henry Wells and William G. Fargo pioneered cross-selling. Not content with a stagecoach transportation company they also wanted to serve customers' banking needs and provide safe keeping; they then went after customers' goods and mail business.

In 1998, the bank was driven by the same desire to supply a wider range of services – to be a financial services company rather than just a bank. The directors reckoned that the 3.2 products per household obtained from Wells was merely one-quarter of the financial service businesses those people consumed; "That means every day our own customers are giving three-fourths of their business to our competitors. That's opportunity."[36]

Wells' services ranged from retail and business banking to investments, insurance, and consumer finance. The variety enabled both revenue opportunities and earnings diversity, providing resilience in economic downturns.

There was a bank even better at cross-selling financial services. Norwest, headquartered in Minneapolis and with branches throughout the land west of the Mississippi, had been labelled by *Fortune* as the best in the country for customer service. It had built superior systems for tracking sales and customer profitability, using technology to personalise services, resulting in a doubling of products sold per household over the 1990s.

Under Richard M. Kovacevich's leadership, Norwest grew organically and through acquisition across 16 western and mid-western states from Montana and Indiana to Texas. Kovacevich pushed relationship banking, focusing on small retail customers and small businesses. This formed the foundation for selling an ever-wider range of services, from mortgages and auto loans to mutual funds and insurance.

Going against the banking fashion of the day, Norwest invested in an extensive branch network, staffed with well-trained bankers and tellers, simply to maintain these relationships. It went against the grain in another way: it had no ambition in investment banking, matching Wells Fargo's attitude.

Norwest was already the 11th largest US bank, roughly the same size as Wells Fargo. The potential synergies of combining were obvious with cost savings to be had, increased cross-selling opportunities and the benefits of having a more diverse streams of earnings in the fast-growing states. This merger would make them the first, second or third in the shares of banking deposits in most of their 21 states.

Wells Fargo had a well-deserved reputation for efficiency, for example, it cost only 54.6 cents to earn a dollar of revenue. Norwest – no slouch – spent 63 cents to generate a dollar. To improve a combined group's efficiency, Wells could offer its 'run it like you own it' and 'know the numbers' culture across all branches.

Wells also brought a superior 147-year-old brand. The name and the stagecoach were two of the most widely recognised brands in the world – in the west of America, consumer awareness approached that of Coca-Cola. "Branding is as indispensable for a national financial services company as it is for a national retailer ... or soft drinks."[37]

Wells Fargo's application of technology to banking was also ahead of Norwest (250,000 internet transactions per week was a lot in 1998) and this advantage could be rolled out to benefit Norwest's customers.

In short, a merger would create the premier banking franchise in the west and mid-west.

Wells and Norwest's merger of equals

In the November 1998 deal, Norwest was technically the acquirer of Wells Fargo. It offered ten shares for each Wells Fargo share of common stock. But the group name was quickly changed to Wells Fargo & Company, and their headquarters was moved to San Francisco. Former Wells Fargo stockholders owned 52.5% of the equity and Paul Hazen became chairman, with Kovacevich becoming president and CEO.

Paul Hazen, 59, ceased executive duties in 2000 once he was assured the merger process was complete. He later said that he stayed at the bank for 26 months after the merger to symbolie equality between the two sides and reassure old Wells hands that they were wanted. He then took on the chairmanship of Accel-KKR, a Palo Alto venture capital firm.

Wells Fargo was immediately one of the giants on the US banking scene, being the third-largest US commercial bank by funding 7.7% of all US home mortgages and being number one for small business and farm lending, and for student loans and insurance agency sales by a bank. It had 6,000 stores.

The annual reports of that period emphasise facts such as only 25% of customers had a Norwest or Wells credit card. "We expect to sell at least one new product to every customer every year," proclaimed the directors.[38] The base for growth was already huge: 15m customers, $202bn in assets and a market capitalisation of $66bn.

The chart of Wells' stock price – see figure 1.17 – illustrates the success of the merger with the stock doubling over eight years. (There was a two-for-one share split in 2006, thus the prices between 1999 and 2006 were in fact trading at double those shown.)

Figure 1.17: Wells Fargo stock price 1999–2021

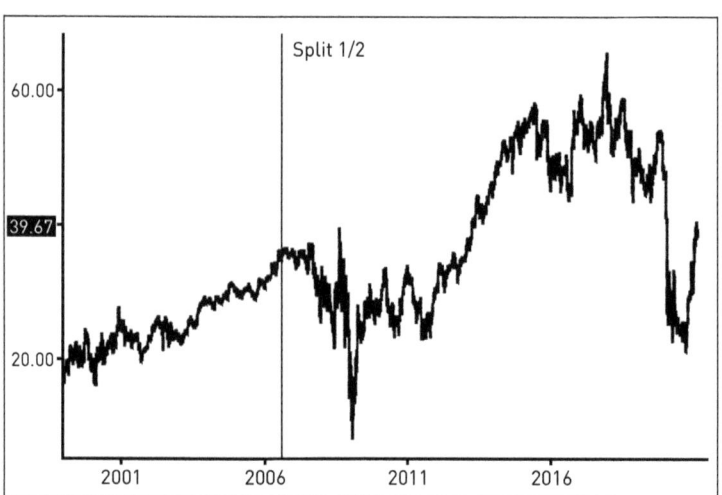

Source: www.advfn.com

Berkshire Hathaway sells

In the stock-market bubble period and its aftermath, between 1997 and 2001, Buffett sold nearly 20m of Wells' shares, raising between $600m and $800m. But Berkshire held on to 53m, worth $2.3bn. The combined purchase cost of those sold and those held amounted to $498m, from which we can conclude that this was a very successful investment for Berkshire over a mere dozen years – even if we leave to one side the annual dividends.

Table 1.3: Berkshire Hathaway's investment in Wells Fargo 1997–2001

	Number of shares	BH's percentage holding of Wells Fargo	Cost	Per share cost (those acquired that year)	Total market value – end of year
1997	BH sold 601,200 shares. Total: 6,690,218	7.8% (WF repurchase about 6% of stock)	Cash released: in the range $246 × 601,200 = $148m to $339 × 601,200 = $204m. Total cost of remaining WF shares: $413m	Sale price: in the range $246–339 per share	$2,271m
1998	BH sold 330,700 old shares or 3,307,000 new shares. Total held (in split shares): 63,595,180	A reverse takeover by Norwest in which WF shareholders end up with 52.5%. Plus, in effect, a ten-for-one split for each of WF's shares	Cash released: in the range $27.50 × 3.3 = $91m to $43.88 × 3.3 = $145m. Total cost of remaining WF shares: $392m	Sale price: in the range $275–439 in old shares or $27.50–43.88 in new shares	$2,540m
1999	BH sold 4.46m Total held: 59,136,680	3.6%	Cash released range: $32.13 × 4.46m = $143m to $49.94 × 4.46m = $223m. Total cost of remaining WF shares: $349m	Sale price: in the range $32.13–49.94	$2,391m

Investment 1. Wells Fargo

	Number of shares	BH's percentage holding of Wells Fargo	Cost	Per share cost (those acquired that year)	Total market value – end of year
2000	BH sold 4.07m shares. Total held: 55,071,380	3.2%	Cash released range: $31 × 4.07m = $126m to $56.38 × 4.07m = $229m. Total cost of remaining WF shares: $319m	Sale price: in the range $31–53.38	$3,067m
2001	BH sold 1.806m shares. Total held: 53,265,080		Cash released range: $38.25 × 1.806m = $69m to $54.81 × 1.806m = $99m. Total cost of remaining WF shares: $306m	Sale price: in the range $38.25–54.81	$2,315m

Looking at the entire period between the dot-com crash and 2013, we find that these dozen years were not nearly as blessed as the first dozen years of Berkshire's association with Wells. While the first few years of the twenty-first century were fine with the economy booming, the banking crisis of 2007–9 caused the Wells' shares to plummet. It lost three-quarters of its market value. The climb back was bumpy and slow – by 2013, the shares were only around 20% higher than they were in 2001.

Phase two: buying by Berkshire

Through those dozen turbulent years, Buffett went back to the market time and again to buy Wells' shares – see table 1.4. This buying was on a much larger scale than the first phase, with $12.4bn spent all told. The big purchases were made in 2007, with 85m shares bought at an average of $34.96, and in 2012, with 56.2m shares bought at an average of $32.40.

Clearly, Buffett trusted Kovacevich. He wrote in his 2005 letter to Berkshire shareholders, "we substantially increased our holdings in Wells Fargo, a company that Dick Kovacevich runs brilliantly".

Table 1.4: Berkshire Hathaway investment in Wells Fargo 2003–2015

	Number of shares	BH's percentage holding of Wells Fargo	Cost	Per share cost (those acquired that year)	Total market value – end of year
2003	BH bought 3.18m shares. Total held: 56,448,380	3.3%	Additional cost: $157m. Total cost: $463m	$49.4	$3,324m
2005	BH bought 38.64m shares. Total held: 95,092,200	5.7%	Additional cost: $2,291m. Total cost: $2,754m	$59.3	$5,975m
2006	WF two-for-one stock split. BH bought 27.98m shares. Total held: 218,169,300	6.5%	Additional cost: $943m. Total cost: $3,697m	$33.7	$7,758m
2007	BH bought 85.24m shares. Total held: 303,407,068	9.2%	Additional cost: $2,980m. Total cost: $6,677m	$34.96	$9,160m
2008	BH bought 0.985m shares. Total held: 304,392,068	7.2% WF issued almost 1bn shares, partly to finance Wachovia merger.	Additional cost: $25m. Total cost: $6,702m	$25.38	$8,973m

	Number of shares	BH's percentage holding of Wells Fargo	Cost	Per share cost (those acquired that year)	Total market value – end of year
2009	BH bought 29.8m shares. Total held: 334,235,585	6.5%	Additional cost: $692m Total cost: $7,394m	$23.22	$9,021m
2010	BH bought 24.7m shares. Total held: 358,936,125	6.8%	Additional cost: $621m Total cost: $8,015	$25.14	$11,123m
2011	BH bought 41.1m shares. Total held: 400,015,828	7.6%	Additional cost: $1,071m Total cost: $9,086	$26.06	$11,024m
2012	BH bought 56.2m shares. Total held: 456,170,061	8.7%	Additional cost: $1,820m Total cost: $10,906m	$32.4	$15,592m
2013	BH bought 27.3m shares. Total held: 483,470,853	9.2%	Additional cost: $965m Total cost: $11,871m	$35.3	$21,950m
2015	BH bought 16.5m shares. Total held: 500,000,000	9.8%	Additional cost: $859m Total cost: $12,730m	$52.06	$27,180m

The run up in price to over $55 in 2015 was starting to confirm that the phase two purchases were wise, even if the share was very slow to get going. Even better, the bank was voted seventh in *Barron's* most respected companies in spring 2015 by professional money managers, providing yet more confirmation.

Riding high, Wells Fargo's Vision and Values document was referred to yet again in its 2015 annual report.

> "We work to make every relationship – new and old – a lasting one by following a few simple principles. We put our customers first and treat them as our valued guests. We are committed to our customers' satisfaction and financial success and to work in their best interest. In short, we are on our customers' side."

But then a scandal broke.

Scandal

As we've discussed, Wells Fargo and Norwest were renowned for selling customers additional financial services. When building those reputations in the 1990s they followed a strict ethical code to genuinely do right by the customer. But something went terribly wrong at some point in the years after 2002. Senior managers set up incentive systems for frontline employees which encouraged them to cross-sell at speed – bonuses were available for those who could obtain customer signatures for additional financial services.

Thousands of employees found an easier way to gain bonuses than actually talking to customers and winning their consent for new accounts; they simply created completely false accounts, often by forging signatures. They also moved customer money into unauthorised accounts and altered contact information in order to open accounts without the knowledge of customers. There was also unfair treatment of customers in both its mortgage and auto-loans businesses.

Employees later said that they felt under extreme pressure from head office to reach daily targets for cross-sales; if they weren't met one day the shortfall was added to the target for the next day. The company eventually admitted that 3.5m accounts were involved in the scandal. Clearly, the culture had gone awry and widespread abuse was taking place.

And yet the abuse was hidden behind the honeyed words of the directors. As late as February 2016, when Buffett wrote his 2015 letter to shareholders, he expressed great faith in Wells' management. He wrote in his letter that his four major investments – American Express, Coca-Cola, IBM and Wells Fargo – "possess excellent businesses and are run by managers who are both talented and shareholder-oriented."

It wasn't long afterwards that the entire nation questioned whether Wells' managers were "talented". Shocked by revelations in the breaking scandal, regulators imposed fines amounting to $185m in September 2016 for phony account openings. Worse for Wells was the limit placed on the total assets the bank could hold. It was set at $1.95trn – their level in 2017. This meant growth was halted at a time when its principal competitors were expanding assets by 4–5% per year. The limit was to remain in place into the 2020s.

As more regulators probed misdemeanours, they too imposed penalties – the total at the time or writing is around $6bn. Over 5,300 employees (out of 260,000) were sacked and Stephen Sanger, chairman of the board, felt he had to write a humiliating admission to shareholders in the 2016 annual report:

> "My fellow Board members and I were deeply troubled that Wells Fargo violated [customers] trust by opening accounts for certain retail banking customers that they did not request or in some cases even know about. We have taken aggressive action to root out these practices and to compensate our customers who were harmed by them. We recognize that these events signalled a need for fundamental changes in Wells Fargo's culture, management systems, and executive leadership."

John Stumpf, CEO since 2007, resigned 12 October, 2016. The following condemnation directed at Stumpf two weeks earlier by Senator Elizabeth Warren at a US Senate inquiry may have contributed to that decision:

> "You know, here's what really gets me about this, Mr Stumpf. If one of your tellers took a handful of $20 bills out of the cash

drawer, they'd probably be looking at criminal charges for theft. They could end up in prison. But you squeezed your employees to the breaking point so they would cheat customers and you could drive up the value of your stock and put hundreds of millions of dollars in your own pocket. And when it all blew up, you kept your job, you kept your multimillion dollar bonuses and you went on television to blame thousands of $12-an-hour employees who were just trying to meet cross-sell quotas that made you rich. This is about accountability. You should resign. You should give back the money that you took while this scam was going on and you should be criminally investigated by both the Department of Justice and the Securities and Exchange Commission."[39]

Buffett said in November that Stumpf was "a very decent man" who made a "hell of a mistake. It was a dumb incentive system. When they found out it was dumb, they didn't do anything about it".[40]

Buffett did not tell Stumpf that he had to go, instead choosing words of powerful understatement to say: "John, I don't think you understand the gravity of this."[41] It was not up to Buffett to say whether he should go or stay because Berkshire was a self-declared passive investor in a bank, and he was being watched by the bank regulators to ensure he did not exert undue influence.

When Buffett was asked about the importance of the culture in the companies he invests in, he said that it was a huge factor. In the case of Wells Fargo:

> "The very act of not correcting the problem affected the culture ... The culture was pretty good, and the incentive system corrupted people. If you leave the petty cash of a large company right near the door where people leave every day, and you don't bother to buy a safe or anything, some people are going to succumb to that who would otherwise behave pretty well. And when other people see other people succumbing to it, they will do it. Cultures shift, and you can affect that culture – that's why they put in cash registers. Any time you get any indication that any policy is leading to bad behaviour, get on it quickly."[42]

He went on to quote one of Charlie Munger's favourite phases, 'an ounce of prevention isn't worth a pound of cure; it's worth a ton of cure.' Buffett says you're going to make mistakes in business (and in investing) and you'd better deal with them. He freely admits he's made a lot of them himself, "it's part of the job".

Following Stumpf's resignation Buffett publicly approved the promotion of Tim Sloan, COO, to CEO after they had lunch together. Unfortunately, Sloan only lasted two and half years after coming under pressure from Congress and regulators – just being a 25-year veteran of the bank raised hackles.

Chronically leaking boats

What to do with an investment when management have erred?

I was listening at the 2018 Berkshire meeting in Omaha when a fellow shareholder reminded Buffett and Munger of one of their time-honoured principles: 'Should you find yourself in a chronically leaking boat, energy devoted to changing vessels is likely to be more productive than energy devoted to patching leaks.' In that context, Buffett and Munger were asked about Wells Fargo. The questioner pointedly asked: "if Wells Fargo company is a chronically leaking boat, at what magnitude of leakage would Berkshire consider changing vessels?"

Buffett admitted that Wells Fargo had the wrong incentives for its staff and that led to some crazy behaviour like opening non-existent accounts, "that is a cardinal sin at Berkshire."

He pointed out that there are 377,000 employees at Berkshire, and he can't expect everyone to behave like Ben Franklin. So the company has to incentivise properly, and find out where things are going wrong and do something about it.

But Buffett rejects the idea of always selling out when there are managerial problems. He said that two of their greatest investments came after the people in charge made similar errors.

> "We bought our American Express stock – that was the best investment I ever made in my partnership years – we bought our American Express stock in 1964 because somebody was incented

to do the wrong thing in something called the American Express Field Warehousing Company. We bought a very substantial amount of GEICO [in 1976] because somebody was incented to meet Wall Street estimates of earnings and growth. And they didn't focus on having the proper reserves. And that caused a lot of pain at American Express in 1964. It caused a lot of pain at GEICO in 1976. It caused a layoff of a significant portion of the workforce, all kinds of things. But they cleaned it up … and look where American Express has moved since that time."

"Look at where GEICO has moved since that time. GEICO … in the early 1970s … charged the wrong price to new customers because they thought their losses were less than they were. And I'm sure some of that may have been a desire to please Wall Street or just because they didn't want to face how things were going. But it came out incredibly stronger. You know, and now it's got 13% of the households in the United States insured. And it came out with an attention to reserves and that sort of thing that was heightened by the difficulties that they'd found themselves in where they almost went bankrupt."

Buffett declared that he could see no reason why Wells Fargo, from both an investment standpoint and a moral standpoint going forward, is in any way inferior to the other big banks with which it competes. And he stated his admiration for Tim Sloan as a manager and the way he was correcting mistakes made by other people. "I see no reason to think that Wells Fargo, going forward, is other than a very, very large, well-run bank that had an episode in its history it wished it didn't have."

Charlie Munger added the thought that Wells Fargo will be stronger in the future than it would have been if these leaks had never been discovered, "but I think Harvey Weinstein has done a lot for improving behaviour, too." He added, "It was clearly an error, and they're acutely aware of it and acutely embarrassed, and they don't want to have it happen again. You know, if I had to say which bank is more likely to behave the best in the future, it might be Wells Fargo, of all of them."

But the Californian shareholder sitting next to me at the AGM was sceptical; he leaned over and pointedly told me that the members of the Wells Fargo board had not changed.

Things did change in October 2019 when Charlie Scharf took on 'one of the worst jobs in banking' (just one of Wall Street's jibes at the time) as the bank's CEO. He was a new brush with a background in east-coast banking, who had a reputation for acute analytical skills and 'getting stuff done', and for being a quiet leader who listens more than he talks as he searches for the unvarnished truth.

When asked whether compliance, efficiency or digitisation was the priority, Scharf said they all were; solving them together was a 'virtuous circle'. But restoring credibility with customers and convincing regulators that it had cleaned up the aggressive sales culture would take some time.

He quickly brought in outsiders to take up senior managerial roles. Perhaps this is a necessary act, but it's one that would have shocked the Reichardt and Hazen team of the 1980s and 1990s who took pride in developing the best managers in banking in-house.

Buffett did not sell any shares when the scandal was a breaking news story, but nor did he buy as the share price declined in 2016. In the following four years, however, he sold about $14–17bn, accounting for the bulk of Berkshire's holding – see table 1.5 (the exact amount raised through sales is not publicly available, but we know the quantity and a rough idea of market prices). That left only $1.56bn invested in Wells Fargo in 2021.

Investment 1. Wells Fargo

Table 1.5: Berkshire Hathaway's dealings in Wells Fargo stock 2017–2020

	Number of shares	BH's percentage holding of Wells Fargo	Cost	Per share cost (those acquired that year)	Total market value – end of year
2017	BH sold 17.46m shares. Total held: 482,544,468	9.9%	Cash released range: $51 × 17.46m = $890m to $59 × 17.46m = $1,030m. Total cost of remaining WF shares: $11,837m	$51–59	$29,276m
2018	BH sold 33.2m shares. Total held: 449,349,102	9.8%	Cash released range: $51 × 33.2m = $1,693m to $65 × 33.2m = $2,158m. Total cost of remaining WF shares: $10,639m	$51–65	$20,706m
2019	BH sold 103.7m shares. Total held: 345,688,918	8.4%	Cash released range: $44 × 103.7m = $4,563m to $54 × 103.7m = $5,600m. Total cost of remaining WF shares: $7,040m	$44–54	$18,598m
2020	BH sold 293.3m shares. Total held in December: 52,423,867	1.3%	Cash released range: $6.9bn – $8.09bn. Total cost of remaining WF shares: $1,067m	$23–53	$1,560m

Not one of Buffett's best investments

The second phase of Berkshire's Wells Fargo investment, starting in 2003, turned out to be poor. It's true, money was not lost, but the $12.4bn spent on shares wasn't even doubled over an 18-year period – even allowing for dividends. The opportunity cost to Berkshire of tying up so much money for 18 years was immense.

Clearly, Buffett lost faith in Wells Fargo. A compounding reason might be that his advice was ignored. In spring 2019 he publicly called for the new CEO to be someone who had not worked in investment banking. "They just have to come from someplace [outside Wells] and they shouldn't come from Wall Street, they probably shouldn't come from JP Morgan or Goldman Sachs," he told the *Financial Times*.[43] He thought a New York investment banker would be like a red rag to a bull in Washington. "There are plenty of good people [from the Wall Street banks], but they are automatically going to draw the ire of a significant percentage of the Senate and the US House of Representatives, that's just not smart."

And true enough, the tough corset on lending was extended for years after Scharf took over and the tension with politicians and regulators continued. Scharf was a New Yorker through and through, having worked at JPMorgan Chase, Citigroup, Salomon Smith Barney and BNY Mellon. On accepting the position at the Wells Fargo, he struck a deal whereby he could continue to live in New York with his family and commute frequently to San Francisco. Charlie Munger regarded this working arrangement as "outrageous … anybody should move for a job like that".[44]

Munger was relatively generous in his comments at Daily Journal's annual meeting (he is chairman) in February 2021, saying that while Buffett became disenchanted with Wells Fargo after it had disappointed its long-term investors, the 97-year-old billionaire blamed the "old management," but said they were not "consciously malevolent or thieving but had terrible judgment in creating a culture of cross-selling." He put this down to error of judgement:

> "I think I'm a little more lenient. I expect less out of bankers than [Buffett] does … The kind of executives that have a Buffett-like

mindset that never get in trouble are a minority group. There's a lot of temptation to do dumb things, which will make the earnings next quarter go up, but are bad for the long term. Some bankers yield to the temptations."[45]

Warren Buffett had misjudged the character of the later leaders at Wells Fargo. When they strayed and covered their tracks with platitudes about customer focus, Buffett was at first unable to detect the cultural deterioration. He places a great deal of trust in key managers. This instinctive stance usually works very well for Berkshire, because the selected corporate leaders respond positively to both being treated as trustworthy and the autonomy it brings. Occasionally hindsight will show that trust to be undeserved and Berkshire will suffer poor returns.

Learning points

1. **When Mr Market rejects an entire sector, the true value investor thinks independently.** Look for sound companies expected to produce high cash flows for shareholders over the long run, as Buffett did when buying Wells Fargo shares in the period 1989 to 1996.

2. **The decisive factor in an investment decision is often a positive qualitative evaluation of the ability of key managers and whether they are shareholder oriented.** Buffett had confidence in the quality of Wells' loan book and its relationships with customers because he trusted the judgement of those who had created those loans and relationships. Reichardt and Hazen believed their role to be the production of high returns for shareholders.

3. **Value investors celebrate when share prices fall.** Decline permits the acquisition of small pieces of good businesses, shares of future income, at even more reasonable prices.

4. **Look for banks which adopt and fully implement sound principles.** In the case of Wells Fargo, this included constant bearing down on costs; disciplined risk management; genuine customer care based on a culture of integrity and professionalism (most of the time); and sticking within a circle of competence.

5. **More of a good thing can be wonderful.** If the economic franchise is intact, the company is generating high returns on tangible capital and the shares are available at a reasonable price, then buying more is smart.

6. **A good reputation takes a lifetime to build and can be lost in a heartbeat.** The hard work of generations of Wells managers creating its reputation for fair dealing was sacrificed for short-term financial targets.

7. **Cultural deterioration must be nipped in the bud.**

Investment 2

USAIR

Summary of the deal

Deal	USAir
Time	1989–1998
Price paid	$358m
Quantity	Convertible preferred stock with a 9.25% annual dividend. Convertible rights to 9.2m common stock (12% of USAir's shares)
Sale price	More than $358m (exact amount undisclosed)
Profit	A double-digit percentage annual return
Berkshire Hathaway in 1989	Share price: $4,700–8,825 Book value: $4,927m Per share book value: $4,296

At one point, Warren Buffett wrote down this investment by 75% and spoke of his bitter regret at having placed Berkshire's money in an industry with such poor economics. He was smarting so much that two years into the investment he said, "Despite the huge amounts of equity capital that have been injected into it, the industry, in aggregate, has posted a net loss since its birth after Kitty Hawk ... it would have been far better if Orville had failed to get off the ground at Kitty Hawk: The more the industry has grown, the worse the disaster for owners."[46]

Three years after that, with things looking even worse: "I have an 800 number now which I call if I ever get an urge to buy an airline stock. I say, 'My name is Warren, I'm an air-aholic' and they talk me down."[47]

Even into the twenty-first century Buffett was feeling the sting. In a 2002 interview with the London newspaper *The Telegraph*, he said: "If a capitalist had been present at Kitty Hawk back in the early 1900s, he should have shot Orville Wright."

And yet a few years later, in 2016, he went back into airlines in a big way, buying around 10% of the common stock of the four largest American airline companies, paying a total of between \$7bn and \$8bn. And he was caught out again – this time because the economics of the industry were hit dreadfully hard by the Coronavirus pandemic and its aftermath, when people refused to fly. (He managed to salvage about \$6bn by selling all those shares in April 2020.)

It would be harsh to criticise Buffett for not allowing for the virus-affliction in 2020. But we can all learn lessons – as he did – from the mistake of investing in USAir in 1989. Back then, the appalling economics of the industry were widely known, with massive over-capacity and cut-throat pricing. And USAir was in a particularly weak position vis-à-vis its larger competitors. Why did he do it?

The making of USAir

In 1937, newly-formed All American Aviation was undertaking daring experiments, swooping its single engine high-wing monoplanes down to grab mail packages suspended from ropes or cables strung across two poles (using a hook). By 1939, they were ready to roll out their airmail pick up service from their Pittsburgh hub, across the Allegheny Mountain Range and down the Ohio River. It wasn't until 1949 that the firm offered a passenger service in the same region.

In 1957, a 31-year-old lawyer joined the company – by then renamed Allegheny Airlines – as assistant to the president and to act as staff attorney. Ed Colodny had spent three years with the regulator, the Civil Aeronautics Board, and so was a game keeper turned poacher; he knew his way around the rules of the highly regulated industry.

Investment 2. USAir

Over two decades, the airline grew through mergers, something that was encouraged by a regulator keen to reduce subsidies handed out to the industry. By the time Colodny was put in charge of the firm as CEO in 1975, the airline business consisted of 12 major trunk airlines, serving larger cities and longer routes, and 12 local service airlines, including Allegheny, which served smaller cities.

As a well-liked and approachable chief, Colodny quickly acquired the sobriquet 'Uncle Ed' around the hangers and offices. Both longstanding employees and those added through acquisitions appreciated their generous wage and benefit package. Colodny really believed that employees were the firm's most important assets: "They're the ones who run the airline. People like myself don't fly airplanes, maintain airplanes, check luggage, or take care of passengers."[48] Even a union official sung his praises: "Ed Colodny was extremely employee friendly. He could meet a flight attendant one time and five years later he would know their name."[49]

In 1979, this profitable airline – now called USAir – was flying hundreds of routes stretching from Canada to the Gulf of Mexico, and from Vermont and Boston down to Florida. It was turning over $729m and making a healthy $33m net income. Shareholder equity was a mere $216m, so it was also making a reasonably good return on equity. At the time its route network was overwhelmingly east of the Mississippi, with just a couple of spokes to Houston and Phoenix.

Momentous change was about to hit the US passenger airline business following the 1978 deregulation of the industry, which resulted in the lifting of barriers to entering the industry and to particular routes and fare restrictions. A silver lining was that greater freedom of entry and exit of routes allowed USAir to expand across the US. On the other hand, it permitted both existing rivals and start-ups to invade the routes USAir was until then serving peacefully and generating good margins from.

As new airlines entered, both the legacy groups and brash start-ups tended to adopt hub-and-spoke systems whereby passengers were taken to a hub airport from a number of outlying airports – the spokes; they then boarded a different plane for the longer-distance flight.

Fares naturally fell as competition heated up. But at least an increase in passenger numbers compensated for that through the 1980s. Indeed, USAir made profits every year up to the time Warren Buffett took an interest in 1989. Returns on capital employed weren't outstanding, but they were good enough.

Colodny's strategy was to 'bulk up', fearing that if he didn't keep up with the big boys in the industry his firm would be vulnerable to being dominated and subservient. This prompted some large deals, including the merger with San Diego-based Pacific Southwestern Airlines in 1987 and one with Piedmont in 1989 (based in Winston-Salem, North Carolina). The latter being the largest deal the industry had seen to that point. The machine Uncle Ed created then offered 5,000 daily flights to 134 airports. Net income in 1988 was $165m on $5.7bn revenue.

However, the very profitability of the business in the 1980s planted the seeds for its near destruction in the coming years. This is because USAir's directors maintained their admiration for and friendship with colleagues throughout the organisation, and provided relatively generous compensation – making it one of, if not the, highest cost operators. This was not a good position to be in when no-frills low-cost operators were poised to take those customers searching for the lowest priced ticket. USAir prided itself on superior service and highly motivated, welcoming employees; the thought being that such differentiation would continue to allow premium prices to be charged.

On top of high fixed costs and high overall running costs, the Piedmont merger, which had doubled the size of the company, ran into a culture clash. USAir folk perceived "emotional resistance"[50] among the former Piedmont people, who resented USAir's people and operating procedures being imposed, and the loss of their identity. Colodny recognised that from a "cultural standpoint, there were differences".[51]

Under attack

Carl Icahn, an activist investor, had gained control of Trans World Airlines (TWA) in 1985 and immediately started calling Colodny to push for the joining of TWA and USAir. "He used to get on the phone and we'd go on for 30 or 40 minutes at a time. He would say we pay employees too much ... and if we merged with TWA he could force us to take the same wage cuts TWA had put on their employees. I told him that, in that case, he would have a lot of very unhappy employees providing very bad service."[52]

Icahn tried to stop the Piedmont merger, finally sending a letter to Colodny on the day the USAir board and the Piedmont board were due to meet to approve the start of the deal process (4 March, 1987). In it he offered to buy USAir for $1.64bn ($52 cash for each of USAir's 31.56m common shares). TWA was already USAir's largest shareholder and Icahn indicated that if his "friendly" deal could not be agreed, he was prepared to go hostile.

Very quickly, Colodny obtained a court order preventing TWA from acquiring more USAir stock.[53] The deal with Piedmont was sealed and TWA withdrew its offer. Before the end of the month, TWA had sold its USAir holding for $180m, having previously paid $178m.

One raider had been stopped but more were waiting in the wings. Michael Steinhardt's $1.3bn fund, with a reputation for aggressive trading, bought a 5.89% stake in July 1989 and seemed poised to mount a hostile takeover bid. Steinhardt's public statements, such as "we might consider seeking control of the rapidly growing airline", didn't help the mood at USAir HQ.

The directors felt the need for defences. One poison pill they approved was to grant the right to existing shareholders to buy USAir shares at *below market price* if a potential raider acquired 20% or more of the group. They also authorised a repurchase of up to 5m shares.

In response, Steinhardt simply bought more stock. Clearly the actions by USAir's board were not enough, they needed a 800lb gorilla to see off Steinhardt.

Buffett, the white squire (or gorilla)

A friend suggested that Colodny go and talk to Warren Buffett, who just might be willing to protect the company/managers from a hostile raid. He made the journey to Omaha with CFO, William Lotus, joining Buffett for lunch at his favourite steakhouse, Gorat's. "We spent a couple of hours talking about the airline, a very friendly casual conversation, and I had a great T-bone steak", recalls Colodny.[54]

Then they got down to business. Buffett was interested in putting Berkshire's money into USAir, but not in the form of common stock – he was fully aware of the growing competitiveness of airlines and considered preferred stock a safer option. Two weeks later they had a deal. On 7 August, USAir sold Berkshire $358m of ten-year convertible preferred stock, paying 9.25% per year.

To reassure USAir's directors that Buffett would not turn raider, he agreed not to participate in any takeover of the airline and pledged not to control more than a 14% voting stake without first obtaining USAir directors' approval. Furthermore, he was denied the ability to dispose of stock without first giving the company or its designee a reasonable opportunity to purchase. In return, Buffett was granted the right to elect two directors.

After two years, the preferred stock could be converted into common stock at $60 a share (in the fall of 1989 the common stock was trading around $52). If converted, they would constitute 12% of the company. Thus, the directors secured a constrained and friendly large shareholder – big enough to be off-putting to all those Wall Street aggressors, and without the threat of Berkshire wanting complete control.

Graeme Browning of *The Washington Post* thought Buffett shrewd, "In securing a 9.25% dividend payment on his USAir preferred and convertible stock at a time when other companies are paying several points lower, Buffett essentially paid a discounted price in return for acting as a friendly investor – or 'white squire'– as such an investor has been called on Wall Street."[55]

Buffett liked the investment, but knew it was not going to produce the exciting level of return he would get if he could put the same money into a common-stock investment in an unappreciated business with wonderful economic prospects. Mediocre returns were all that could be expected if "industry economics hinder the performance".[56] And such hinderance seemed distinctly possible in the rivalrous airline sector. But at a time when common stock bargains were rare, at least Berkshire had put $358m of its money to some use.

He did allow himself to hope that the USAir preferred stock might produce a reasonably attractive return if industry conditions were not too harsh:

> "Under almost any conditions, we expect these preferreds to return us our money plus dividends. If that is all we get, though, the result will be disappointing, because we will have given up flexibility and consequently will have missed some significant opportunities that are bound to present themselves during the decade. Under that scenario, we will have obtained only a preferred-stock yield during a period when the typical preferred stock will have held no appeal for us whatsoever. The only way Berkshire can achieve satisfactory results from its four [convertible] preferred issues is to have the common stocks of the investee companies do well."[57]

The track record of 13 years uninterrupted profits at USAir and the prospect of synergies by combining the original USAir with Pacific Southwest and Piedmont supplied reasons to believe that there were some strong positive profit forces countering the overall industry economics.

Buffett was convinced that a combination of good USAir management and the presence of a large, stable and interested shareholder, whose chairman and vice chairman each had a very significant proportion of their net worth's committed to USAir through their Berkshire holding, would benefit all USAir shareholders.

Furthermore, as a responsible dominant holder, he promised that both his and Munger's interactions with the company, and with the other companies in which Berkshire held preferred stock, will be "supportive, analytical, and objective … We recognize that we are working with experienced CEOs who are very much in command of their own businesses but who nevertheless, at certain moments, appreciate the chance to test their thinking on someone without ties to their industry or to decisions of the past."[58]

Unfortunately, Buffett's optimism proved to be misplaced.

Kamikaze pricing

It took only months after Berkshire had bought into USAir for the airline's managers to indicate that losses were on their way for both 1989 and 1990. That news sent the common stock to around $30, far below the $60 required to make it worthwhile for Berkshire to convert the preferred stock to common.

Writing his 1990 letter, wrapping his embarrassment in irony, Buffett told his shareholders that in making the USAir purchase he had "displayed exquisite timing: I plunged into the business at almost the exact moment that it ran into severe problems". He added that no one had pushed him; in tennis parlance, "I committed an 'unforced error'". Almost everything that could go wrong went wrong:

- **Low morale**

    The resentments of ex-Piedmont employees kept coming to the boil. "An affliction I should have expected since almost all airline mergers have been followed by operational turmoil",[59] mused Buffett.

    The resulting operational and service hiccups caused USAir to fall so far from grace that it was ranked as the worst in the industry for on-time performance. Ed Colodny, acknowledging the problems, told the *Washington Post* in September 1990: "When the economy is growing, growth covers up a lot of sins."[60]

- **Increasingly commoditised industry structure**

    Buffett blamed the "kamikaze pricing tactics of certain carriers"[61] for accelerating the deterioration in airline industry economics. It was impossible for any airline to escape the downward pressure on fares because the flying public can easily observe numerous rivals each desperate for their dollar – airlines tend to offer much the same service and therefore passengers shop around for low prices.

    When some in the industry are stupid enough to offer prices below operational costs it's difficult for more rational players to stand apart and try to sell tickets at higher prices. "The trouble this pricing has produced for all carriers illustrates an important truth: In a business selling a commodity-type product, it's impossible to be a lot smarter than your dumbest competitor."[62]

Bankruptcy law made matters worse because airlines continued to operate under bankruptcy court protection, including reducing or eliminating their previous debt burden. Thus surplus capacity was not eliminated and, relieved of the cost of debt, the zombie companies tended to price fares aggressively.

- **Fatal crash**

  On 20 September, 1989, an inexperienced pilot overran the runway on take-off at LaGuardia airport, resulting in 21 injuries and two deaths. There was plenty of bad publicity and employee morale was damaged.

- **Recession**

  To squeeze inflation in 1989, the Federal Reserve pushed up interest rates. This resulted in the real estate boom going into reverse and widespread loss of business and consumer confidence, followed by recession.

  The poor outlook was worsened by oil prices more than doubling following Iraq's invasion of Kuwait on 2 August, 1990. The combination of higher fuel costs and slackened consumer demand was a dreadful mix. Recently-added airline capacity was met with little or no growth in demand, resulting in carriers facing the dilemma of flying empty or battling to fill seats with discounted fares.

USAir cut its workforce by 7% and implemented other cost-saving measures but still it racked up losses both in 1989 ($63m) and in 1990 ($454m). Of course, common stock nosedived all the way to $14.

Despite the troubled first year, Buffett – writing in February 1991 – was convinced that "our investment should work out all right", but he acknowledged it was less secure than at the time he made it.

Things can only get worse

1990 was a bad year, but 1991 was terrible. In fact, it was the worst year in the history of the airline business. Big beasts were forced into bankruptcy, including Pan Am, TWA, Continental, Midway and America West. Some were kept alive and then they too lowered fares so much that airlines like USAir, which had not sought protection of the courts, were forced to price fares below cost.

Buffett recognised that the preferred shares were no longer worth the $358m Berkshire had paid for them and so he marked them down to $232.7m. He placed a high probability on the industry remaining unprofitable, worsened "by the fact that the courts have been encouraging bankrupt carriers to continue operating. These carriers can temporarily charge fares that are below the industry's costs because the bankrupts don't incur the capital costs faced by their solvent brethren and because they can fund their losses – and thereby stave off shutdown – by selling off assets. This burn-the-furniture-to-provide-firewood approach to fare-setting by bankrupt carriers contributes to the toppling of previously-marginal carriers, creating a domino effect that is perfectly designed to bring the industry to its knees."[63]

Fed up with the airline industry, Buffett couldn't resist making his now-famous jibe about the disfavour the Wright Brothers did for shareholders (notwithstanding the enormous social benefit coming from flying). Buffett was spitting feathers when he thought of the madness of the airline industry's lemming-like drive for yet more empty turnover when he wrote his 1992 letter:

> "Business growth, per se, tells us little about value. It's true that growth often has a positive impact on value, sometimes one of spectacular proportions. But such an effect is far from certain. For example, investors have regularly poured money into the domestic airline business to finance profitless (or worse) growth."

This observation led to some thoughts on what rational capital allocation looks like, both when conducted by an intelligent investor and by a corporate officer.

What is value?

When judging the value of a share, a bond or a business, Buffett encourages us to go back to basics as set out in John Burr Williams' book *The Theory of Investment Value* (1938). He endorses seeing value as being determined by estimated future cash inflows and outflows, with each forecast net cash flow for a period being discounted at an appropriate interest rate.

The logic of using discounted flows of cash applies to shares, where there is greater uncertainty over what cash will be generated in, say, five or ten years, as much as it does to bonds, with their defined payment amounts and dates.

Of course, the analyst has a tougher job estimating the cash attributable to shareholders than for bondholders. Equity flows are subject to significant variability due to a whole host of qualitative factors, from the morale of the workforce and the behaviour of competitors to customers changing preferences and the competence of managers. "The quality of management affects the bond coupon only rarely – chiefly when management is so inept or dishonest that payment of interest is suspended. In contrast, the ability of management can dramatically affect the equity 'coupons'."[64]

Despite the difficulties with equity valuation, it is better to think through the issues within the framework of discounted cash flow, with its forward focus and its discounting discipline, rather than lazily adopt measures such as multiplying last year's profits or, worse, using EBITDA or, more frighteningly, adjusted EBITDA.

Managers and discounted cash flow

In addition to investors valuing shares using the discounted cash-flow method, corporate managers should also apply it when considering growth in the company's asset base. This will bring them to a deeper understanding that "growth benefits investors only when the business in point can invest at incremental returns that are enticing – in other words, only when each dollar used to finance the growth creates over a dollar of long-term market value. In the case of a low-return business requiring incremental funds, growth hurts the investor."[65]

Airline growth was certainly hurting investors. Acutely so for the common stockholders, but it was also bad for preferred stockholders because operating losses were so poor that there was doubt that USAir would be able to maintain the preferred dividend, hence Buffett's estimated 35% drop in the value of Berkshire's holding to $232.7m.

Applying discounted cash-flow logic to building a portfolio

The investment to be bought is the one that is cheapest relative to its value determined by discounted-flows-of-cash calculation, "irrespective of whether the business grows or doesn't, displays volatility or smoothness in its earnings, or carries a high price or low in relation to its current earnings and book value."[66]

I've found to my cost the impossibility of disabusing many managers from the notion that their shareholders want turnover growth and earnings-per-share growth prioritised regardless of value creation. These managers often operate in industries where any newly allocated capital is destined to generate a rate of return which is both below the required rate of return in the stock market generally, and below the rate of return the company has generated in previous years on its current stock of capital. For example, the 200 stores it has been operating in California might produce, say, 40% returns on capital whereas retained earnings allocated to opening identical stores in Ohio would generate an unacceptable 2% per year because the franchise – the quality of the brand in people's minds – is weaker there.

So many managers feel the imperative to do something, to show that the company is moving forward – look turnover is up overall due to the opening of the Ohio stores, look earnings per share are up because of the extra profit from those stores, and book value is up, they say. They forget that investors could have gained a much better return on that Ohio money if it had been handed to them, maybe 8%, in the equity markets. Plainly, rational investors would far rather have spare cash distributed to them to allocate elsewhere than for it to be applied to projects with ever-decreasing rates of return below the opportunity cost of that money.

> "Leaving the question of price aside, the best business to own is one that over an extended period can employ large amounts of incremental capital at very high rates of return. The worst business to own is one that must, or will, do the opposite – that is, consistently employ ever-greater amounts of capital at very low rates of return. Unfortunately, the first type of business is very hard to find: Most high-return businesses need relatively little capital. Shareholders of such a business usually will

benefit if it pays out most of its earnings in dividends or makes significant stock repurchases."[67]

How do you simplify the complexity of estimating future cash which might flow to equity?

It's all very well saying that we should obtain intellectually-sound estimates of future cash flows and then discount them at the opportunity cost of capital, but for the investor this is often a daunting task. What is the cash flow of General Motors or Tesla going to be in five years from now? This is tough. Buffett has two suggestions for easing the burden.

1. **Stick to businesses you have a reasonable hope of understanding.**

   "That means they must be relatively simple and stable in character. If a business is complex or subject to constant change, we're not smart enough to predict future cash flows."[68] So your typical biotech company or Silicon Valley start-up is very difficult to understand, whereas companies with proven records in a stable environment such as Coca Cola or Disney are much more straightforward. You do not have to be knowledgeable about all industrial sectors; you need to know the boundaries of your knowledge base: "What counts for most people in investing is not how much they know, but rather how realistically they define what they don't know. An investor needs to do very few things right as long as he or she avoids big mistakes."

2. **Make sure the gap between your estimate of intrinsic value and Mr Market's price is large.**

   This allows for errors to be made in the estimation process and still for safety to be built in. "We insist on a margin of safety in our purchase price. If we calculate the value of a common stock to be only slightly higher than its price, we're not interested in buying. We believe this margin-of-safety principle, so strongly emphasised by Ben Graham, to be the cornerstone of investment success."[69]

The Seth Schofield years

Colodny's chosen successor, Seth Schofield, became chairman as well as CEO when Colodny retired in summer 1992. Schofield had come through the ranks, starting at 18 as a ramp agent: loading bags, selling tickets and boarding aircraft. He was a popular 'blue-collar guy' with a reputation for caring about his employees and a strong rapport with union bosses. Buffett really liked him and his actions:

> "Seth Schofield is making major adjustments in the airline's operations in order to improve its chances of being one of the few industry survivors. There is no tougher job in corporate America than running an airline: Airline managers need brains, guts, and experience – and Seth possesses all three of these attributes."[70]

But Summer 1992 was a bad time to take on the leadership of a firm which only weeks before had reported a massive $305m loss. It was still reeling from two fatal crashes[71] which sapped the spirit of employees and damaged the company's image with passengers. Even worse was the perennial problem of carrying much higher wage costs than competitors, and the unions' imposition of crippling work rules.

The unions had been faced down through the 1991 strike, but this was not enough to save USAir from continuing to report losses exacerbated by yet more strikes and yet more competition. The biggest blow was the entry of low-cost Southwest Airlines to Baltimore routes in 1993. They hammered fares. USAir, not to be outdone in its home market, pitched its tickets below Southwest, which prompted another round of fare reductions. The ratcheting-down didn't stop until it was only $19 to fly from Baltimore to Cleveland. Of course, the result was a lot of red ink. To make matters worse, Continental Airlines started offering low fares out of North Carolina. And American, Delta and United Airlines kept adding capacity and discounting fares too.

A helping hand from the Brits

Fully aware of growing losses and balance-sheet debt ballooning to $2.2bn, the board found a way of gaining some cash and customers. It agreed in 1993 to sell a 44% ownership stake to British Airways in return for $750m (BA's votes were limited to 21% due to federal rules on foreign investment).

This alliance brought together the largely domestically focused USAir, carrying 55m passengers annually, with the internationally focused BA, serving 24m flyers. Each airline could feed customers into the other's network, expanding the range of destinations to 77 countries, and they could integrate marketing and some other functions. Schofield said the deal will "ensure our survival".[72] Buffett agreed it would help it dodge bankruptcy and hoped the path was now "eventual prosperity".[73]

BA took four seats on USAir's board, and they considered it "particularly important"[74] that Buffett and Munger join the board too. Buffett thought that this fifth board position was more than he judged advisable when he was trying to concentrate on being an active CEO of Berkshire. But he nonetheless agreed to join saying, "there are times when large owners should do their bit."[75]

Even though Wall Street recognised the benefits of the BA deal and duly nudged up USAir's stock price, this was only temporary, as investors put much more weight on their worries of seemingly never-ending value-destroying industry economics. Thus, USAir's common stock was traded at a mere $14 – far below the $52 in 1989 when Berkshire bought the preferreds and even further below the conversion price of $60. Clearly, the value of the right to convert just got smaller and smaller as the airline reported losses in 1992, 1993 and 1994.

Value disappearing

Matters became so bad that in September 1994 USAir's board decided that it could not afford the dividend on the preferred stock issued to Berkshire Hathaway. Buffett and Munger faced reality and determined that the fair value of the preferred was now $89.5m – that is, 25 cents on the dollar of what they paid. Their reasoning was that such a low valuation reflected both a possibility that full value will one day be restored "and an opposite possibility that the stock will eventually become worthless".[76]

Fortune wrote in November 1994:[77]

> "Quick: What's the fastest way to become a millionaire in the airline business? Answer: Start with a billion. So goes a joke from Warren Buffett, who, by *Fortune's* estimate, is sitting on a paper loss of about $200m on his $358m investment in the embattled USAir Group."

Because Buffett was then a famously successful investor his misstep with USAir caused quite a stir in the investment community – perhaps he wasn't invincible after all? Had the old man really lost it? At 65, perhaps he should retire?

He poked fun at himself. In response to students' question as to why he had invested in USAir (at Columbia University) he quipped: "My psychologist asks me that too. Actually, I have an 800 number now which I call if I ever get an urge to buy an airline stock. I say: 'My name is Warren, I'm an air-aholic' and they talk me down."[78]

He may have joked in public, but behind the scenes he was furious that USAir had failed to lower costs to give it at least a fighting chance to make a profit – it spent 10.5 cents for each available seat-mile on its flights compared with 6.5 cents at some other operators. He threatened that he and Charlie would resign from the board if the executives failed to win concessions from the unions. It needed to slice $1bn out of its overhead to have a hope, with $500m coming from labour (estimated by *Fortune*).

It was plain to all – analysts, journalists, shareholders, executives and many rank-and-file employees – that unless costs were lowered the company would sail into the sunset. And yet the pilots' union just kept demanding more. Then, in the autumn yet another fatal crash resulted in months of diminished ticket sales as worried flyers avoided the airline perceived as having a poor safety record.

A confession of investor failure

An exasperated Buffett wrote in his 1994 letter to Berkshire shareholders his list of 'mistakes du jour', which he would've liked to pass off as Charlie's but "whenever I try to explain things that way, my nose begins to grow".[79] Top of the list was his $358m purchase of USAir preferred stock. This error was the result of his "sloppy analysis". This was put down to the fact that he was purchasing a more "senior" security (safer than common stock) or to his own "hubris".

He kicked himself for paying insufficient attention to the problems bound to beset an airline with high costs that were extremely difficult to lower. In the 1970s, these costs were not too much of a problem because the carriers were protected from competition by regulation and so could pass on the extra expense to customers.

Even in the 1980s, the newly formed low-cost competitors were small and attacking only a few routes, allowing the legacy companies to continue with profitable pricing in their home markets. But "during this period, with the longer-term problems largely invisible but slowly metastasizing, the costs that were non-sustainable became further embedded".[80]

The problem was made worse by bankruptcy laws which allowed bust carriers a fresh start with lowered debt, "as Herb Kelleher, CEO of Southwest Airlines, has said: 'Bankruptcy court for airlines has become a health spa.'"[81]

The real trouble came in the early 1990s, as the capacity of the low-cost operators grew to be enormous and fares fell across the nation. "In an unregulated commodity business, a company must lower its costs to competitive levels or face extinction. This principle should have been obvious to your Chairman, but I missed it."[82]

By spring 1995 they had had enough, and Charlie and Warren stated their intention to resign from USAir's board. "Should Seth wish to consult with us, however, we will be pleased to be of any help that we can".[83]

The turnaround

Having presided over losses accumulating to $2.4bn in five years, Seth Schofield led the company back to profits in 1995. But unfortunately he had still not gained enough concessions from the intransigent unions to give any surety of future profits. The *Washington Post* commented that ironically the first sight of a profit became a problem because when the airline began to make money, "the union membership saw less need to grant concessions."[84] Schofield was constantly up against this catch-22. Through much of 1995 Buffett tried to sell Berkshire's preferred stock at 50% of face value but couldn't find any takers.

In September 1995, with the common stock down to $8, a frustrated Schofield resigned as chairman and CEO. A few months later there was yet another blow: British Airways was forming an alliance with American Airlines, tying up the lucrative US-London market and excluding USAir. AA and BA were to share passengers; coordinate fares, schedules and ticketing; and pool profits on some routes.

The people at USAir felt betrayed and sued to break its deal with BA. The arrangement had, after all, bought BA a great deal of power in the US boardroom but little for USAir in the way of access to European markets, as BA blocked its efforts to go there. Acrimonious divorce proceedings slogged their way through 1996.

The leadership of USAir was taken up by Stephen M. Wolf in January 1996. A former chairman of United Airlines, Wolf was determined that USAir would no longer muddle along as a medium-sized airline with high costs and negative margins. It would either shrink back to being a regional carrier or, his preferred option, modernise and grow to become major global competitor with the most up-to-date fleet, manageable costs and profitable routes.

These are the options he presented to the unions. To show what he was aiming at with the growth option, he made arrangements to buy 400 new jetliners from Airbus worth $15bn over the following decade, replacing the hodgepodge fleet of older planes from several manufacturers (the old fleet was expensive because each type required separate maintenance procedures, spare parts inventories and crew training).

So this was the shiny new vision of the future that pilots, cabin crew and ground staff were invited to gaze upon. And as they excitedly pondered that sunny picture, the wily Wolf completed his offer: the planes were on order but could be cancelled at the drop of a hat. If the unions refused to be reasonable then Wolf would take the firm in the opposite direction, resulting in closed routes and massive redundancies. The choice was theirs: be reasonable on salaries, work rules, etc. (for example, pilots were on $120,000 per year on average), or risk seeing most of your colleagues disappear.

Oh, and there was a third option: Wolf let it be known that he was in discussions with both United and American Airlines to sell the company to one of them. Do you, union leader, want to be run by their executives, who might have a view on cutting overlapping routes following a merger?

Wolf was looking for annual $500m concessions to lower costs per available seat from the highest in the industry, at 12.69 cents, to nearer Southwest's 7.5 cents.

The blink

Negotiations dragged on so, in early spring 1997, Wolf warned that he would begin laying off pilots and other employees unless agreement had been reached by 30 June. If things were still not headed in the right direction after June, then on 30 September, when Airbus will demand affirmation of the order or cancellation, Wolf would recommend withdrawal.

The *Washington Post* wrote: "The moment of truth is at hand. Wolf has determined that the carrier cannot make its aircraft purchase without cost cuts that would allow it to compete with new low-cost rivals that are blanketing its core markets in the East".[85]

In April, Jim Gardner, a spokesman for US Airways (it had recently changed its name) pilots' union told the *Washington Post* that "the pilots share management's belief that the only path for the company is to grow, not downsize."[86] Despite this desire, they still would not permit changes to allow US Airways to compete with Southwest and others.

Wolf pointed at a list of defunct airlines that waited too long to save themselves by negotiating concessions, but still the standoff continued.

A 'consolidation programme' was revealed in May involving the closure of three maintenance facilities and two reservation centres, and the loss of flights to nine cities. Buffett tried to cajole in a public statement in May, "If the labor groups have the will, I know management has the ability to make this airline into the global competitor everyone wants it to be."[87]

Finally, in July 1998, the unions blinked: the pilots overwhelmingly approved a new pay scale and to run operations more efficiently. The following day, Wolf pressed ahead with the order of the first 30 A330s to follow through on his plan to compete in the transatlantic market. The common stock jumped to $73.

The preferred stock now had value in its $60 conversion right. Also, the skipped dividends were made up. Furthermore, because of the lateness in paying the dividends, US Airways was obliged by a term shrewdly inserted by Buffett and Munger when the preferreds were issued to add compensatory payments.

> "The resuscitation of US Airways borders on the miraculous. Those who have watched my moves in this investment know that I have compiled a record that is unblemished by success. I was wrong in originally purchasing the stock, and I was wrong later, in repeatedly trying to unload our holdings at 50 cents on the dollar."[88]

As always Buffett praised his key manager: "Two changes at the company coincided with its remarkable rebound: 1) Charlie and I left the board of directors and 2) Stephen Wolf became CEO. Fortunately for our egos, the second event was the key: Stephen Wolf's accomplishments at the airline have been phenomenal."[89]

The preferreds were called by US Airways for redemption 15 March, 1998. In spring 1998 Buffett wrote in his Berkshire letter that "It is now almost certain that our US Airways shares will produce a decent profit ... and the gain could even be indecent ... hefty." He has not publicly disclosed the dollar gain, but we can surmise that it amounts to an annual gain of more than 9.5%. On top of annual dividends, US Airways would have paid Berkshire Hathaway the value of the conversion rights, so the annual return would have been well into double percentage figures.

Buffett's conclusion was that they got very lucky. "In one of the recurrent, but always misguided, bursts of optimism for airlines, we were actually able to sell our shares in 1998 for a hefty gain. In the decade following our sale, the company went bankrupt. Twice."[90]

Shareholder value destroyed completely

In the two years after Berkshire's sale of its preferred shares, US Airways' common stock dwindled to $26 from a peak of $83 in 1998. Then the 11 September, 2001, Twin Tower attacks reduced passenger demand and the company entered Chapter 11 bankruptcy in 2002, exiting it 2003.

Failing to cut enough costs, it again entered bankruptcy in 2004. In a greatly weakened state, in 2005 it merged with America West Airlines. The old US Airways shareholders did not fare well; they were shut out and lost all value, while its debtholders obtained 11% of the equity of the new group. But at least the US Airways brand lived on as it was used for the combined fleet.

In December 2013, American Airlines merged with US Airways to create the world's biggest airline. In the same year Buffett told Berkshire shareholders at the annual meeting that "Investors have poured their money into airlines and airline manufacturers for 100 years with terrible results. [The industry is] a death trap for investors."

Ed Colodny, then aged 89, flew on the last flight branded as US Airways on Friday 16 Oct, 2015. A year later, Berkshire Hathaway bought stakes in the four largest American carriers, including American Airlines. These investments, and the thinking behind them, are a story for another chapter.

Learning points

1. **If the industry economics are appalling, then walk away.** Despite the excellent yield on the preferred stock Buffett came close to losing the entire investment because intensified rivalry caused severe operating losses.
2. **Industry economics can change, so you need to keep up to date.** In the 1980s/90s, the impetus for change was regulatory; in 2020, it was a virus. Other potential causes are social shifts (e.g., greening), technological disruption (e.g., online conferencing) and economic (e.g., relative costs of manufacturing and shipping for different countries).

3. **Mergers often lower shareholder value.** Mergers bring many opportunities for things to go wrong, such as staff resentment and overpaying.

4. **Growth is not important, value is.** Many company directors feel it is their duty to grow the top line (revenue) and expect that to feed through to large increases in the bottom line. But lots of growth destroys value. The key factor is the amount of shareholder money needed to achieve growth relative to the earnings that it generates. Often the present value of all the incremental earnings is much less than the amount taken from shareholders to satisfy managerial growth goals. The airline industry was even worse than that: shareholder money was used, but losses were generated on existing and incremental capital devoted.

5. **Value is the estimated future cash inflows and outflows with each forecast net cash flow discounted at a discount rate that allows for risk of the venture/asset.** The investor looks for the cheapest asset relative to its value.

6. **Be familiar with your circle of competence.** What counts for most investors is not how much they know, but how realistically they define the boundaries of what they do and don't know.

Investment 3

AMERICAN EXPRESS

Summary of the deal

Deal	American Express
Time	1991–Present
Price paid	1991: $300m ($21.43 per share) 1994: $423.9m ($30.81 per share) 1995: $669m ($30.83 per share) 1998: $77m ($71.57 per share)
Quantity	1991: "A modified form of common stock" bought. These "PERCS" were converted to 14m common stock in 1994. 1994: additional 13.8m of common stock (taking total to 5.5% of Amex) 1995: 21.7m bought (taking total to 10%) 1998: 1.08m bought (Total: 11.3%) Berkshire's now has 18.8% of Amex following buy backs
Sale price	Still held
Profit	Over 2,000%, and counting
Berkshire Hathaway in 1991	Share price: $6,550–9,100 Book value: $7,380m Per share book value: $6,437

What attracted 33-year-old Warren Buffett to American Express in 1964 was the undeniable strength of its business model and the quality of the brand in the minds of customers. These franchise qualities persisted despite the loss of a significant sum in an obscure branch of the company – a fraudster had left American Express with a $60m bill to pay (volume one, investment eight). Buffett turned a $13m investment (5% of Amex and one-third of the Partnership's fund) into about $33m.

A similar logic applied in the early 1990s when Buffett, not slowing one jot as he approached the standard retirement age, put a big chunk of Berkshire Hathaway's money to use. Amex had muddled through years of wasting money on ventures outside of the core business of charge cards, travellers' cheques and related services, and now faced the growing competitive might of Visa and Mastercard.

Mr Market viewed the company with suspicion, wondering how it could stem the bleeding from some of its arms, and doubtful that it had the leadership to come up with a credible plan.

And yet underneath the rubble was the ever-shining high-quality franchise. Cardmembers remained loyal, still liking the convenience of carrying the card, drawn by the psychic benefit of membership to a special club of cardholders, linking their sense of self (having 'made it') with the brand, and still valuing the imprimatur of American Express on a range of other financial services. Holidaymakers and executives trusted Amex's travellers' cheques to deliver when they pitched up at any one of thousands of places around the globe.

Wall Street focused on the recent blunders; Buffett saw the franchises.

Wall Street looked at immediate numbers; Buffett peered to see where the profit levels could be in ten and 20 years given the right steer.

Wall Street examined the company's shape as it was; Buffett saw that its firm foundations, built on a reputation for integrity and service, would allow focused expansion within America and globally.

It's all about the economic franchises

By the 1990s, American Express had built two major franchises, both of which were based on customers' need to pay for goods and services in a safer and more efficient way than carrying cash.

The card franchise

The American Express charge cards, first used in 1958, evolved to solve a number of problems.

First, people with the income or wealth to spend above-average amounts on restaurant meals, hotels, clothes and flights needed a way of paying which did not involve carrying hundreds of dollars around. It is so much more convenient to pay with a card when at home or abroad for goods, experiences, or services, and then to receive an itemised bill from Amex to pay the outstanding amount a month or so later. It's all the better if everyone knows that American Express would only grant such a card to a person of some standing in terms of financial status and reliability – it doesn't hurt one's self-esteem to flash a card with such exclusive cache.

Then there are merchants – the hotels, shops, car-rental outfits, airlines, etc. – faced with the problem of attracting the higher-spending holders of the American Express card. They knew that Amex would charge them a hefty percentage (e.g., Amex would reimburse the amount of a purchase minus 2.5% or so), but that was okay if offering to accept the Amex card would make the difference between making a sale or losing it. Retailers refusing the card take a gamble that an executive looking to buy a couple of suits might just walk down the street to another shop with a prominent sign in their window proclaiming: "American Express accepted here".

The third problem it solved was for business owners who suffered the administrative hassle that comes when hundreds of members of staff are encouraged to buy services or goods when out in the field or back at base. They welcomed the innovation of the corporate version of the American Express card, which could be handed to key employees who could then rack up expenses for hotel stays or office supplies over a month. The various costs were amalgamated by Amex and all the company had to do was pay the total in one go a month or so later. No more tedious paper for the salesforce to reclaim scores of expenses, nor for board executives as they criss-crossed the world.

Better yet, the companies (or employees) were given perks by American Express, the amount of which varies depending on spending levels; for example, 0.5% of spend is rebated in cash, or airmiles are accumulated.

The Membership Rewards Loyalty Program is a great draw for the general public as well as for corporates. They earn points when using the card which can then be redeemed on a broad range of goods and services, or cash.

Gold and platinum members obtain a wider range of benefits, from access to airport executive lounges and room upgrades to a line of credit, but Amex charges hundreds of dollars per year for such memberships compared with well under $100 for the standard card.

Cardholders could also benefit from the 'free' Business Travel Accident Insurance Plan or the Global Assist Hotline.[91] There is also Car Rental Loss and Damage Insurance Plan (cover for damage or theft, accidental injury, death, etc.) and the Purchase Protection Plan (reimbursement by Amex for items stolen or accidentally damaged within 90 days of purchase).

Buffett explained the importance of the card operations to American Express at Berkshire's 1995 AGM: it remains "synonymous with financial integrity and money substitutes around the world … By far the most important factor in [Amex's] future for a great many years to come will be the … card. We think American Express's management thinks well about … how to keep the card special."[92]

The travellers' cheque franchise

Before the invention of the travellers' cheque there was an awkward choice for those touring a foreign country when it came to paying for services such as a hotel stay: carry large amounts of cash or arrange letters of credit through your bank back home so that you could pick up cash or make payments through a local bank.

The first induced the fear of theft and the second was cumbersome and restrictive (you had to go to that bank).

An American Express employee invented the travellers' cheque in 1891. One hundred years later the company was the world's leading issuer. A book of travellers' cheques could be organised ahead of your trip. You hand over cash to American Express and they print the cheques in your name, which can be denominated in any one of dozens of currencies. When they arrive you sign each one.

Then, when you buy something abroad, you sign a cheque again in the presence of the hotelier, shop keeper, car rental company. They check that your two signatures match. These organisations have the reassurance of American Express's guarantee to pay, known the world over to be trustworthy.

Customers who lose their travellers' cheques, or have them stolen, may obtain a refund or replacement from American Express.

American Express benefits from the fees it charges buyers of travellers' cheques, from the exchange rate and from the cash float. The existence of a cash float was an intriguing quality of the company for Buffett – all that money collected from buyers of the cheques sitting within the company until they go abroad and spend the cheques and they are redeemed. At the very least it offered a great cash flow opportunity for the Group. On top of that, it could generate interest: the float was/is typically invested in safe sources of income (usually highly rated debt securities – primarily medium and long-term US government – or municipal notes and bonds).

The information edge

American Express serves millions of customers, and their spending patterns generate a mountain of data. Data crunching allows both a ratcheting-up of the service by tailoring offerings and the opportunity to sell customers new products and services. Amex has long segmented customers into groups based on a variety of characteristics, from income and lifestyle to food preferences and flying patterns, so that it can pitch services and goods appropriate to each.

The data helped Amex, even before the 1990s, to sell more consumer products than many major retailers. It also assisted the growth of a $150m publishing arm producing dozens of magazines. Then there was the substantial financial services division which used the information to cross-sell an array of products.[93] In the early 1990s, this division generated 22% of Group sales. It was called Investors Diversified Services (but later American Express Financial Advisors and later still spun off as Ameriprise Financial) and offered financial planning, wealth management, mutual funds, insurance, etc., through thousands of financial planners.

American Express Bank could also draw on the customer database to promote itself. While the bank only accounted for 5% of Group sales it had over 80 offices in 37 countries and acted as the local representative for other businesses. Its focus was on high-net-worth entrepreneurs.

Yet another business offered travel arrangements – trip planning, reservations, ticketing, trip expense management, etc. – similar to travel agents.

Reinforcing the franchises through a quality emphasis

For decades Amex employees have been inculcated in the culture of always striving to deliver the highest quality of service possible. James D. Robinson III, who led the company from 1977 to 1993 frequently stated: "Quality is the only patent protection we've got". He also liked to say: "Promise only what you can deliver and deliver more than you promise".

Robinson introduced quantitative measures of quality such as the number of seconds it takes to answer the phone (an average of seven seconds in the 1980s) and how many hours passed between a customer notifying Amex of a lost card and the replacement arriving (the standard was 48 hours even in the 1980s). In the same way that McDonald's set up the McDonald's Hamburger University, American Express established the Quality University.

Stories abound of staff going the extra mile to help a customer. Sometimes this is literal, as when a Boston employee got up in the middle of the night to deliver a card to a stranded customer at the airport.

This relentless attention to quality and extensive marketing (costing over $250m a year in the late 1980s – twice as much as Visa and Mastercard spent combined) resulted in American Express being one of the ten most recognised brands in the world by the 1990s. Positioned with an image of security, integrity and customer service, the brand was endowed with a competitive edge.

These factors allowed American Express cards to be highly profitable even in a world where Visa and Mastercard controlled over three-quarters of the card market. It could get away with obtaining half its revenue from merchants by charging them hefty 'discounts' on transactions. It could also ask customers to pay significant annual fees, while Visa and Mastercard did not. It leaned on its exclusive, prestigious brand – if you could get past the door then a great array of targeted services could be yours, as well as the satisfaction of being in an elite club. On average, members annually spent around four times that of the customers of Visa and Mastercard.

The network effect and economies of scale

American Express established a global payment network with tens of thousands of merchants offering to take its cards (in the early 1990s it operated in 160 countries and 32 currencies). This gave it an incumbency advantage. That, combined with continued improvements to the offering, made it extremely difficult for a new entrant to create a parallel network.

Also, the cumulative impact on the psychology of members or aspiring members of advertising and other brand building over decades was extremely difficult to compete against. And then the ecosystem of partnership programs with the likes of Delta, British Airways, Hilton Hotels, etc., built on reinforcing quality images and tailored discounts, would be hard for an entrant to replicate.

Blunders

The core American Express businesses threw off so much cash in the early 1980s that James D. Robinson III eyed an opportunity to create a 'financial supermarket', offering customers an increasing range of services. Surely, there would be synergies, not least from being able to market additional products to cardholders and travellers' cheque clients?

It stands to reason that customers would welcome access to half a dozen different services without needing to step outside the Amex family of companies. And surely there would be economies of scale in back-office work?

Thus it was, in 1981, that investment bank and retail brokerage firm Shearson Loeb Rhoades, the second largest securities firm in the US, was acquired for $932m. In 1983, the Swiss private bank, Trade Development Bank, was added for $550m. And, in 1984, Investor Diversified Services was bought for $790m.

To beef up even more, investment bank Lehman Brothers was purchased in 1984 for $360m, followed by E.F. Hutton, a retail brokerage house, for $962m in 1987.

That is a lot of spending for a $10–14bn market-capitalisation company.

Maybe not such a great strategy

Many of the once-fashionable financial-services conglomerates of the 1980s turned out to be failures. The American Express experiment was partially successful – for example, IDS was a good fit – but mostly there was disappointment.

The various parts did not mesh into a coherent whole. Executives at the card division did not want to tie their valuable brand to Shearson's investment banking adventures, suspicious that their buccaneering style and regular slip-ups would tarnish their image. They were also reluctant to hand over their precious customer list, created through patient relationship building, to Shearson's or Lehman's hard-selling transaction-focused guys.

Besides which, most cardholders quite liked shopping around for value in financial services, rather than buying all from one organisation.

The conglomerate became unwieldly. In the sprawl, division chiefs were allowed to grow their domains unimpeded, and power seeped from the centre. Some bosses, freed of constraint and with an over-abundance of self-confidence, made errors that had a large impact on the Group.

Losses sprung up at the insurance subsidiary, the Fireman's Fund, and at the Trade Development Bank, when risks were not carefully controlled. Shearson exposed the Group to enormous risks and losses, from underwriting gaffes and commercial real estate asset errors to poorly priced bridging loans and Latin American loan debacles.

So much was lost that Robinson was in no position to refuse to pump more money into Shearson to keep it afloat. And so much senior management attention was devoted to fire-fighting problems at various loss-making arms that the core card and travellers' cheque businesses were neglected.

Other ways of losing money

As if these problems were not enough, Group strategy included escapades into businesses that did not even offer financial services, such as the over-priced Beaver Creek Conference Centre and an art gallery.

And there was unethical behaviour, the Safra affair being an outstanding example. Edmond Safra was head of the Trade Development Bank when it was sold to Amex. He was led to believe that he could run the bank under the Amex umbrella in his way. However, two years later, in 1985, dissatisfied with the restrictions under which he had to operate, he resigned.

When Safra tried to establish a new bank, he became the subject of a smear campaign. To discredit him, Amex's people planted false rumours in newspapers. This unprofessional and unprincipled conduct received considerable press attention to the detriment of American Express's public image. An embarrassed and humbled American Express agreed to pay $8m to charities chosen by Safra in 1989, as well as offer an apology.

Then there was more intense competition from credit cards issued by a wide variety of organisations – led by Visa and Mastercard, but including powerful groups such as Sears (Discover Card), General Electric, Ford and AT&T – which made headway difficult for the Amex charge card or their credit card.

There were widespread protests about the merchant fees charged by Amex. These were led by the Boston Fee Party group of restaurants. In one particularly memorable episode, a chef stuck a knife through an

Amex card on national TV. Amex had been able to get away with high merchant fees because its cardholders spent so much more than holders of other cards, and so retailers etc., were particularly keen on their custom. But in the late 1980s, Amex arguably went too far and suffered 'suppression' as a result, meaning merchants would ask customers to use another card or cash. Amex lost market share.

Shareholders were not happy

John J. Byrne – the same 'Jack' Byrne who saved GEICO in 1976[94] – summarised the story of the 1980s when he spoke as a director of American Express in a September 1992 board meeting: "$3 billion to $4 billion of the shareholders' money had been lost during Robinson's tenure."[95]

So, despite the profits and high returns on capital flowing from the core businesses, the share price went nowhere over the eight years to the summer of 1991 – see figure 3.1.

Figure 3.1: American Express shares $ (summer 1983–summer 1991)

Buffett's two deals

The Shearson-Lehman losses and the worsening position in other parts of the business left American Express with a weakened financial structure. This led, in July 1991, to Standard and Poor's downgrading its senior debt from AA to AA-, sending a very negative signal about a company which had, in the past, been regarded as having a rock-solid business and balance sheet. Its cost of borrowing the money needed to grant grace periods to cardmembers rose, and financial markets were less receptive to its commercial paper, notes and securitisations.

By mid-July 1991, Robinson knew he had to do something to raise cash and improve the capital structure. He had to sell shares. Jack Byrne, attending American Express's finance committee, immediately thought of his friend Warren Buffett. Robinson agreed to Byrne's idea. Recalls Buffett: "I told Jack that I would be interested, and he had Jim call me."[96]

The conversation with Robinson went well and a week later (1 August) Berkshire Hathaway invested $300m in American Express (he would have invested up to $500m but Robinson was only looking for $300m). Buffett was fully aware of the historic strength of the franchise, but in 1991 he, like the rest of the investing community, was nervous about the pile of problems the company had made for itself. It had losses that needed stemming – if they were not stopped, they might overwhelm the Group.

More significantly, American Express was not as dominant as it once was. Rival credit card providers were growing rapidly with consumers attracted by the absence of an annual fee and long grace periods for cardholders to pay (naturally with a high interest rate attached). They also courted merchants with lower fees.

The uncertain future of the franchises left Buffett unable to commit to owning common stock in 1991. Instead, he bought an unusual type of preferred stock called PERCS – that is, preferred equity redemption cumulative stock. These carried a fixed dividend of 8.85%, which was high relative to what would have been available on standard preferred stock.

The PERCS had to be converted three years later into a *maximum* of 12.245m common shares of American Express.[97]

If, however, the market value of that common stock in August 1994 exceeded $414m, there would be a downward adjustment in the conversion ratio such that Berkshire would not receive more than $414m worth of shares.

Buffett laid out the reward profile of the PERCS in his 1991 letter: "Though there is thus a ceiling on the value of the common stock that we will receive upon conversion, there is no floor."

But at least the conversion date could be extended by one year if the common stock was below $24.50 on 1 August 1994 (this is the breakeven level: $24.50 × 12.245m shares = $300m).

It was unusual for Buffett to accept such limits on the upside, but Robinson was insistent. Buffett had few alternative avenues to invest money at this sort of rate of return (the dividend rate was raised precisely because of the loss of much upside) and he hoped that the franchise could be made yet stronger in the future.

He also had an attachment to the company that had helped him make a fortune and reputation a quarter of a century before. The Berkshire chairman joked in an *Omaha World-Herald* interview that Jim Robinson had not offered to let him pay for the transaction with his credit card.

While Buffett did not take up a board seat – perhaps because he was already on Salomon's board, a Wall Street rival – he told the *Associated Press* that he would "speak when spoken to".

The second deal

In August 1994, American Express mandatorily redeemed the PERCS through the issuance of 13,997,141 common shares to Berkshire (the additional shares, above the originally specified 12.245m were to compensate for the earlier spin-off of Lehman Brothers).

At this point, Buffett needed to make a decision: hold on to the 14m shares or sell them and invest in other opportunities. On the one hand "was Amex's outstanding CEO, Harvey Golub [Robinson's replacement], who seemed likely to maximize whatever potential the company had"[98] as well as the attraction of the franchise in the core business. On the other hand, "the size of that potential was in question: Amex faced relentless competition from a multitude of card-issuers, led by Visa."[99]

As Buffett weighed the arguments, he leaned toward sale. But during that month of pondering, he played golf with Frank Olson, CEO of Hertz.

> "Here's where I got lucky … Frank is a brilliant manager, with intimate knowledge of the card business. So from the first tee on I was quizzing him about the industry. By the time we reached the second green, Frank had convinced me that Amex's corporate card was a terrific franchise, and I had decided not to sell … I naturally feel very grateful to Frank. But George Gillespie, our mutual friend, says that I am confused about where my gratitude should go. After all, he points out, it was he who arranged the game and assigned me to Frank's foursome."[100]

Focus on the franchise restored – so Buffett buys more

Long before the golf game Buffett had observed a return to rationality.

First, there was a change at the top. After Robinson was pressed by investors and the board to resign, Harvey Golub stepped up to fill his position in February 1993. Golub was an experienced Amex man, having been boss of the very successful IDS Financial Services Division since 1984, and of the card and travellers' cheques businesses since November 1991. He had a three-part strategy:

1. build the core franchises, with a particular focus on the 'brand value' – music to Buffett's ears
2. raise money by selling underperforming divisions, and
3. cut costs.

Second, a bunch of non-core businesses were sold in rapid succession, raising billions. In April 1992, a 46% stake in First Data – the information service subsidiary (card processing operations for many card companies including Visa and Mastercard) – was sold in a public offering, raising almost $1.1bn. The next March saw the First Data stake reduced to approximately 22%, raising another $1.1bn.

In 1993, Shearson Lehman's retail brokerage and asset management business was sold for $1bn plus a portion of future profits from that business. And the Boston Company, a private banking, trust and mutual fund administration businesses, combined with Shearson Lehman Hutton Mortgage Corporation, which engaged in mortgage banking, was sold for $1.45bn.

In May 1994, the Lehman Brothers division was spun off to American Express's shareholders in a tax-free distribution (a special dividend: one share of Lehman for five of American Express). Prior to that, the company stated its 'investment' in Lehman was $2.4bn.

These actions were designed to achieve the targets Golub had set:

1. achieve an annual return on equity of 18–20%, and
2. increase earnings per share by 12–15% per year.

In 1995, the revitalised card business expanded to 27 countries. The company started the drive to strengthen its credit-card offering (branded the Optima card to distinguish it from the charge card) to compete with Visa and others. They also entered a foreign country, Britain, for the first time that year.

Sending money to shareholders

The third part of Golub's strategy must have been the clincher for Buffett because it gave insight into the degree to which the directors were shareholder oriented.

Between 1992 and 1994 the directors did so well in improving the core business, raising capital through non-core sales and cutting costs that American Express was clearly generating cash flow greater than that needed to maintain the economic franchise. And it looked as though it would continue to do so for as far as the eye could see.

Instead of hoarding the money or going on a wild spending spree of acquisitions – as far too many managers do – American Express quietly returned it to shareholders via the repurchase of common stock.

They understood their circle of competence and that any additional dollar invested must generate a good rate of return. The directors expressed their intent in the 1994 annual report:

> "To the extent retained earnings exceed investment opportunities, the Company will return excess capital to shareholders in the form of share repurchases. During 1994 the Company has moved from the point several years ago when it needed to strengthen its capital position to where the Company has the capital to support its credit ratings, fund growth opportunities in its core businesses and return capital to shareholders through a share buyback program."

The stream of cash to shareholders started in September 1994 with a buyback of 14.6m shares at an average of $30.37. Large repurchases have taken place in most years since, reaching as much as $1.89bn in 1998 and $4.6bn in 2019.

Berkshire becomes the largest shareholder

All these encouraging signs led to Buffett becoming increasingly convinced that American Express was on track to be a superb investment. In 1994, Berkshire not only held on to the 14m shares coming from the conversion of the PERCS, but bought a further 13.8m (average price $30.81). This raised Berkshire's stake to 5.5% of the company.

At $724m, Amex was Berkshire's largest spend on a non-controlled company except for the amount devoted to Coca-Cola, at $1,298m.

Then, in March 1995, BH bought another 21.7m shares at an average of $30.83, taking the holding to just shy of 10%. Buffett had spent $1,393m, more than even the Coca-Cola stake at the time.

Banking regulators take a dim view of non-banking organisations holding sway over a bank due to potential conflicts of interest (American Express's bank and other financial sector operations raised the possibility of Berkshire firms being offered preferential treatment on, say, loans). Berkshire pushed up against the threshold of what was considered an influential stake in 1995 and so Buffett felt obliged to weaken Berkshire's ability to exert control.

In February, he wrote a letter to Golub stating that "if Berkshire should acquire 10% or more of the voting securities of American Express ... (1) Berkshire will not dispose of any shares ... without the prior consent of American Express [to anyone who held more than 5%], (2) So long as Harvey Golub is Chief Executive Officer ... Berkshire shall vote ... in accordance with the recommendation of the Board of Directors."

Buying on the dip in 1998 after American Express was hit by the Asian financial crisis, BH topped up with another 1.08m shares, costing $77m. At $71.57 for each share, this was more than twice as much as previous purchases. The higher price was easily justified, given that 1998 was the sixth year in a row that the EPS growth target of 12–15% and return-on-equity target of 18–20% were exceeded.

A growing business

By the late 1990s, the directors had changed the dynamic of the business from expense reduction with low revenue growth to one with core business revenue growth rates ranging from 10–13%. They succeeded in encouraging a significantly increased use of Amex cards beyond travel and business to everyday spending at such places as gas stations, supermarkets, retailers, and for telecommunications.

Another shift: in 1995 just 4% of US card billings came from credit cards; by the end of the decade it was 19%.

The number of currency denominations of American Express cards rose to 50 in 1999 with 46m cards in force – see figure 3.2. Profit after tax grew from under $0.5bn in 1992 to almost $2.5bn in 1999 – see figure 3.3. The shares responded by rising six-fold over the 1990s – see figure 3.4.

Figure 3.2: Cards in force issued by American Express (m)

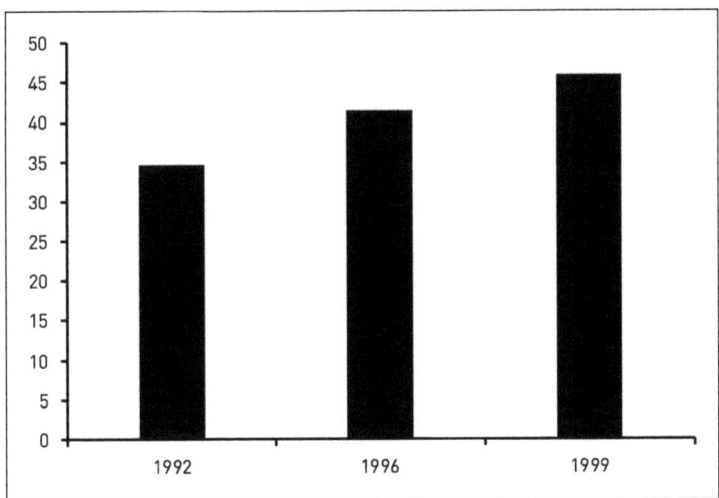

Source: American Express annual reports

Figure 3.3: American Express net income ($bn)

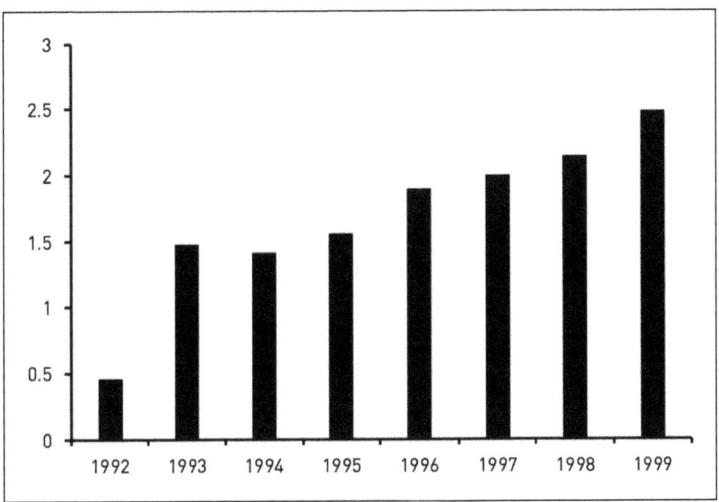

Source: American Express annual reports

Figure 3.4. American Express share price $ (July 1991–December 1999)

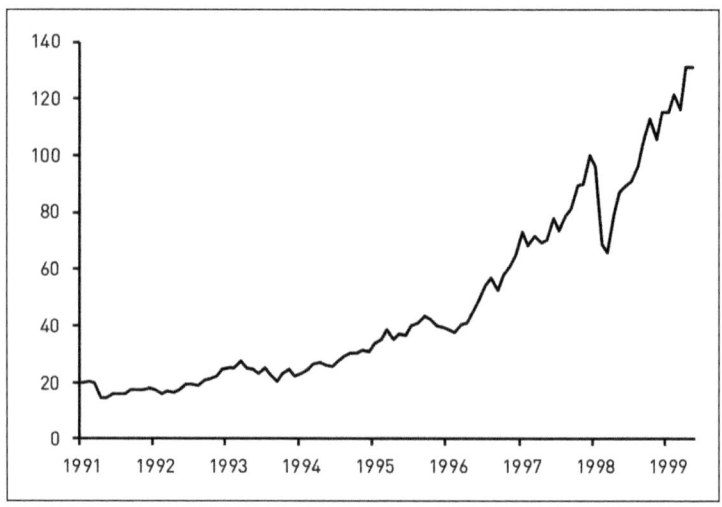

Source: ADVFN

Intrinsic value – a calculation based on perfect foresight

On 1 August, 1994, when Berkshire bought its first common stock in American Express, the company's market capitalisation was $12bn. Was Mr Market too optimistic, too pessimistic, or about right? To try to answer that I'll estimate annual owner earnings and from those derive possible intrinsic values.

In the following calculations I make a simplifying assumption, but one that is not too far from the truth: the amount American Express needed to spend annually on capital items and increases in working capital to maintain its economic franchise and volume and invest in value-adding projects amounted to roughly the same as the non-cash charges in the accounts (e.g., depreciation and amortisation).

With this assumption in place, owner earnings equals net income.[101] This allows us to estimate intrinsic value by using published net-income figures rather than making the adjustments to published earnings which might otherwise be necessary to obtain owner earnings estimates.

To calculate intrinsic value, the investor needs to look at the financial record of the company and its qualities in terms of strategic position and management to gauge likely earnings power in the future. This is a process Buffett went through in 1994 as he grasped for estimates of future owner earnings.

His starting point might have been observing 1993's owner earnings/net income of approximately $1.5bn and the expectation of $1.4bn for 1994. It is likely he also examined a number of years before that and separated income from the core economic franchise businesses and that of non-core activity, which often produced write-offs and losses.

If he took a conservative approach and assumed no change in future years, i.e., a perpetuity of say $1.4bn, and used a discount rate of 10%,[102] he would calculate an intrinsic value of $1.4bn/0.10 = $14bn, slightly higher than the $12bn market capitalisation.

But that estimate does not allow for the elimination of drag by selling the investment bank and brokerage businesses. If he could allow himself some optimism, imagining that the new managers would effectively refocus the business on its core and would raise capital by selling underperforming units, then perhaps owner earnings would rise from one year to the next. Let's assume an estimate of average annual growth of owner earnings of 5%.

In this case, estimated intrinsic value would be $1.4bn/(0.1 − 0.05) = $28bn, providing a very large margin of safety on the market price.

We have the benefit of hindsight as we know the net earnings *after* 1994 – see table 3.1. Our perfectly foresighted selves can use actual future owner earnings/net income to calculate intrinsic value in 1994. The final column of table 3.1 shows the present value of net income if discounted to 1994.

Table 3.1: American Express, net income, discounted net income

Year	Net income, $bn	Discount factor (10% per year)	Discounted net income, $bn – to present value in 1994
1995	1.56	0.9091	1.42
1996	1.90	0.8264	1.57
1997	2.00	0.7513	1.50
1998	2.14	0.6830	1.46
1999	2.48	0.6209	1.54
2000	2.81	0.5645	1.59
2001	1.31	0.5132	0.67
2002	2.67	0.4665	1.25
2003	2.99	0.4241	1.27
2004	3.45	0.3855	1.33
2005	3.73	0.3505	1.31
2006	3.71	0.3186	1.18
2007	4.01	0.2897	1.16
2008	2.70	0.2633	0.71
2009	2.13	0.2394	0.51
2010	4.06	0.2176	0.88
2011	4.94	0.1978	0.98
2012	4.48	0.1799	0.81
2013	5.36	0.1635	0.88
2014	5.89	0.1486	0.88
2015	5.16	0.1351	0.70
2016	5.41	0.1228	0.66
2017	2.75	0.1117	0.31
2018	6.92	0.1015	0.70

Year	Net income, $bn	Discount factor (10% per year)	Discounted net income, $bn – to present value in 1994
2019	6.76	0.0923	0.62
2020	3.14	0.0839	0.26
Assume perpetuity thereafter	6.76 (6.76/0.1) = 67.6	0.0839	5.67
Intrinsic value estimate in 1994 (total of discounted earnings)			$32bn

Source: American Express annual reports

Clearly, the conservative assumption of a constant $1.4bn net income turned out to be way off the mark. It doubled to $2.8bn in as little as six years – a compound growth rate of 14.9% per year.

Admittedly, American Express was hit hard by the post-dotcom recession (compounded by the 9/11 attack on the Twin Towers in 2001, in which 11 Amex employees died) and the global financial crisis of 2008. Nevertheless, income did not fall too badly even after those shocks and recovery was rapid.

In 2019, American Express generated $6.76bn in net income, and paid out to shareholders – in both dividends and share repurchases – $6bn. Berkshire now has 'look-through earnings' of 18.8% of American Express's profits, an *annual* share almost equalling the *total* Berkshire 1990s investment of $1.47bn.

Return on equity

The key element leading to the outstanding success of Berkshire's American Express investment was the ability of the Amex managers to exceed even the ambitious return-on-equity targets set by Harvey Golub in 1994 of 18–20% per year.

You can see the amazingly high percentage returns in figure 3.5. In only four years has RoE fallen below 20%, a target that executives and shareholders in more humdrum companies can only dream of.

American Express's senior team deliberately kept the amount of equity capital in the business very tight – they were determined not to have any dollar kept within the business which could not earn at least 20 cents each year. Money unable to earn its keep at that level was sent to shareholders either through share buybacks or dividends.

Figure 3.5: American Express return on shareholders' equity held within the business (%)

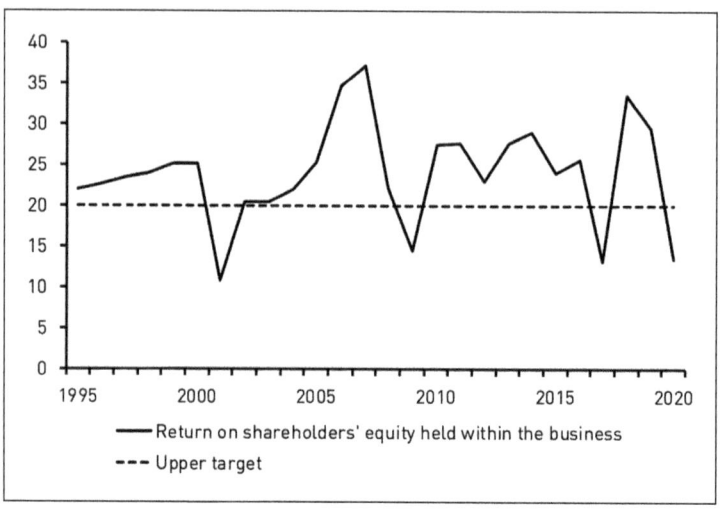

Source: American Express annual reports

The share price response

The market value of Berkshire Hathaway's holding rose from a buying price of $1.47bn to $18.3bn by the end of 2020 – see figure 3.6.

Figure 3.6: Market value of the American Express shares held by Berkshire Hathaway $bn (1998–2020)

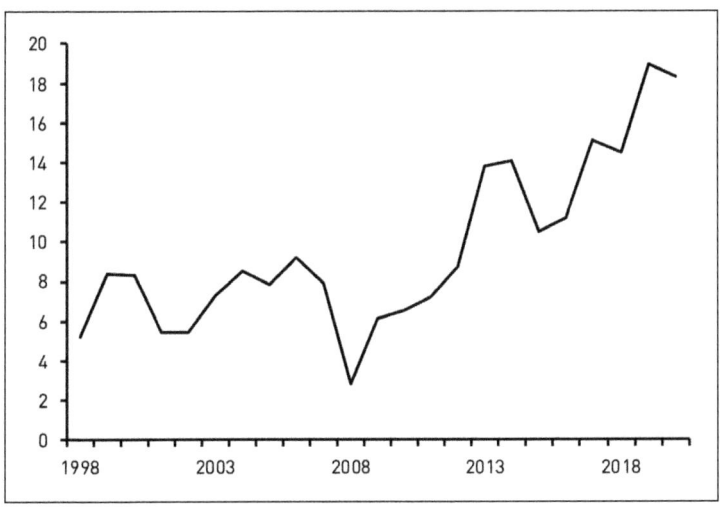

Source: Warren Buffett's letters to Berkshire Hathaway shareholders

In addition to share price appreciation, Berkshire has received in dividends nearly twice the amount it paid for the shares. And it received shares in the spin-off in September 2005 of American Express Financial Advisors as Ameriprise Financial. Berkshire became the owner of 30.3m shares or 12.2% of Ameriprise, worth about $1.1bn. (They were all sold by May 2008.)

In 2020, Berkshire received $1.72 in dividends for each American Express share, totalling $261m.

Don't sell wonderful franchises

Note in figure 3.6 the one-third drop in price in 2001 and the two-thirds fall in 2008. And yet Buffett chose not to sell in anticipation of these two economic downturns, despite the obvious likely impacts of recession on travel, card spending, bad debts and net income.

He regarded American Express as one of his "big four exceptional companies",[103] those he would never sell. As always, he reverted to his love of long-term partnership-type relationships in business and in investment, saying: "We view these holdings as partnership interests in wonderful businesses, not as marketable securities to be bought or sold based on their near-term prospects."[104]

In the long run, his steadfastness was vindicated. Such dedication and loyalty not only reinforced the strong relationship Buffett had with Amex's board, but avoided the trap of trying to guess market tops and bottoms.

The shares now trade at over $140 each. Note, this price is after the three-for-one share split in 2000, so each 'old share' has effectively risen from around $30 in 1994 to over $420 today. (In 2000, Berkshire's holding went from 50.54m shares before the split to 151.61m shares afterwards.)

Change, but continuity

Harvey Golub, aged 60, announced in 1999 that he did not want to go on working full-time until he was 65. His work was done, "the company is in terrific shape: robust growth engines have been built; our brand and our reputation are stellar; our people and intellectual capital are outstanding; and our customer base is large and loyal."[105]

He allowed plenty of time for the transition to a new CEO. Golub chose, and the board and shareholders approved, the highly respected Ken Chenault, who had been his trusted number two since 1993. He became only the third black CEO of an S&P 500 company in 2001.

Buffett said, in his 2006 letter, that he greatly admired Chenault. He went on to note the different skill set required to run a company compared with being an investor:

> "I don't think I could do the management job they do. And I know I wouldn't enjoy many of the duties that come with their positions – meetings, speeches, foreign travel, the charity circuit and governmental relations. For me, Ronald Reagan had it right: 'It's probably true that hard work never killed anyone – but why take the chance?' So I've taken the easy route, just sitting back and working through great managers who run their

own shows. My only tasks are to cheer them on, sculpt and harden our corporate culture, and make major capital-allocation decisions. Our managers have returned this trust by working hard and effectively."

Chenault retired in 2018 to be succeeded by another American-Express lifer, Stephen Squeri. In May 2020, Buffett offered the same advice to Squeri when Covid-19 was raging that he had 56 years earlier at the height of the salad oil scandal: "The most important thing about American Express is the brand and the customers that aspire to be associated with the brand".[106] Squeri doubled down on maintaining customer relationships when many faced financial difficulties. Amex waived late fees, lowered interest rates and cut monthly payments. It also helped customers obtain refunds.

Moats and castles

This emphasis on building the brand has always been to deepen the moat around the economic franchise castle:

> "A truly great business must have an enduring 'moat' that protects excellent returns on invested capital. The dynamics of capitalism guarantee that competitors will repeatedly assault any business 'castle' that is earning high returns. Therefore, a formidable barrier such as a company's being the low-cost producer (GEICO, Costco) or possessing a powerful world-wide brand (Coca-Cola, Gillette, American Express) is essential for sustained success."[107]

Buffett warns us to beware of illusionary economic franchises. You will come across many 'Roman Candles', those companies where the moat loses its effectiveness and thus the economic franchise fizzles out as determined rivals succeed.

An economic franchise, by definition, has to be enduring, which is unlikely to occur in industries prone to rapid and continuous change. A lot of 'creative destruction' is going on out there. While this is great for society, it precludes investment certainty. As Buffett says, "A moat that must be continuously rebuilt will eventually be no moat at all".[108]

An illusion arises where the outstanding success of the business depends on a great manager leading the enterprise:

"Of course, a terrific CEO is a huge asset for any enterprise, and at Berkshire we have an abundance of these managers. Their abilities have created billions of dollars of value that would never have materialized if typical CEOs had been running their businesses. But if a business requires a superstar to produce great results, the business itself cannot be deemed great. A medical partnership led by your area's premier brain surgeon may enjoy outsized and growing earnings, but that tells little about its future. The partnership's moat will go when the surgeon goes. You can count, though, on the moat of the Mayo Clinic to endure, even though you can't name its CEO."[109]

Economic franchise investing does not necessarily prioritise earnings growth within the identified wonderful business; rather, it puts high returns on equity capital employed first. Whether the cash the business throws off is invested within its own operations allowing growth or is taken by investors to redeploy in high RoE situations elsewhere is determined by the return on the marginal dollar:

"Long-term competitive advantage in a stable industry is what we seek in a business. If that comes with rapid organic growth, great. But even without organic growth, such a business is rewarding. We will simply take the lush earnings of the business and use them to buy similar businesses elsewhere."[110]

American Express required some investment to grow its business, but not very much relative to the cash it was generating. Thus, it pumped cash to shareholders amounting to many times its early-1990s market capitalisation. Buffett has allocated the billions Berkshire has received from American Express to some other wonderful business – stories saved for later chapters.

Learning points

1. **Focus on the economic franchise.** Is it still strong even though managers have wasted time and money on other ventures?
2. **If the company has gone off-track, does it have the capability to get back on it?** Does it now have managers able to both rationally choose the right way forward and to implement the change?

3. **Business reputation is worth much more than the millions that might be obtained in the short run through meanness, insensitivity or cheap service.** Buffett advised Amex's directors in the 1960s to forgo quibbling regarding paying those who had lost money in the salad oil scandal. He emphasised spending on quality of service and marketing in the 1990s. In the Covid-19 crisis he advised generosity, flexibility and excellent service to cardmembers facing a period of financial embarrassment.

4. **A company generating high returns on equity should not expand/diversify unless the extra dollar of investment is likely to produce a good rate of return.** When all value-enhancing investments are financed, a well-run company returns any further cash to shareholders.

Investment 4

THE SHOE GROUP – H. H. BROWN, LOWELL, DEXTER

Summary of the deal

Deal	The Shoe Group
Time	1991 - Present
Price paid	**H. H. Brown**, July 1991: $161m **Lowell**, December 1992: $46m **Dexter**, November 1993: 2.14% of Berkshire's shares, worth $433m
Quantity	All their shares
Sale price	Still held
Profit	Not disclosed, but acknowledged to be disappointing
Berkshire Hathaway in 1991	Share price: $6,550–9,100 Book value: $7,380m Per share book value: $6,437

This story covers what Buffett himself declared as his "most gruesome error".[1] Within a few short years the value of $433m paid for the third company bought, Dexter, had evaporated completely. It wouldn't be quite so painfully seared on Buffett's mind if he had paid cash. Okay, that's $433m lost, but in the context of a company with a market capitalisation of $10bn it would be bearable.

But he agreed to pay with 25,203 Berkshire Hathaway shares, around 2.14% of the 1.177m shares in public issue. Thus, Berkshire shareholders swapped 2.14% of their company for something that would soon be slaughtered by the blows of competitors. The shares they sacrificed are today trading over $390,000 each. So effectively, Dexter has cost almost $10bn.

The shoe adventure wasn't all bad by any means. The specialist manufacturers H. H. Brown and Lowell continued to be able to charge prices which allowed a reasonable profit. Customers of these products, e.g., telegraph pole climbers, soldiers and nurses, needed good quality boots with steel toe caps or indoor comfortable shoes that they could wear all day. They were more than willing to pay a premium price to get the right fit and performance – going cheap would be an obvious false economy. And so it is that Berkshire Hathaway has enjoyed a flow of profit from shoes and boots selling in niche areas for over three decades. It is just a pity that two-thirds of the money laid down to create what Buffett named the 'Shoe Group' turned out to be wasted.

Still, we investors can learn much from errors, especially when made by a then very experienced 63-year-old investor.

H. H. Brown

Henry H. Brown opened his first shoe factory in 1883, adding to the 23 already in the town of Natick, Massachusetts. Two years later the company was employing 175 people and producing 2,000 pairs daily.

In 1927, Henry H. Brown sold his company to 29-year-old Ray Heffernan for $10,000. He was to run the firm for 62 years, during which time it earned a reputation for producing rugged boots.[112] For example, the Corcoran boot was the original jump boot for paratroopers in the second world war, and its combat boots have been used by infantry soldiers in many theatres. It collected other famous brands through takeovers, such as the Double-H western boot.

It's not just the military who are willing to pay up to $300 for a pair of boots (average prices are $120–160). Builders, farmers and lumberjacks need long-lasting strength, steel toe caps and all-day comfort, as do police and firemen. Miners, postal workers, bikers and search-and-rescue teams not only value resilience but water resistance.

Then there is the built-in-America cachet meshing with the proclivity of US government organisations at all levels to favour home manufactured goods.[113] Also, many key customers require short lead times, and sometimes small batches, which mean there is an advantage to manufacturing in America rather than far-away Asia.

These factors allowed H. H. Brown to both grow its market and achieve good margins. By 1991, operating profit was 12% of over $200m revenue. Pre-tax profits were about $25m, and after-tax profit attributable to shareholders was around $15m.

Frank Rooney

Ray Heffernan managed the four factories, employing around 1,800 employees and a direct sales force of over 100 people brilliantly. Under his management, the company supplied hundreds of small independent retailers and wholesalers, who then sold to workers required to wear safety shoes or boots because of the nature of their work in, say, heavy manufacturing, construction or steel. Then there were the special relationships he built with the likes of the army, police force or fire service.

Over a lifetime of endeavour, he created the leading domestic producer of safety work shoes and boots, and established a significant presence in other markets too, such as the western-boot and casual-shoe market. But in early 1990 he was ailing and was forced into retirement. Heffernan turned to his son-in-law, Frank Rooney, to keep things going.

Frank Rooney was no married-the-daughter inheritor of a great business. He had already made his name far away from Heffernan and long before his call to the company. After securing a degree from Wharton School of Finance and Commerce, the 22-year-old served in the Pacific in 1943.

Investment 4. The Shoe Group – H. H. Brown, Lowell, Dexter

His business career started at the bottom, as a sales trainee at the John Foote Shoe Company in Boston in 1946. Eighteen years later he became CEO, aged 42, of the parent company, Melville, which he took from annual revenue of $180m in 1964 to $7bn on his retirement 23 years later. Melville's earnings averaged over 20% on the equity capital employed in the business. Between 1964 and 1987 its common stock rose from $16 to $960 (19.5% average increase per year compounded).

By then, the company was much more than a manufacturer and seller of shoes. It had thousands of stores, including Thom McAn shoe shops, discounted-clothing stores, toy outlets and a home-goods chain. But the leading retail business in the group was CVS, which retailed drugs, cosmetics and other personal products.

Rooney's managerial approach was to push responsibility down the organisation. He kept an executive staff of only seven even as sales multiplied, and he liked to communicate face to face or over the telephone – not through memos, to which he said he was allergic. As a result, he would travel 50,000 miles a year to visit stores across North America.

Even his children were recruited (there were eight). His son Stephen remembers many a Saturday being bundled into the family car with one or two siblings to check on some stores. Rooney would quiz the local store assistant or manager on what was not working and what customers were seeking. "The manager of the store just would start talking, and some would think he was just a curious customer," Stephen Rooney said. "When it would come out in the conversation that it was his business, of course the guy would be a little bit shocked."[114]

In 1996, a spin-off from Melville became CVS Health Corporation, which today is a 300,000-employee company, ranking fourth largest in the US by revenue – just behind Walmart, Amazon and Apple. Its market capitalisation is $97bn.

Back when Rooney was a 29-year-old marrying Frances Heffernan, he was abruptly told by his future father-in-law that he had better forget any ideas of working for Ray Heffernan at H. H. Brown. Given the record Rooney notched up over the next three decades, Buffett described that rejection as "one of Mr Heffernan's few mistakes".[115]

The deal for H.H. Brown

Ray Heffernan died in December 1990, aged 92. Early in 1991, his family concluded that it was best if the company were sold, and Frank Rooney took up the task of finding a buyer with the help of Goldman Sachs, which carefully put together a pack of material to give to potential buyers.

But real progress began on the golf course. A long-time friend of Buffett, John Loomis, was out on the links in Florida in spring 1991 playing against Frank Rooney. The conversation turned to the sale of H. H. Brown. Immediately Loomis thought the company a good fit for Berkshire Hathaway. "John told Frank that the company should be right up Berkshire's alley, and Frank promptly gave me a call", Buffett recounts in his 1991 letter.

The conversation went well. According to Rooney, "Warren said 'Well, that sounds interesting. Don't send me any of that stuff from Goldman Sachs, just send me the audited numbers for the last couple of years.'"[116] Buffett came away from the call thinking "that they would make a deal".[117]

Rooney sent the accounts and they agreed to meet in New York. At lunch, Buffett asked Rooney and his brother-in-law whether, if Berkshire agreed to their asking price, they would stop talking to other potential buyers. "I said 'Yes' and he said, 'Okay, we got a deal.' So my brother-in-law and I took a walk around the block and came back and said, 'Okay, that's it.'"[118]

Rooney was astonished that Buffett had agreed without having yet seen a factory or met any of the H. H. Brown people. "Why the hell did he buy a shoe company? I asked him later, and he said … 'because of you'."[119] Berkshire paid $161m cash for 100% of H. H. Brown shares on 1 July, 1991.

Why buy?

Apart from the proven earnings there were three key reasons why Buffett wanted H. H. Brown, each linked directly to the likelihood of the profits continuing to rise:

1. **Frank Rooney was prepared to carry on running the show.** "Much of my enthusiasm for this purchase came from Frank's willingness to continue as CEO. Like most of our managers, he has no financial need to work but does so because he loves the game and likes to excel. Managers of this stripe cannot be 'hired' in the normal sense of the word. What we must do is provide a concert hall in which business artists of this class will wish to perform."[120]

2. **It had an excellent managerial team.** "Shoes are a tough business – of the billion pairs purchased in the United States each year, about 85% are imported – and most manufacturers in the industry do poorly. The wide range of styles and sizes that producers offer causes inventories to be heavy; substantial capital is also tied up in receivables. In this kind of environment, only outstanding managers like Frank and the group developed by Mr Heffernan can prosper."[121]

3. **A brilliant way of compensating managers.** Only a small proportion of overall pay was fixed, most of a manager's income depended on achieving good company profits relative to capital devoted to making those profits. "A distinguishing characteristic of H. H. Brown is one of the most unusual compensation systems I've encountered – but one that warms my heart: A number of key managers are paid an annual salary of $7,800, to which is added a designated percentage of the profits of the company after these are reduced by a charge for capital employed. These managers therefore truly stand in the shoes of owners. In contrast, most managers talk the talk but don't walk the walk, choosing instead to employ compensation systems that are long on carrots but short on sticks (and that almost invariably treat equity capital as if it were cost-free) … Managers eager to bet heavily on their abilities usually have plenty of ability to bet on."[122]

Who gained from the deal?

Rooney reckoned both Berkshire and H. H. Brown benefitted from the sale. Berkshire acquired a consistent profit-maker and people at H. H. Brown retained the freedom to focus on pursuing high-return business in the way they thought fit. As usual, Buffett wanted his key manager to feel and think like a proprietor, to run the business as though it was still 100% family owned.

In addition, H. H. Brown could now access a very deep pool of money, useful for strengthening the Shoe Group through acquisition of footwear manufacturers. Rooney judged being part of Berkshire as "the next best thing to being in business for yourself".[123]

And he got to join Buffett's inner circle:

> "[Buffett's] an unusual personality, like an old shoe. He is fun. He is bright. He is funny. He is enjoyable. He is crazy … When he comes to visit, he makes his own breakfast, which is a ham sandwich and a Cherry Coke. It seemed to me that he only does the things that are fun for him to do. It's the people and associating with the people that he enjoys."[124]

The pleasure that comes with running his own show and working with Buffett kept Rooney working long past the conventional retirement age. When 78-years old he said in an interview with Bob Miles for his book *Warren Buffett CEO* (August 2000) that Buffett gave him "purpose, and I run H. H. Brown in order to make him proud." At that stage he was still chairman and CEO but was grateful for the strong support he got from his number two, Jim Issler.

How to run a business

Rooney's management philosophy was heavily influenced by management guru Peter Drucker, with whom in the old days running Melville he would have had monthly meetings. His key rules were: keep it simple; clearly define the business; focus on customer satisfaction (even at the expense of short-term numbers); be a people person to attract and keep the best, those who show passion for the business; always exhibit integrity; delegate and let your people have fun.

> "We have a strategy. We have a mission," he says. "It's not very fancy – just more blocking and tackling, getting out there, defining the business. We talk a lot about the need to define one's business. It's not as easy as you think. Some people think it is just to make a profit, but we know that our business is one of satisfying customers. And we believe that if we stick to it, we'll be successful."[125]

Rooney was still overseeing that success in his eighty-ninth year in 2011.

Lowell

After a satisfactory second half of 1991 for H. H. Brown, in the first full year under Berkshire's ownership the company earned $17.3m on revenue of $215m, which was a steady increase and a decent income on the $161m Berkshire had laid out.

Rooney and Buffett made their next move to create the Shoe Group on the penultimate day of 1992 by acquiring Lowell Shoe Company for $46.2m.

This act is an example of a BH principle: subsidiaries are encouraged to make small add-on acquisitions if at least a dollar of value is created for each dollar spent. Such moves could be used to extend product offerings or distribution capabilities. "In this manner, we enlarge the domain of managers we already know to be outstanding – and that's a low-risk and high-return proposition."[126]

Lowell, also located in New England but with one of its manufacturing plants in Puerto Rico, had a niche business supplying nurses (and some doctors) with shoes. Nurse Mates are anti-slip, lightweight and comfortable with their broad heel. With a reputation established over decades, most US nurses today wear Nurse Mates or shoes from their rival, Dansko. Turnover in 1992 was $90m. This was boosted by the sale of other kinds of women's shoes, but the reputational competitive advantage lay with nurses' shoes.[127]

Buffett joked about a limitation on potential candidates for acquisition:

> "a trend has emerged that may make further acquisitions difficult. The parent company made one purchase in 1991, buying H. H. Brown, which is run by Frank Rooney, who has eight children. In 1992 our only deal was with Bill Kizer, father of nine. It won't be easy to keep this string going in 1993."[128]

A significant pattern

So far in the story of the development of the Shoe Group, I've described two companies with one thing in common – they served niche markets in which customers were willing to pay a premium for work-related design, quality and comfort. The price premium was not large, but it was enough to provide healthy profit margins and returns on capital. With that in mind, let's turn to the third company to join, Dexter.

Dexter

Harold Alfond, the son of blue-collar Russian-Jewish immigrants, worked his way up from 25-cent-an-hour shop-floor work making shoes in the Depression to factory superintendent. Then, in 1939, aged 25, he picked up a hitchhiker when driving to the county fair in Maine. In passing, the hitchhiker mentioned an idle shoe factory in nearby Norridgewock. Intrigued, Alfond skipped the fair to look over the factory. He wanted it but didn't have the $1,000 asking price. However, a year later he sold his car and partnered with his father to buy it. That $1,000 was turned into $1.1m when, in 1944, the Norrwock Shoe Company was sold to a rival for that sum.

In 1956, Alfond put down a bet ten times as large as his first by creating another shoe company and spending $10,000 buying an abandoned wool factory in his hometown of Dexter, Maine. In 1958 he was joined by his nephew Peter Lunder, who was to become his valuable right-hand man.

At first, the Dexter Shoe Company concentrated on making own-label shoes for department stores such as Sears, JCPenny and Montgomery Ward. It wasn't until 1962 that Alfond, Lunder and the team developed the 'Dexter brand' of reasonably priced yet stylish shoes for men and women. Dexter was aiming at the volume market. With the help of a crack sales and marketing team, these shoes were sold to independent stores all over the US.

The innovation of the 1980s was the purchase of malls along highways in New England. Dexter turned these into factory outlet malls selling seconds (new shoes with slight imperfections) and discontinued lines.

The company would take some space for their own shoes – the units looked like log-cabins – and rent out units to other manufacturers.

By 1990, Dexter owned more than 80 factory outlets, employed 4,000 employees, and annually turned over $250m through selling 7.5m pairs of shoes. It had also branched out into moccasins, boat, golf and athletic shoes.

Warren Buffett's deal to buy Dexter

In early 1993, Buffett was excited by the way Frank Rooney and Jim Issler were managing "superbly-run"[129] H. H. Brown, "a real winner … expectations have been considerably exceeded".[130] Confidence was boosted further when Rooney and Issler deftly implemented a 'fixing' plan at Lowell and again surpassed Buffett's hopes.

So, when Rooney suggested to Buffett that Dexter would fit the Shoe Group well, and that he should meet his old friends Alfond and Lunder to discuss buying it, Buffett jumped at the chance.

An airport in West Palm Beach, Florida, was the chosen location. "We went to some little restaurant based on a World War II theme, had a hamburger, and talked about shoes" Buffett recalls.[131] He made a cash offer there and then.

But Alfond and Lunder were not interested in cash. After all, one-third might be taken by the government in capital-gains tax. They wanted to hold Berkshire shares. This is not something Buffett could easily agree to, he needed time to think about it. There had to be a very compelling reason for cutting out a significant portion of the future rewards accruing in Berkshire's stock and handing it to someone else. Alfond would become the largest shareholder in Berkshire outside of the Buffett family.

In subsequent months Berkshire's shares rose, making the swapping of shares more palatable. And so, another meeting was arranged, this time in Lunder's apartment in Boston. Neither side thought it necessary to invite lawyers, accountants or investment bankers. They didn't need to consult those experts, nor pay their fees.

The businessmen struck a simple deal: Berkshire Hathaway would issue 25,203 shares, 2.14% of the shares in public circulation, in return for all of Dexter's shares. This deal was completed on 7 November, 1993, by which time those Berkshire shares had a market value of $433m.

Buffett saw many virtues in Dexter. It was run in a lean and efficient way by experienced family members. It had a good profit record and, apparently, some marketplace power from its branding and customer relationships. In his 1993 letter, Buffett was effusive in his praise: "Dexter, I can assure you, needs no fixing: It is one of the best-managed companies Charlie and I have seen in our business lifetimes."

He was grateful that Alfond and Lunder were keen on continuing to run the show: "of paramount importance, Harold and Peter can be sure that they will get to run their business – an activity they dearly love – exactly as they did before the merger. At Berkshire, we do not tell .400 hitters how to swing."[132]

Fully aware of the might of the Chinese factory, able to pay wages one-tenth of those in the US, Buffett acknowledged that, in general, American shoe manufacturers were under threat. But, while "the domestic shoe industry is generally thought to be unable to compete with imports from low-wage countries … someone forgot to tell this to the ingenious managements of Dexter and H. H. Brown and to their skilled labor forces, which together make the US plants of both companies highly competitive against all comers." (Buffett writing to Berkshire shareholders spring 1994.)

Even when the year was only a couple of months old, Buffett's projections for 1994 were for a great leap in Berkshire's shoe sales, from the $372m achieved in 1993 to more than $550m, implying a rise at all three shoe companies.

In the event, his expectations were far exceeded with $609m coming in, producing $55.8m in after-tax profit for Berkshire. "Five years ago we had no thought of getting into shoes. Now we have 7,200 employees in that industry, and I sing "There's No Business Like Shoe Business" as I drive to work. So much for strategic plans."[133,134]

But 1994 was the high point for the Shoe Group

Profits from the Shoe Group jumped from $28.8m in 1993 to $55.8m in 1994, with about nine-tenths of the increase down to Dexter being brought into the fold. And Buffett and Munger were looking forward to 1995:

> "Management was pleased with Dexter's 1994 performance and better results are anticipated during 1995. This optimism results from the fact that recent wholesale price adjustments should help mitigate the effects of prior years' increases in Dexter's costs. Additionally, operating efficiencies are anticipated in connection with the start-up of Dexter's new computerized distribution center and from advanced manufacturing technologies."[135]

But rather than profits moving up another notch they fell, down to $37.5m. Buffett put a brave face on it, pointing to the even worse performance of other US manufacturers. "Our shoe business operated in an industry that suffered depressed earnings throughout last year, and many of our competitors made only marginal profits or worse. That means we at least maintained, and in some instances widened, our competitive superiority."[136]

And he looked forward to a climb back to top-grade earnings in 1996, as the managers capitalised on opportunities resulting from loss-making competitors closing, and lowered production and administration costs.

He asked Berkshire shareholders to view the 1995 result as a cyclical problem – just a bad year in a cycle of good and bad – and not as a secular one, a long-term trend.

He was right, to some extent, as profit crawled up to $41m in 1996; managers exploited a slightly improved marketing environment and had indeed cut costs. Buffett anticipated further operating profit increases during 1997.

But it wasn't to be, the trend was very much secular for Dexter after all. For the Shoe Group, profits fell to $32.2m in 1997 and operating-profit margin fell to 7.4% on revenues, which were down by $18.9m to $542m.

Dexter was now clearly identified by Buffett in the annual report as the problem area. Its sales were down about 12% in one year. But, nevertheless, Dexter's management were "repositioning its brand to be more competitive in a highly discount-oriented retail environment."[137] Berkshire's shareholders were told that Dexter's managers anticipated a recovery of a substantial portion of the lost volume in 1998.

After waiting another year, shareholders were shocked to discover that shoe profits were down yet again. They were now less than half those of 1994, at $23m from sales of only $500m. "The unfavorable results represent a continuation of a trend which began three years ago. Manufacturers such as Brown, Lowell and Dexter are facing reduced demand for their products. Additionally, major retailers are offering promotions to generate sales which is resulting in an ongoing margin squeeze."[138]

Still Buffett gave the benefit of doubt to the people running these operations, saying they were working to align production activity to the reduced sales level. Hopefully, their genius at an operational level would cause profits to rise to a satisfactory level.

Despite their efforts, 1999 was dreadful. Profits halved again to $11m. Buffett noted that all businesses in the Berkshire stable had "excellent results in 1999" except Dexter.

He identified the problem not as one of managerial capability. Dexter's managers were every bit the equal of the other Berkshire managers in terms of skills, energy and devotion. No, the core of the issue was that "we manufacture shoes primarily in the U.S., and it has become extremely difficult for domestic producers to compete effectively. In 1999, approximately 93% of the 1.3 billion pairs of shoes purchased in this country came from abroad, where extremely low-cost labor is the rule."[139] Thus, the issue was strategic; Dexter lacked competitive advantage to contest overseas producers.

Belatedly, the reluctance of the Shoe Group to manufacture a significant proportion of output in low-cost countries dissolved. "We have loyal, highly-skilled workers in our U.S. plants, and we want to retain every job here that we can. Nevertheless, in order to remain viable, we are sourcing more of our output internationally," Buffett wrote in his 1999 letter. Some US plants were closed in 1999 and the Group had to bear the costs of severance and relocation.

Figure 4.1: Berkshire's after-tax earnings from the Shoe Group $m (1994–1999)

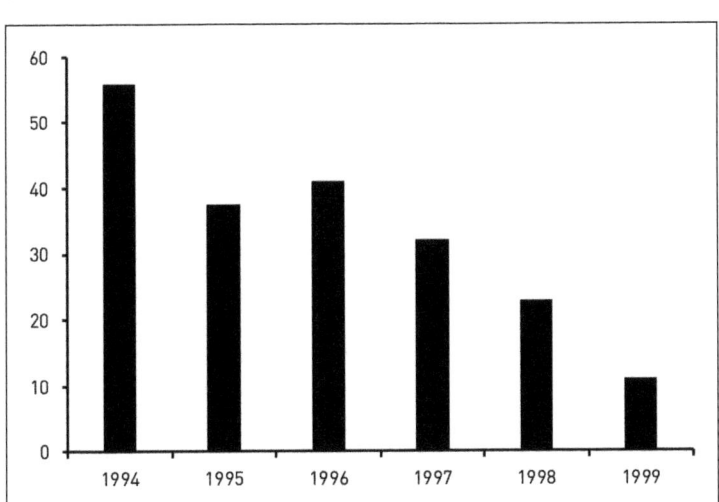

Buffett is not perfect

In 2000, all the remaining goodwill attributable to Dexter was written off and more factories were closed, with others scheduled to close in 2001. Buffett took the blame on himself for the tragedy. His *mea culpa* drew attention to mistakes across his career. "We try ... to keep our estimates conservative and to focus on industries where business surprises are unlikely to wreak havoc on owners. Even so, we make many mistakes: I'm the fellow, remember, who thought he understood the future economics of trading stamps, textiles, shoes and second-tier department stores."[140]

He was being far too hard on himself. While there were errors in these areas, we know that successes elsewhere far outweighed those mistakes. Equally, resources from Blue Chip Stamps, Berkshire's textile business and Diversified Retailing were taken from unproductive areas and allocated to highly profitable investments in other industries, such as candy (See's Candy), insurance (e.g., National Indemnity), and in stock-market-listed shares, such as Capital Cities and Coca-Cola, which went on to multiply six- or 20-fold.

What Buffett was doing by dwelling on mistakes was impressing on himself and others the need to remember the logic-path that led to the error. We all need post-mortems to learn how to advance the quality of our thinking in our investment journey.

The error of keeping too much shoe production in America was compounded by paying too much for Dexter in the first place. Even more frustrating for Buffett was that the payment was in Berkshire shares, which were later worth billions of dollars.

Keeping faith with boots and shoes

Berkshire Hathaway's shoe businesses were joined by Justin Boots in 2000 (one of the subjects for volume four), a purchase which clearly indicated Buffett had not given up on the sector. Both Justin Boots and H. H. Brown were profitable in 2001. But a massive loss from Dexter resulted in an overall loss of $46.2m pre-tax for Berkshire's shoe businesses.

Frank Rooney and Jim Issler were asked to take over the management of the now much diminished Dexter. They greatly helped the Dexter operation in 2001, but sadly the emphasis was on sharply reducing activity rather than reaching out to new customers. In Maine, the last three remaining Dexter plants were closed.

Buffett expected that, after an awful year in 2002, Berkshire's shoe business as a whole "will be reasonably profitable"[141] thereafter. But when it came to Dexter, he didn't express any optimism.

It wasn't killed off completely. Bits of the business – one or two brands/lines and some facilities – were absorbed into H. H. Brown's operations. The impact was devastating for employees. In just one small Maine town, 1,600 staff were put out of work.

In his 2007 letter, Buffett declared Dexter a worthless business and the worst deal that he'd made "to date". All experienced investors know that they will make numerous errors over the years. Buffett is no exception, but he might be unusual in being so honest about it in public: "I'll make mistakes in the future – you can bet on that. A line from Bobby Bare's country song explains what too often happens with acquisitions:

'I've never gone to bed with an ugly woman, but I've sure woke up with a few.'"[142]

Through the noughties, Jim Issler and Frank Rooney continued to run a tight ship at H. H. Brown, with sales and profits rising through the decade (helped by selling over 1,000 pairs each year at Berkshire's annual meeting).

While revenue rose, the number of employees did not. This was partly because it increasingly bought in components and finished shoes from abroad, and partly because rapid expansion was eschewed because high rates of return on capital were not available on the marginal dollar of investment. Thus, the vast majority of profits made by the shoe businesses flowed to the Berkshire centre for Buffett and Munger to allocate elsewhere.

That pattern continued in the next decade – by 2021 H. H. Brown staff numbers had fallen to below 830 (from around 1,250), again indicating tight rules on expansion beyond the profitable core.

Despite the continuing flow of cash from shoes and boots to Berkshire's bank account, Buffett will forever feel sore about the major slip-up at Dexter. "As a financial disaster, this one deserves a spot in the *Guinness Book of World Records*," he wrote in his 2014 letter.

What became of the key characters?

Frank Rooney

Frank Rooney had not only built Melville/CVS into one of the top-10 US companies and been Buffett's right-hand man in the Berkshire shoe operations but, active into his 90s, was a renowned philanthropist serving as a trustee of at least eight charities including the Inner-City Scholarship Fund, United Cerebral Palsy and the Smithsonian Institution. He died in 2015, aged 93, to be succeeded by his wife of 65 years, the former Frances Heffernan; four sons; four daughters; 27 grandchildren; and five great-grandchildren. Warren Buffett and Charlie Munger will be forever grateful for his friendship and for coming out of retirement to serve the shareholders of Berkshire Hathaway.

Harold Alfond

Harold Alfond held onto his Berkshire Hathaway shares. After retiring from Dexter in 2001, his main focus was on philanthropy, donating millions of dollars to universities, schools and hospitals in Maine. The Harold Alfond Foundation remains the largest private foundation in Maine, with much of its money held in Berkshire Hathaway stock. It offers a $500 college scholarship to every Maine-resident baby at the moment of birth. This is designed to encourage the child's family to start saving for college. Thus, we see that Berkshire shareholders' loss is Maine's children's gain, so maybe it's not such a bad deal after all.

Back in 1978, Alfond acquired a minority interest in the Boston Red Sox which he greatly enjoyed. He passed away in 2007, aged 93, leaving most of his fortune to his four children who, in turn, are philanthropic billionaires. Two sons continue the family interest in the Red Sox. Even today his family are worth perhaps $4bn, mostly thanks to Harold's insistence on holding Berkshire Hathaway shares, which have risen 27-fold since 1993.

Peter H. Lunder

Peter Lunder helped his uncle Harold build Dexter into something Buffett would find attractive, serving as co-chairman, president, and CEO. He is now retired but still has interests in many businesses and is a former limited partner of the Boston Red Sox. The Lunder Foundation supports arts, education, and healthcare institutions in Maine and Massachusetts.

Jim Issler

Jim Issler still loyally serves Buffett and Munger as president of the Berkshire Hathaway Shoe Holdings, which is made up of 22 brands distributed throughout the US, as well as Europe and Asia (most notably Justin, Tony Lama, Chippewa, Børn, B.ø.c, Carolina, Eurosoft, Söfft, Double-H Boots, Nurse Mates and Comfortiva). It has two retail chains and some US manufacturing facilities but mostly purchases from overseas, generating over $350m of revenue. Year after year it transfers money for Warren Buffett to invest.

Learning points

1. **Past business performance does not always predict future earnings power.** Until it was bought, Dexter showed good profit numbers. But the oppressive competitive forces from overseas in mid-market shoes were reaching renewed heights, ensuring a dire future.

2. **Even in sectors in general retreat there might be companies with market-beating competitive strengths allowing good returns on capital.** H. H. Brown and Lowell dominated niche markets with strong brands attracting consumers willing to pay premium prices for performance, comfort, or just because they were American made.

3. **If you swap equity in your company for equity in another, consider the value of what is given away as much as what you get.** Two percentage of Berkshire became worth billions. It was sacrificed to buy what became a worthless business. Cash payment would have limited the damage.

4. **When the writing is on the wall concerning the competitive dynamic act quickly.** Buffett continued to praise the work of Dexter's managers despite their failure to position the business to produce shoes as cheap as overseas competitors.

5. **The competence and character of business leaders sits alongside strategic strength as vital in assessing long-term prospects.** The decisive factor in purchasing H. H. Brown was the willingness of Frank Rooney to continue as CEO.

6. **When you have a business 'artist' on your team, do all you can to help but don't try to manage them.** They need the freedom to act. Buffett simply provided a concert hall for Frank Rooney to perform.

7. **Tie the pay of managers to shareholder returns.** At H. H. Brown, managers received a small, fixed salary and a large bonus which depended on returns per dollar used in the business.

Investment 5

HELZBERG DIAMOND SHOPS

Summary of the deal

Deal	Helzberg Diamond Shops
Time	1995
Price paid	Undisclosed. Estimated $165–183m in Berkshire shares
Quantity	100% of the equity
Sale price	Held today
Profit	Still flowing
Berkshire Hathaway in 1995	Share price: $20,500–32,000 Book value: $17,217m Per share book value: $14,426

On a sunny May morning a week or so after Berkshire's 1994 annual meeting in Omaha, Warren Buffett was about to cross near the corner of 58th Street and Fifth Avenue, New York, when he was stopped by a woman who just wanted to say how much she had enjoyed the annual meeting.

Barnett C. Helzberg Jr., who was in New York to talk to Morgan Stanley about selling his business – a 143-jewellery store chain carrying his family name – was 30–40 feet away when the woman in the bright red dress shouted across to Buffett. On hearing the name of the chairman of the company in which he held four shares, he stopped and waited for the woman to say her goodbyes.

As Buffett went to cross the street again, Helzberg grasped his opportunity. He thrust out his hand and said: "Hello, Mr Buffett. I'm Barnett Helzberg of Helzberg Diamonds in Kansas City."[143]

Helzberg looked for some recognition on Buffett's face. But none was forthcoming, despite Helzberg Diamonds then being one of the largest jewellery chains in the country. But Buffett was polite and shook his hand, said "Hello" and graciously accepted more compliments about the annual meeting.

Then, in 30 seconds flat, "right there on the sidewalk, as busy New Yorkers rushed past us and street traffic buzzed around us, I told one of the most astute businessmen in America why he ought to consider buying our family's 70-year-old jewellery business … I believe that our company matches your criteria for investment."[144]

As Buffett recalls the encounter, his first thought was that he was hearing yet again that phrase about a 'good fit' when the business hawker hasn't really understood the acquisition criteria applied by Buffett and Munger, "it usually turns out they have a lemonade stand – with potential, of course, to quickly grow into the next Microsoft."[145]

Given the probability that this was yet another dead-end, Buffett cut short the conversation by civilly asking if Helzberg could write to him with the particulars, "that, I thought to myself, will be the end of that."[146]

Helzberg went home and sent Buffett nothing. He later said he was "afflicted by hang-ups about confidentiality. I'm the kind of guy who asks for someone's Social Security number before I tell them the time."[147] Then one night he re-read Berkshire's annual report and paid particular attention to the section where Buffett invites companies that meet his criteria to send him information.

Buffett's acquisition criteria

Here is the regular 'advertisement' included in Berkshire annual reports. This one is from 1995:

"We are eager to hear from principals or their representatives about businesses that meet all of the following criteria:

(1) Large purchases (at least $25m of before-tax earnings),

(2) Demonstrated consistent earning power (future projections are of no interest to us, nor are 'turnaround' situations),

(3) Businesses earning good returns on equity while employing little or no debt,

(4) Management in place (we can't supply it),

(5) Simple businesses (if there's lots of technology, we won't understand it),

(6) An offering price (we don't want to waste our time or that of the seller by talking, even preliminarily, about a transaction when price is unknown).

The larger the company, the greater will be our interest: We would like to make an acquisition in the $3–5bn range. We are not interested, however, in receiving suggestions about purchases we might make in the general stock market.

We will not engage in unfriendly takeovers. We can promise complete confidentiality and a very fast answer – customarily within five minutes – as to whether we're interested. We prefer to buy for cash, but will consider issuing stock when we receive as much in intrinsic business value as we give."

Helzberg slept on it. In the morning Buffett's promise of complete confidentiality hit him on the head. "While shaving I looked at the slow learner in the mirror and began to scold myself for procrastinating. 'He told you in person it would be confidential. He told you in writing. Do you want it set to music? Send him the information.' So I finally did."[148]

Merger principles

There is more to the rational buying of companies than the above acquisition criteria. Some more fundamental philosophical principles need to be followed. In his 1995 letter, Buffett – having bought Helzberg and R.C. Willey (investment six) and recently agreed to buy the second

Investment 5. Helzberg Diamond Shops

half of GEICO (volume two, investment one and investment ten in this volume) – set out his thoughts on the dangers inherent in acquisitions and put forward his ideas on the thought process needed.

The first thing to acknowledge is that, while some mergers/acquisitions do benefit business owners, the majority damage the interests of the acquiring company's shareholders. This has been shown in study after study by academics across the globe. Buffett and Munger had seen it time and again in front of their eyes. Understanding why company directors are inclined to destroy value this way will help us stay on the right track.

One factor is that those selling will present glowing financial projections which will fool some people, even highly paid directors. As Buffett said, "In the production of rosy scenarios, Wall Street can hold its own against Washington."[149] "Too often, the words from *HMS Pinafore* apply: 'Things are seldom what they seem, skim milk masquerades as cream.'"[150]

Buffett urges us to treat such projections as having more entertainment value than educational value. Buffett and Munger do not understand why potential buyers look at financial forecasts. They are frequently offered them, but don't give them a second glance.

Instead, they bear in mind the old story about the owner of a lame horse: "Visiting the vet, he said: 'Can you help me? Sometimes my horse walks just fine and sometimes he limps.' The vet's reply was pointed: 'No problem – when he's walking fine, sell him.'"

Another problem is the siren call of the fun aspect of acquisition. "Talking to *Time Magazine* a few years back, Peter Drucker got to the heart of things: 'I will tell you a secret: Dealmaking beats working. Dealmaking is exciting and fun, and working is grubby. Running anything is primarily an enormous amount of grubby detail work … dealmaking is romantic, sexy. That's why you have deals that make no sense.'"[151]

Acquisitions are often driven by a strategic plan which states that the company must grow in a particular way, say, buying up other players in one industry, or moving into particular growth areas. This can lead it to paying silly prices to fulfil the plan.

Buffett and Munger's advantage is that they simply do not have a strategic plan. This frees them to change direction at will, to wherever the greatest value might come from, be that adding to the Berkshire family a firm from yet another new industry, say shoes or candy; buying more minority holdings of listed companies such as Coca-Cola; or buying more wholly-owned businesses.

> "We always mentally compare any move we are contemplating with dozens of other opportunities open to us, including the purchase of small pieces of the best businesses in the world via the stock market. Our practice of making this comparison – acquisitions against passive investments – is a discipline that managers focused simply on expansion seldom use."[152]

Buffett and Munger are very aware of their opportunity cost. They already have under their wing some excellent companies which are constantly being examined for potential to absorb more of Berkshire's investment capital, which means they can generate high rates of return on that money. The obvious consequence of any new venture outside of the existing set is that it will take cash from one of these internal investments (including the adding of more shares to existing holding such as American Express). These are tough benchmarks to beat, so Buffett and Munger rarely buy into new companies – perhaps only once or twice a year.

The wherewithal to buy

Dividends and interest from investing insurance float poured into Berkshire Hathaway in the early 1990s – see table 5.1. An astonishing $283–351m per year was coming from this source. In addition, Buffett and Munger were selling shares at profit – in 1993, for example, over $357m capital gains were realised.

While income and capital gains on insurance float were the big earners, the operating businesses – from See's Candies to Scott Fetzer – were nicely profitable. More importantly, they were very profitable relative to the amount of capital they used.

Table 5.1: Berkshire's share of net earnings (after taxes and minority interests) 1990–95 ($m)

	1990	1991	1992	1993	1994	1995
Insurance underwriting	-15	-77	-71	20	81	11
Insurance net investment income	283	285	306	321	351	418
Realised security gains	23	124	60	357	61	125
Buffalo News	26	22	28	30	32	27
Fechheimer	7	7	7	7	7	9
Finance Businesses	-	-	-	14	15	13
Home Furnishings	8	7	8	10	9	17
Jewellery	-	-	-	-	-	19
Kirby	18	23	23	25	28	32
Scott Fetzer Manufacturing	18	16	20	24	25	21
See's Candies	24	26	26	24	28	30
Wesco – other than insurance	10	9	9			
Shoe Group	-	7	17	29	56	38
World Book	20	15	20	14	17	7
Other	26	38	23	1	3	1
Interest on debt	-50	-57	-63	-36	-37	-35
Charity donations by BH shareholders	-4	-4	-5	-6	-7	-7
Decline in value of USAir preferred stock					-173	
Tax accruals caused by new accounting rules				-146		
Total earnings	**394**	**440**	**407**	**688**	**495**	**725**

Sources: Warren Buffett's Letter to Berkshire Hathaway shareholders (1991–95)

Book value (net asset value) per share rose from $4,296 at the end of 1989 to $14,426 at the end of 1995 (to total over $17bn). It's no wonder that the share price rose above $30,000 – see figure 5.1.

Figure 5.1: Berkshire Hathaway shares $ (1990–1995)

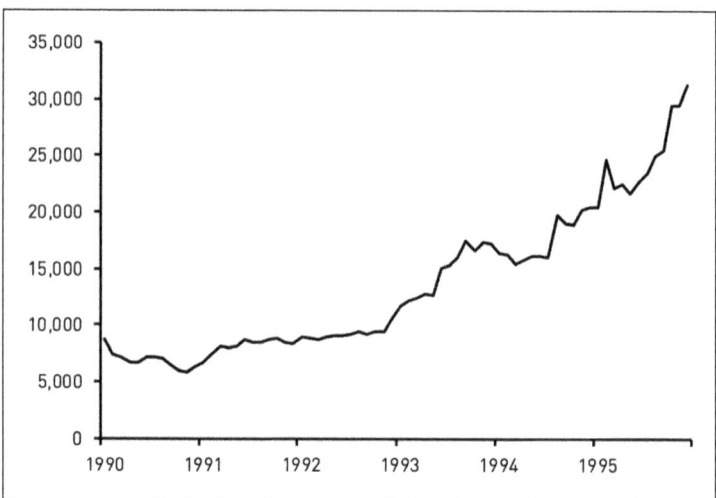

A short history of Helzberg

Russian immigrant Morris Helzberg, grandfather of Barnett Jr., opened a small jewellery store in Kansas City in 1915. All five of his children not only helped out at the store but were involved in its decision making – there was a family tradition of long discussions. It was a great blow to the family when, two years after opening, Morris had a serious stroke, making him unfit to work. Eldest son, Morton, was in dentistry school and another, Gilbert, was soon to fight in the first world war. That left two girls and 14-year-old Barnett.

Despite his young age, Barnett Sr had already shown a great deal of enthusiasm for the business and so the family decided that he was to take over. One problem: he still had to attend school. The solution was that an uncle would run the store during the day and when Barnett got out of school at 3pm, he would take over. It was assumed that when Gilbert returned to the USA he would become the leader.

But Barnett was having a whale of a time. He had a natural talent for retail. A born salesman he was, full of exciting plans. In 1920, now all of 17, he opened his own store in a more expensive location in Kansas City while Gilbert ran the original shop. It wasn't long before Barnett's grander place was outselling Gilbert's, so Gilbert shut his store and joined Barnett.

Sadly, Gilbert Helzberg died in a motor accident in 1934, just as the firm was expanding as far as Wichita. By 1940, the chain of five stores was the largest in the Midwest. In 1950, Barnett Jr. – aged 15 – was given summer work. He says he was a rather timid child, but soon grew to love building relationships with customers and the thrill of selling. After graduating in business from the University of Michigan, Barnett Jr. joined full-time in 1956, at a time when the company was set for a period of rapid expansion throughout the Midwest. By 1962, when Barnett became president of the firm aged 29, it had 39 shops.

Things seemed to be going well in the 1960s but there was a flaw: the majority of Helzberg stores were located in downtown districts, whereas people were now flocking to the new suburban shopping malls. Barnett Jr. remembers this period with feelings of fear and regret because Helzberg came close to complete business failure following its strategic wrong turn. It was stranded with high downtown costs, dwindling customer flow and a cash crisis. He decided to close the older stores, causing the chain to shrink to only 15 outlets, and by 1970 all except one outlet were in suburbs and shopping centres.

Barnett Helzberg Jr. nurtured the company's reputation for selling only internally flawless diamonds, putting it a cut above most competitors. Associates (employees) took pride in knowing the firm refused to lower the quality in terms of colour, cut or clarity.

Now that the formula – in terms of the target customer (middle and upper-middle-class), location and marketing (Barnett Jr.'s idea of the 'I am loved' campaign became a national phenomenon) – was in place, Helzberg decided it was time to grow at a steady rate of around three stores per year. By the end of the 1970s, there were 42 stores in 16 states. The pace was stepped up in the 1980s, taking the chain to 101 stores in 22 states in 1990.

While Helzberg remained at the helm, Jeff Comment was brought in as president in 1988. Comment was an outsider who previously ran a Philadelphia department store. He stepped up customer engagement, e.g., asking customers for birthdays to put on a database for later marketing use, and opened larger stores. By 1995 the average store turnover was nearly $2m, almost double the industry average. And considering there were then 143 stores, that meant that company turnover was $282m.

Barnett's reasons for selling

As Barnett Helzberg Jr. passed his 60th birthday he thought about the future of the firm. He had long subscribed to the philosophy that leaders must so design their businesses that they thrive when they are no longer there: "If you can say that if you fell down dead tomorrow, your company would prosper quite nicely without you, it's a sign you have been a good leader."[153]

With the company's growth he found himself working harder and travelling more in his quest for new locations and to bolster morale at existing stores. He was missing his family. He also felt uncomfortable in heading a business which had grown beyond his ability to know every store manager by first name. Barnett Helzberg Jr. loved the business, but he needed to step off the treadmill.

And he had to think of the next generation, which then had all its eggs in one basket; they needed to diversify the family's holdings. Also, Barnett was itching to spend more time – and money – on his many charitable activities.

Helzberg was determined to stay off the stock market: "We didn't want to be pressured to pay more attention to quarterly earnings and stock price than to the long-term operational health of the company and the well-being of our associates. We certainly didn't want some financial butcher carving up this jewel and selling it piecemeal. I also didn't want my associates spitting on my grave."[154]

Prior to searching for a new home for the company he set other criteria. First, the owner must continue to employ the current associates. Second, the buyer must appreciate and reinforce its unique culture with its focus on doing right by the customer. Finally, corporate headquarters must remain in the Kansas City area.

The deal

As Buffett read Helzberg's financial statements a few things struck him. First, sales had grown from $10m in 1974 to $53m in 1984 to $282m in 1994. Clearly the company was on an impressive growth path; "we weren't talking lemonade stands", Buffett noted in his 1995 letter.

Second, it exhibited remarkable productivity per-store. Turning over an average of around $2m was far superior to competitors operating similar-sized stores. Buffett told Berkshire shareholders, "If the company continues its first-rate performance – and we believe it will – it could grow rather quickly to several times its present size".[155] The high sales per square foot contributed greatly to the key element Buffett looks for: good returns on invested capital.

Third, the seller, Barnett Helzberg Jr., loved the business and cared deeply about what would happen to his people and customers under a new owner. The character of the seller, including what motivates him, provides clues on whether a good deal can be struck. For example, as he isn't obsessed with accumulating money, he will be unlikely to hide problems, prettify accounts or fail to engender good morale.

Fourth, Buffett could see quality managerial leadership was supplied in the form of Jeff Comment. So, even though the patriarch was not going to be around much the managerial team would remain solid.

> "There was never any question in my mind that, first, Helzberg's was the kind of business that we wanted to own and, second, Jeff was our kind of manager. In fact, we would not have bought the business if Jeff had not been there to run it. Buying a retailer without good management is like buying the Eiffel Tower without an elevator."[156]

A meeting

Buffett called Helzberg and told him that he would like to talk. He also paid what Barnett thought was the "ultimate compliment"[157] by saying that Helzberg Diamonds was a lot like Berkshire. It wasn't long before they met in Buffett's Omaha office to negotiate the sale. As well as Jeff Comment, Helzberg brought along a consulting accountant who had crunched some numbers to come up with a very high price (it was supposedly based on what Buffett had paid for another company). Despite it being obviously absurd, even to Barnett, Buffett was diplomatic in choosing to show no reaction at all.

Morgan Stanley had put together a pile of material on Helzberg Diamonds, so naturally Barnett took a copy along to the meeting and offered it to Buffett. He declined to take it. "I'm not interested in books. I'm not interested in working with Morgan Stanley. Why do you want to sell it?"[158] For ten to 15 minutes Barnett explained his need to do other things in life. This made sense to Buffett. After all, he'd witnessed similar motives in many sellers.

Buffett then asked Comment to tell him about the business and why he should buy it. Comment spoke for about an hour and half, answering a dozen questions along the way.

Who needs due diligence?

Buffett said that the deal could be "the fastest in history".[159] Helzberg was taken aback. How can it be done so quickly? What about the time it normally takes for a buyer to carry out due diligence? He said that "most suitors demand to see every scrap of paper you've ever generated and to interview every top manager."[160] Buffett's response was that he could "smell these things. This one smells good."[161]

It is also usual to include a clause preventing vendors or senior managers from quitting and then competing with the firm. Helzberg asked about that. But Buffett had already sized up Barnett and concluded, "You wouldn't want to do anything to hurt this company."[162] A response that engendered even greater admiration, loyalty and reciprocating trust in Helzberg. "When a guy says that to you, he has you on your honour for the rest of your life."[163]

One price only

Buffett's approach is to state a price, one that he regards as fair to both sides. This is then non-negotiable. One of Barnett Helzberg's guiding management principles, inherited from his father, was always to offer fair contracts rather than ones where the other party thinks you are playing 'gotcha'. He understood Buffett's insistence that he arrive at a fair price.

At the 2015 annual meeting, Charlie Munger commented on a pattern he had observed with business sellers, or at least those that wanted to hold Berkshires shares in return, as Barnett Helzberg did.

> "We frequently find that owners of entire businesses have schizophrenia. They want to sell their business for a little more than it's worth, taking stock, so they don't have to pay taxes. And they want the stock to be in a kind of business that will make just one dumb acquisition — theirs. And thereafter will guard the stock like gold, making no more dumb acquisitions. Needless to say, the world is not that easy. And I think over time, we've made acquisitions that were fair on both sides, and averaged out, they've worked well for Berkshire. And I think a company that behaves that way is giving the best long-term value to the private owner who wants to sell. You do not want to sell your business for stock to a firm that likes issuing stock."

Drawing it out

Buffett concluded the meeting by saying he would call in a couple of days "and tell you what it's worth".[164] The amount offered turned out to be about half the accountant's number. It wasn't a done deal at that point. There was much toing and froing because Helzberg had not fully absorbed the lesson about Buffett's negotiating approach. But it gradually sunk in and he later passed on the message to others but saying, "Basically the way to negotiate with Warren Buffett – you don't negotiate. He tells you the deal and that's the deal."[165]

In fact, it wasn't until 30 April, 1995, that the exchange of Berkshire shares for 100% of Helzberg shares took place. The exact number of Berkshire shares exchanged is obscure, but we know that 15,762 shares were issued during 1995 in exchange for the both R.C. Willey and Helzberg. We are also told that those given for R.C. Willey were valued at around $175m when Berkshire's shares traded in the range $21,650–24,200. Thus, between 7,231 and 8,083 shares were given for R.C. Willey. Leaving between 7,679 and 8,531 shares given for Helzberg, worth $165–183m.

Barnett chose to share a significant part of the proceeds with associates, an act of generosity that Buffett took as a very positive indicator, "when someone behaves that generously, you know you are going to be treated right as a buyer."[166]

Estimating the intrinsic value of Helzberg, the Buffett way

When asked at the annual meeting in May 1996 for detail on his discounting method, for example, how many future years does he extend the calculation to, Buffett explained that, yes, the discounted owner earnings method is the framework at the heart of investing or buying businesses, but, no, there are no calculations written down at Berkshire with cut-off dates for calculating what is called the terminal value.

He said that though the equation is simple and direct, "we've never actually sat down and written out a set of numbers to relate that equation. We do it in our heads, in a way, obviously. I mean, that's what it's all about. But there is no piece of paper. There never was a piece of paper that shows what our calculation on Helzberg's or See's Candy or The Buffalo News was, in that respect."

Buffett and Munger fear that people get hung up on the illusory appearance of 'scientific' quality when using apparently sophisticated numerical analysis. Inputs to the formula are of an imprecise nature. What you need are good ballpark estimates after taking on board the all-important qualitative factors that create shareholder value (quality of franchise and management).

> "We are sitting in the office thinking about that question with each business or each investment. And we have discount rates, in a general way, in mind. But we really like the decision to be obvious enough to us that it doesn't require making a detailed

calculation. It's the framework, but it's not applied in the sense that we actually fill in all the variables."[167]

Charlie Munger added:

> "Berkshire is being run the way Thomas Hunt Morgan, the great Nobel laureate, ran the biology department at Caltech. He banned the Friden calculator, which was the computer of that era. And people said, 'How can you do this? Every place else in Caltech, we have Friden calculators going everywhere.' And he said, 'Well, we're picking up these great nuggets of gold just by organized common sense, and resources are short, and we're not going to resort to any damn placer mining as long as we can pick up these major aggregations of gold.' That's the way Berkshire works. And I hope the placer mining era will never come. Somebody once subpoenaed our staffing papers on some acquisition. And of course, not only did we not have any staffing papers, we didn't have any staff."

The Jeff Comment era

The sale to Berkshire met all of Barnett Helzberg's criteria. He was able to step back from the business and devote more time to his family and philanthropic pursuits. The family were diversified now with a large holding in Berkshire which gained income from a broad spread of business sectors; and they could sell the highly liquid Berkshire shares at any time to diversify further.

Most importantly, the future of the company was in good hands. There was a solemn commitment from Buffett and Munger to continue the firm's business philosophy, to retain the current associates and to maintain the corporate HQ in the Kansas City area.

Jeff Comment expected his new boss to give him some instructions. Buffett did indeed ring him up the day after the sale, but all he said was, "Guess what you get to do today. Start breaking all your banking relationships, because from now on I'm your bank."[168] Thus Buffett required control of capital allocation across the group. But apart from that, Comment was free to manage the business how he thought best. "Berkshire hasn't asked me to do anything that's really changed the business".¹⁶⁹ He told the *Kansas City Star* that Buffett had said that he doesn't call his presidents but he likes "hearing from you guys once in a while."¹⁷⁰

Jeff Comment says that Buffett and he are very different people, but they really trust one another and have a high degree of mutual respect. He thinks that is the case with all of Buffett's managers – there is a sort of chemistry. "That chemistry is missing in a lot of businesses today. They're functional, they're tactically correct, but boy do you lose the passion, and you lose the love of the business. That doesn't happen here … Warren is an incredibly cordial, warm, personable person."¹⁷¹

Why not put Borsheims and Helzberg together?

Most business groups already holding a jewellery retailer would instinctively look for synergy, such as buying economies or rationalising the store estate, when adding another. They would put them under the same management. But Berkshire is no ordinary group.

First, Buffett had promised that the businesses would be largely autonomous, each with their distinctive culture and leadership. Second, the synergistic gains would be pretty small compared with the loss of focus, damage to the *esprit de corps* and confusion over strategy. On the latter point Buffett wrote in his 1995 letter that "Helzberg's … is an entirely different sort of operation from Borsheim's, our Omaha jewellery business, and the two companies will operate independently of each other."¹⁷²

He expanded on that thought at the 1995 meeting:

> "Both [Borsheims and Nebraska Furniture Mart] offer this incredible selection, low prices brought about by huge volume, low operating costs, and all of that. Operating multiple locations … you would lose something, in terms of the amount of selection that could be offered. There's $50 million-plus at retail of jewellery at Borsheims' one location. Well, when someone wants to buy a ring, or a pearl necklace, or something of the sort, they can see more offerings at a place like that than they possibly could at somebody who is trying to maintain inventory at 20 or 50 locations. Similarly, that gives us a volume out of a

given location that results in operating costs that, again, can't be matched if you have an enormous number of locations. So, I think those businesses tend to be more successful in that particular mode as one-location businesses. Now, Helzberg's will be bringing merchandise to people all over the country at malls. And through that mode of operation, they perform that exceptionally well. But Borsheims can't be Helzberg's, and Helzberg's can't be Borsheims."

Each business is going after different groups of customers. It's important that a Berkshire subsidiary figure out what it's good at and who they can really offer something special to. Borsheims offers something very special to people in having the widest selection in the world in one place and having low prices due to driving operating costs 20 percentage points below competitors. "It's very hard to replicate something like that. And trying to do it in 10 spots probably wouldn't work well."[173] So it is best to leave Helzberg to use its special culture, knowledge and experience to operate in 200 malls nationwide and for Borsheims to keep improving its one-shop model.

The 1996 shock

In spring 1996, Buffett was full of optimism regarding Helzberg's prospects: "we believe it could grow to several times its present size," he wrote to shareholders. But he was brought down to earth only a few months later. Jeff Comment had gone for growth to such an extent that store numbers went from 166 to 181 in 12 months, costs spiralled, and the managerial team simply could not cope. "We had a serious downturn in 1996 … We overexpanded. We outran our people", says Comment.[174]

On top of these operational problems its biggest competitor, Zales, was permitted to come out of bankruptcy with a clean balance sheet (little debt) and Signet, another big player, was pumping money into jewellery retailing.

Early in 1996, Comment called Buffett to give him the bad news. Buffett merely asked what he, Comment, wanted to do. He requested 30 days to come up with a plan and then to meet Buffett in Omaha for him to explain it. The general tone of the meeting was not one of a subordinate trying to gain approval but of a trusted manager just telling Buffett what he was doing. Buffett did however quiz him on when the firm would get back to being the business Berkshire had bought. Comment was confident that he would stabilise it in 1997 and produce a significant turnaround in 1998.

And that is what he did. In fact, it was a quicker turnaround than he anticipated, allowing Buffett to tell Berkshire shareholders that profits had improved in 1997 and were gaining real momentum by the crucial Christmas season and through into the first part of 1998. It wasn't long before expansion was back on the agenda, and by September 2000, Helzberg Diamonds had 236 stores in 38 states, making it the fifth largest jewellery chain in the country.

Moreover, store efficiency was great, with a per-store turnover averaging close to $2.2m compared with competitors' $1–1.5m. Helzberg Diamonds were noted for their determination to open only in premium locations. To secure the best stores, it helped that they had built strong relationships with premium shopping-mall developers.

We do not have published numbers after Helzberg was absorbed into Berkshire, but Comment did say when interviewed in September 2000 that he anticipated sales in 2001 of $500m (up 77% since the Berkshire purchase) and annual pre-tax profits of $50m.[175] Such a profit from a company that cost less than $200m must have greatly pleased Buffett.

Steady state

Sadly, Jeff Comment died suddenly aged 60 in October 2004. He was succeeded by H. Marvin Beasley, who five years later resigned without a reason being made public.

In 2009, highly regarded jewellery expert and retail executive Beryl Raff was handpicked by Warren Buffett to take the leadership of Helzberg. She came from JCPenney, where she had been executive vice president and general merchandise manager for their fine jewellery operations, following a few years as Zales' CEO. On her appointment Buffett wrote that she was "an outstanding merchant and strong multi-store retail executive [with a] finely balanced blend of merchandising instinct and analytical sharpness."[176]

In 2000, there were over 3,000 associates working for Helzberg in 236 stores. But that was the high point. Store numbers did rise to 270 when Raff took over, but employee numbers were down to 2,147. Today there are less than 2,000 employees running only 210 stores.

To shrink a company like this is unusual. Buffett and Munger are in charge of capital allocation, and I can only suppose that they are unconvinced that additional stores will generate the high rates of return on capital that other uses of that money could do within the Berkshire family.

This does not mean that the current Helzberg shops are in any way suffering. They, like See's Candy stores, are likely to be producing high rates of return. It is just that the team have a clear vision of the boundary lines of their circle of competence and their circle of competitive advantage. The existing stores lie within those circles. It is rare that a proposed new store would command sufficient competitive power to generate high returns.

Learning points

1. **Apply rationality to mergers and acquisitions.** Most do not generate value for acquiring shareholders. Reasons include belief in rosy scenarios; managers falling in love with buying companies rather than day-to-day management; and managers too enamoured with a strategic plan so they overpay to fulfil the plan.
2. **Good sellers are not motivated by money alone.** Barnett Helzberg cared deeply about what happened after the sale in terms of employee and customer welfare, culture and loyalty to Kansas City. This reduced the risk of buying from him.
3. **Search for good returns on capital.** Buffett thought Helzberg's high revenue per square foot combined with the experienced and able management, sound culture and reputation created superior rates of return on invested capital.
4. **There must always be high quality leaders in place.** If Jeff Comment was not there Buffett would not have bought the company.

5. **Think for yourself about the decisive qualities of a business.** Investment bankers and accountants tend to be too quantitative – when the really important factors in business success are qualitative – and only put forward positive scenarios when acting for the seller.

6. **The character of certain key people is far more important than conventional due diligence.** Look for integrity, honesty, competence, values and rationality.

7. **The most meaningful intrinsic value (discounted cash flows/owner earnings) estimates do not need to be set down on paper with precision.** All you need are good ballpark estimates that allow sufficient margin of safety from purchase price. The decision must be so obvious that there is no need for detailed calculations.

Investment 6

R.C. WILLEY[177]

Summary of the deal

Deal	R.C. Willey
Time	1995
Price paid	$175m in BH shares
Quantity	100% of the equity
Sale price	Held today
Profit	Over five times the purchase price already handed over to Berkshire, and we're still counting.
Berkshire Hathaway in 1995	Share price: $20,500–32,000 Book value: $17,217m Per share book value: $14,426

The R.C. Willey story is one of mid-western values of hard work, decency, business-smarts and devotion to community leading to outstanding success. It is the story of three men who epitomised those values: Rufus Call Willey, Bill Child and, of course, Warren Buffett.

Rufus Call (or R.C.) Willey sold electrical appliances in 1932 from the back of a pickup truck in the area north of Salt Lake City, Utah. A consummate salesman, he had the amazing ability to engage with people, often to sell them things they thought they didn't need. When people in the farming community around his hometown of Syracuse said they could not afford a refrigerator, he would gently suggest that they try it for a week without charge, "and if you don't want it after a week I'll come back and take it out – no obligation".[178] Naturally, once they experienced the benefits they generally found the money from somewhere.

When competitors complained to manufacturers that R.C. had a competitive advantage in avoiding the overheads of a store, and therefore they should stop supplying him, R.C. built a simple 600-square-foot cinderblock store next to his house and stocked it with fridges, stoves and other appliances. His 22-year-old son-in-law Bill Child helped out in the evenings and Saturdays when he wasn't studying at the University of Utah in preparation to take up a teaching position at the junior high in nearby Clearfield.

When R.C. died suddenly in 1954 the responsibility for the tiny store landed in Bill Child's lap. And while it had a tremendous reputation with customers, there were piles of debt and it was touch and go as to whether it could survive.

With tremendous resolve, ingenuity and a family pulling together, it got through. Over time extensions were added to the single-storey building. Low prices and great customer service drew customers back time and again, despite being located down a side road. Then a second store was added. Eventually there were six, all in Utah. By 1995 annual revenue was over $250m, profits and return on capital were great, and there was little debt. R.C. Willey then accounted for half of the furniture sold in Utah and one-third of the electrical goods.

Bill Child, at 63, looked to secure the future of the enterprise beyond his tenure as CEO. Remembering that R.C. had died at a much younger age, he was concerned that his own death might result in enormous taxes to be paid which the family would only be able to afford by selling a large portion of their shares. A much better solution was to swap those R.C. Willey shares for Berkshire Hathaway shares. Not only would the tax burden be better managed, but the team and its unique ethos would be preserved.

Warren Buffett could see the values he most admired lodged in Child. He wrote:

"Bill Child represents the best of America. In matters of family, philanthropy, business, or just plain citizenship, anyone who follows in his footsteps is heading true north ... By doing the right things for his customers and associates, he eventually left once-strong competitors in the dust ... He just applied the oldest and soundest principle ever set forth: Treat the other fellow as you would like to be treated yourself".[179]

Buffett advises us to examine the lessons from Child's life and apply them to our own to lead a happier, more productive life. This chapter describes those lessons and values, and why Buffett was more than willing to pay $175m for the company.

Rufus Call Willey

Rufus Call, born in 1900 in Syracuse, 25 miles north of Salt Lake City, was one of 11 children in a Mormon farming family. At 17 he found work in the exciting field of electricity, which was then only just reaching rural areas. He did the backbreaking work of erecting poles and stringing wire across Utah. In 1922 he married Helen Swanker and took night classes to become a certified electrician; he was later made substation manager.

A few years later he surprised Helen with a refrigerator. She loved it – as did many neighbours, who kept stopping by just to look and wonder how it worked. They could see the advantages of having one in their homes. The idea for a business on the side sprung into R.C.'s mind. His employer, the Utah Power and Light Company, were only too happy for him to sell refrigerators and other appliances to his neighbours. After all, they wanted people to use their electricity.

In 1932, R.C. set up properly and, with a line of credit from the Barnes Banking Company, bought a range of appliances to go on the back of his pickup truck – and off he went to sell door to door. R.C. could wire the home and even offer credit so that farmers did not have to pay until after harvest.

The business was run by only two people: R.C. and Lamar Sessions (who delivered and repaired the various machines). When competitors complained about R.C.'s business, the Hotpoint representative didn't want to lose his top salesman in the area and so suggested that R.C. build some sort of store. Which he did, in the corner of his farm next to his house, off an old track with no foot traffic. An electricity cable ran from R.C. and Helen's house. The store lacked plumbing and had four parking spaces. But, through word of mouth, acting with integrity and salesmanship, annual revenue was about $50,000 in 1950.

Bill Child

Bill Child, in 1951, married R.C. and Helen's youngest daughter, Helen Darline (they were sweethearts from childhood). Bill had recently gained a scholarship to study at the University of Utah, greatly helping him in his ambition to become a teacher. A few months later, when Darline was expecting a child, R.C. and Helen gave the young couple a small piece of land 50 yards from the store to place a modular house on.

Bill worked the summer at the store, and in the evenings and on Saturdays during term time. Not only was he strong and worked hard, but he had a natural, caring way with people, putting them at their ease, and went out of his way to serve their needs.

Here's an indicator of the nature of the community; on many Saturdays R.C. and Child would go off to the local baseball game, leaving a message on the open door saying: "Gone to the ballgame … Come in and look around".[180]

Trouble

In spring 1954 R.C. felt discomfort in his stomach. Thinking he had ulcers brought on by the stress of coping with annual revenue of $250,000 with only him and Sessions as full-timers, he continued to soldier on. When the discomfort didn't get any better, R.C. announced that he really needed a vacation. He booked two weeks in California and asked Sessions to keep the business going while he was away. At first Sessions protested, saying there would be too much for him to do, but something R.C. said stunned him. "You know, Lamar, when you think you're going to die, you'll do most anything to prolong your life."[181]

Around that time, Child was offered a secure job as a teacher in North Davis Junior High. All he had to do was sign the school contract and his work life was set. On Child's graduation day (1 June, 1954) R.C. went to Bill and Darline's house to explain his need for a vacation, and handed the keys to the store to Bill, asking him to oversee it while he was away.

Ominously, R.C. and Helen returned a week early because R.C. was feeling too ill to continue. Then the bad news: he was diagnosed with pancreatic cancer and was unlikely to leave the hospital.

Bill Child faced a dilemma. On the one hand he could take up the teaching contract he had always wanted. On the other, there was a business that really needed him, a business that supported the family. The store had obligations to customers, suppliers and to Sessions. Perhaps the school principal would allow him time to get the business on the right path before he entered the classroom?

But there was more bad news to come. First, the tax man arrived at the store to conduct an audit. The 22-year-old hadn't a clue as to what was happening. It turned out the business' accountant had not been making any tax payments for years – over $10,000 was due.

Then the bank called and told Bill to stop writing cheques at once; there weren't funds to cover them.

Then R.C. died on 3 September.

After the funeral, the bank manager called a meeting with Bill and Helen to explain just how bad the finances of the business were. R.C. had borrowed $9,000 and the unpaid interest was mounting up. In addition, the bank had been financing credit given to customers. That finance was guaranteed by the business. It turned out that two-thirds were behind on their payments. Of those, one-half had failed to pay anything in nine months. For a business with a turnover of $250,000 and $150,000 on credit, that is a lot of money to have outstanding. The bank manager wanted the store to immediately repurchase $50,000 of delinquent accounts.

The bank clearly had little faith in a 22-year-old business ingénue with teaching ambitions. "Helen", the banker said, "you need to sell the business and let Bill go teach school."[182]

They agreed the family needed a little time to discuss what to do. Bill had only taken on the task of running the business because he had assumed it would be for a short period of time. He still had the school job lined up, so why not just sell up? But, because of all the debt, the company was unlikely to fetch a good price. Furthermore, R.C. had not saved any money for Helen. As profits came in, he would spend it freely on his family and give it away to needy people he met. If the business were to close his widow would have little to live on, and no one in the family could support her. Bill had to turn the business around. And given the enormous goodwill it had built up over the years it still had potential.

The accidental businessman

Bill Child spoke with the school principal who instantly understood that he had to get the business straight. Still hankering after the classroom, Bill asked: "If you have a teaching position open in the future, would you please consider me?"[183] Prophetically, the principle replied: "Bill, I would love to have you teach for me. However, my intuition tells me that if you get into business, you'll never teach."

Child next went to see the bank manager to plead for time, saying, "If we close the business, there'll be no funds to pay you. If we remain open, we will be able to pay everything off."[184] Given the lack of assets it could seize, the bank reluctantly agreed.

Then Child visited a different bank to see if they would advance a loan. They wouldn't. After all, the inventory was purchased on credit and the store didn't have a separate deed as it was attached to the family home. There was no cash either. The only real asset was a pickup truck.

R.C. had built customer loyalty partly by selling appliances at low prices, sometimes below cost. It was not that he consciously aimed at a loss, just that he was first and foremost a salesman and keen to treat his customers well. Near term profits were an afterthought.

Then Child had a break. He tried one more bank, First National Bank of Layton. It was a rival of R.C.'s bank and, in its keenness to poach a client, it agreed to provide R.C. Willey with a $10,000 line of credit. But that still left the daunting tasks of paying off the old $9,000 loan and $50,000 of customer debts.

Another break: the Utah Power and Light Company incentivised appliance retailers with $35 bonuses each time they persuaded a customer to replace their gas-fired boiler with an electric one and $25 when they switched to an electric stove. Bill set a target for himself and Sessions of 150 water heaters and 150 ranges, which would raise the $9,000. Slowly but surely the mortgage was repaid.

As for the delinquent credit accounts, Child took a different approach. He learned a finance company, Commercial Credit, specialising in what we might today call subprime lending, might be willing to purchase the delinquent contracts from R.C. Willey and then collect what they could from customers, charging a higher interest rate along the way.

It was important that the non-paying customers gave their consent for the transfer. Child would visit them to push. Even though he wanted to remain friends he would, in the end, firmly state that either they signed the agreement or the appliance would be repossessed. Most signed, and cash flowed to the company while responsibility for collecting debts flowed away from the company.

Business began to pick up. To cope, Child hired Connie O'Brien part-time to handle phone calls and administration while he concentrated on sales. The relationship with Commercial Credit blossomed, allowing Child to offer credit to customers without much paperwork or use of R.C. Willey's capital.

Bill was working 12-hour days but enjoying it. He and his family lived frugally, reinvesting the money they had into the business. He paid himself the same as his repairman Sessions, $100 per week. But for the first couple of years, because of the tight cash situation, he would only draw it about half the time. He said it didn't cost him much to live; he was working so hard that he had little time to spend it.

Acting decently

In 1954 and 1955 a big seller was Hotpoint's automatic washing machine – 400 were sold at a gross margin of $40 each. But a year or so later calls came in that the spin mechanism had failed, leaving clothes wet. The manufacturer was obligated to replace the defective parts with R.C. Willey funding labour costs. Hotpoint supplied the parts, but absurdly they were the defective ones again. And the manufacturer was only required to repair once.

Naturally, after another year customers would be complaining again, only this time Hotpoint could disavow any responsibility. R.C. Willey would have 400 dissatisfied customers. Child complained to Hotpoint, asking for better replacement mechanisms, but this was to no avail.

So after two and a half years of hard slog getting the business out of debt and finally seeing a possible profit in 1956, Bill had to bear the cost of those repairs if the company's reputation was not to be trashed. He wavered in his commitment to carry on. Should he close up and go and teach? Doing so would leave hundreds of neighbouring families with defective washing machines. Bill thought, "That's not the R.C. Willey way".[185] Besides, he had done the heavy lifting; this was clearly a business with potential.

He braced himself and decided to take the hit on the warrantees to do right by the people of his community, despite there being no legal obligation. It cost thousands of dollars. This act of service and generosity did not go unnoticed. Word spread, and people decided not to shop anywhere else.

Expansion

Child looked for ways to build profits and, in 1956, hit on the idea of selling furniture – items, thankfully, without the burden of moving parts or onerous warranties. At first, a few pieces were placed in Child's personal double garage and customers in the main store were encouraged to take a 50-yard stroll to take a look. In particular, the sofas were a great hit, selling out very quickly. A decision was made in 1957 to add 1,800 sq ft to the store's footprint.

Bill really needed help in the showroom now. His 18-year-old brother, Sheldon, enthusiastically accepted the offer to work part-time. When Sheldon went to Utah State University, he would drive home to work Saturdays. This was mostly deliveries and installations with Roy Hodson, the recently hired deliveryman. Sheldon was superb at demonstrating the workings of the appliance. He moved into R.C. and Helen's old home right next to the store so he could work more hours at a job he loved.

The move into furniture worked and company revenue doubled in a year. Both a full-time and a part-time salesman were hired, and the store was extended again. Sheldon was approached to take on a salesman's role. He accepted the role to pay his way through college, but he too had retained ambitions to be a teacher. As his final year approached in fall 1959, Bill said to his brother, "I'm not going to tell you what to do. But if you're going to teach, then you ought to go back to school. But if you're going to stay in the furniture business, I don't think a degree will make a difference … You could spend a year working and then decide whether to go back to school".[186] Sheldon agreed.

That year was one of rapid expansion, with more product lines added and more salesmen coming on board. It was exciting. Sheldon and his wife built their own home next to Bill's and were starting to accept that Sheldon was unlikely to return to college.

More extensions to the store were added to make it, by 1965, the largest furniture store in Utah outside of Salt Lake City. Their out-of-the-way position was even turned to an advantage with advertising slogans such as, 'Lower overhead means lower prices because of our country location'. People drive a long way to find a bargain. Employee numbers rose to 50 full-timers.

Sadly, in spring 1965, Bill's wife Darline died aged 31 from a rare condition causing blood clots, leaving a devastated Bill and two boys and two girls behind. The whole family were rocked to the core, but found some strength from their Mormon faith, which has a strong belief in families reuniting in heaven. Bill kept himself extraordinarily busy to avoid thinking too much.

Diversification

Near to Syracuse was the Hill Air Force base, which employed more than 20,000 civilians and 3,000 military personnel. Not only did R.C. Willey benefit from the wealth brought to the area via wages for civilians, but air force people were moved around, and they tended to buy furniture and appliances when they set up home in Utah.

The base was a blessing, but also posed a threat. It was possible – and there were rumours to this effect – that the base could be downgraded, resulting in fewer people. Bill saw that R.C. Willey's income was over-concentrated in one place. As much as two-thirds of revenue could be linked to the base.

The solution was to replicate the low-price/excellent-service formula in another store sufficiently far away that it pulled in different customers. A four-acre site at Murray, south of Salt Lake City and 36 miles from Syracuse, seemed ideal. A successful TV campaign had already raised the company's profile through the area, so the brand was well-known in Utah way beyond Syracuse.

It took until 1969 to open the 20,000 sq ft store, by which time Bill had married Patricia and their first child was one year old. They eventually had four, so there were eight children in the family home.[187] It was a time of exceptional hard work for Bill and Patricia as they juggled the needs of the business and those of the children.

Thankfully, the new store was a great success and over the next decade no less than eight extensions were added, and Murray staff numbers rose from 20 to over 200.

Going into finance

In 1975, R.C. Willey started issuing its own credit cards. This took a lot of capital and presented considerable risk, but it was a way of building the brand and they could earn substantial interest (even at rates lower than customers would be charged by banks or other financial institutions).

Providing financing also maintained R.C. Willey's relationship with its customers. This allowed the company to take more time than a bank would to understand the circumstances leading to a missed payment – say the loss of a job or illness – and be more compassionate and patient than an anonymous financial institution, leading to long-term loyalty.

In the mid-1980s over $7m profit was being made from credit interest. In the early 1990s that rose to over $18m.

Doing the right thing

At its stores R.C. Willey would offer warrantees for the year or two after the manufacturer's first year warranty ran out, for a fee. R.C. Willey would repair or replace at no cost to the customer. The company later passed on the responsibility for the cost of the repairs or replacement to an insurer. R.C. Willey would pay the insurer slightly less than the customer paid for the extended warrantee.

Then one day the insurer declared bankruptcy. R.C. Willey was not legally obliged to honour the warranties because that was the responsibility of the bust insurer. But the Child brothers felt they could not tell customers they were out of luck (as some other retailers with a relationship with the same insurer did). That decision cost the firm $1.5m. "We felt it was the right thing to do. Customers trust us enough to purchase products from us. So we felt we should cover the guarantees."[188]

Getting big

With annual revenue from the two stores totalling over $50m in 1985, a third was opened only eight miles to the west of the Murray store. Then, in 1990, on a 13-acre block of land in South Salt Lake City (about seven miles north of Murray), a 180,000 sq ft warehouse, 30,000 sq ft of corporate offices, and a 70,000 sq ft furniture display were opened.

Company sales rose to $85m. Just as things were really happening at R.C. Willey, the man Bill most leaned on in the business, his brother Sheldon (then sales director and president), was asked by the Church of Jesus Christ of Latter-day Saints to become the full-time president of the Church's proselytising mission in New York City. He accepted the calling.[189]

Despite the loss of Sheldon, the company continued to grow at a tremendous rate, achieving a turnover of $257m in 1995, by which time there were five stores in Utah with a sixth on the way.

Guiding principles

For Bill Child to succeed he had to follow sound principles to gain the trust of customers and the admiration and loyalty of employees. Fortunately for us he has written about his rules for success:[190]

1. **Be motivated by excellence, not money.** If you are better than your competitors, the profits will come.
2. **Offer customers true value on quality products.** A low price on a cheap piece of furniture is not value.
3. **Think like a customer and treat them as you would like to be treated.** They can take their business elsewhere at any time. (Associates witnessed daily the commitment of Bill and Sheldon to customer service. They too went out of their way for people.)
4. **Enjoy your business and know the industry and its future.**
5. **Avoid unnecessary debt.** When the economy takes a downturn, excessive debt will sink you.
6. **Be efficient.** Nothing drains a business like waste.
7. **Treat your associates with respect.** Otherwise employees won't treat customers with respect. (An example: the company ran a generous profit-sharing plan.)
8. **Pay attention to details.** To borrow a phrase from Warren – in retail, you need to be good every day.
9. **Be honest!** Nothing sinks a reputation faster than dishonesty. It takes years to build a reputation, but it can be destroyed in one day over one misdeed. (Sheldon's motto was, "If you always tell the truth, you never have to remember what you said".)
10. **Hire good and capable people.** People you respect and will enjoy working with.
11. **Make decisions with an eye on the future.** Not just what is good for today.
12. **Differentiate your company with marketing; don't always follow the crowd.** At times you must go outside the box.

13. **Most important, be able to adapt to changes in the marketplace and don't be afraid to change when circumstances demand.** We live in a changing world.

He adds that there is one other crucial lesson: **the importance of saying thank you** – to associates, to people who help you along the way and to family.

From this list, and from the story of his life, perhaps we can conclude that Bill Child really did turn out to be a teacher after all, just not in the way he originally intended.

The deal with Warren Buffett

At the start of 1995 an investment bank approached Bill Child with an offer to buy R.C. Willey. The headline figure mentioned was $200m. This followed separate approaches by two publicly traded retailers. These were totally unsolicited offers. After looking around the stores of the two retailers and being unimpressed by the way the furniture was presented, Child decided they were a poor fit for R.C. Willey.

As for the investment bank, the $200m was not all it seemed. The bank would only put up $100m in cash, borrowing the other $100m using R.C. Willey's assets as collateral. The company would thus deteriorate from having a very conservatively managed balance sheet to a risky one. True, Bill and Sheldon would walk away with a lot of money, but their creation would be lumbered with debt, making it and all the livelihoods that depended on it vulnerable. They hated that thought.

Bill was 63 and, cognisant of his father-in-law's death at 54, was fully aware that there was a possibility of him suddenly leaving a mess for his survivors to sort out. He wanted the business, with its loyal associates, customers and suppliers, to go on decades after his lifetime. This outcome was unlikely if he sold to one of Wall Street's financial engineering players or to a less able retailer. Sheldon was six years younger and would be a natural successor, but he was increasingly drawn to the Church.

While pondering this problem in January 1995, Bill attended the San Francisco Furniture Mart Trade Show, where he met his old friend Irv Blumkin, CEO of Nebraska Furniture Mart (volume two, investment three). The Blumkin family had faced a similar issue in 1983 and found the solution to be to sell most of the shares in NFM to Berkshire Hathaway.

Bill was curious as to what life was like over the intervening 12 years. Irv responded in such positive terms – Buffett had kept every promise and was the best of business partners, and the family were still in managerial control – that Bill asked him, "do you think Warren would be interested in buying our company?"

Irv greatly respected R.C. Willey as one of the best-managed furniture businesses in the country, and considered Bill to be an excellent and principled manager. He said that Buffett would, most likely, be interested and offered to introduce Bill to Warren to explore the possibility.

Bill talked it over with Sheldon, who immediately agreed that a sale to Berkshire would be an excellent solution. A few days later Bill asked Irv to please go ahead and contact Buffett. Irv was due to have dinner with Buffett a few days later and promised to raise R.C. Willey then.

It wasn't the first time they had discussed R.C. Willey because for years Buffett had probed Irv with the question, "Are there any more at home like you?" To which Irv had responded that scattered around the country were three other very well managed furniture retailers, one of which was R.C. Willey (the other two come into the Buffett story later). In his 1995 letter Buffett said that over the years Irv had told him about the company's strengths, so he was already familiar with the firm.

Warren and Bill speak

In mid-February Irv rang to give Bill the good news. Buffett was really interested and would call. Only a few minutes later he did. "This is Warren Buffett, Bill. I just talked to Irv, and I understand you have an interest in selling your company."[191]

Buffett was particularly keen to know why Bill wanted to sell. Child replied: "I want to be sure the company continues beyond my lifetime. Second, if anything were to happen to me or my wife the business would have to be sold at a fire-sale price to pay the estate tax."[192]

Buffett needed good management in place and so asked how long Bill planned on remaining CEO. From Buffett's standpoint the response was terrific: "For as long as I can be productive and make a contribution. I can promise you at least seven years."[193]

Final key question: "How much?"

Bill answered, "Just a fair price ... We want whoever buys it to be just as happy two, three and five years from now."[194]

Buffett said he would love to look at it and asked for the previous two to three years of accounts along with some history.

Buffett liked what he saw: 17% annual sales and profit growth, dominant market share in Utah, and a profitable finance business. Its balance sheet was rock solid, with all land and buildings paid for and no debt apart from that to help finance some of the credit given to customers.

Four days after receiving the package from Salt Lake City, Buffett wrote to Child saying that he had "a jewel of a company" and would have a purchase price within three days. Buffett's second letter promised that the company would be run just as before the sale, and it would retain its identity as a local institution just as most Californians thought of See's Candy as a strictly Californian institution. Bill would be CEO and never be required to travel to Omaha. The price offered was $170m either in cash or Berkshire stock.

There was much for Bill and Sheldon to discuss, not least the $20–30m discount compared with selling to a Wall Street firm. But Buffett's offer had the offsetting positives of the family continuing to run the business and no disruption for customers or associates. Buffett had shown time again, from Borsheims to Scott Fetzer, that he kept his word on continuity – in the case of See's Candy for over two decades.

Bill called Irv Blumkin who advised that "no matter what you do, take stock. Had we taken stock instead of cash – and held it – it would have been worth over a billion dollars today" (90% of NFM's shares were sold to Berkshire for $55.35m).

An investment banker friend advised that the offer was on the low side and so Bill should negotiate. But Bill said, "If Warren buys the company

I'm going to be working with him and for him. I'm not too comfortable in negotiating with him."[195]

He called Warren and said that the offer was very fair and invited Buffett to come and look over the operation. "I don't need to come and look at it," Buffett replied, "You have a wonderful reputation. I know that if you say the assets are there, then they are there, plus some."[196]

"Warren, there's no way I could sell this company to you without you first seeing what you are buying. It just wouldn't be fair."

Buffett said he could call in when on his way to Palm Springs to play golf with Bill Gates. While touring the stores and stopping for a Coke and Hamburger the subject of payment in Berkshire stock was raised by Bill. He noted that the value of a Berkshire share fluctuated, making it difficult for him and Sheldon to value. Where would the value be at the time that the sale closed?

"I can understand your concern," Buffett said "the stock is now at $22,000 a share. I'll tell you what I'll do. I'll lock it in at $22,000 if we do the deal. If it goes up that's to your benefit."[197]

"What if the value goes down?" Bill asked.

"Then we'll talk about it", Buffett replied, which seemed fair to Bill.

For the next few weeks, the Child family tied themselves in knots trying to minimise tax on the deal. Buffett called regularly to see if they had a solution. In the end he said that, while he couldn't guarantee that taxes won't be paid if it helps resolve the situation, he would throw another $5m into the pot.

Berkshire Hathaway's stock had recently risen to $24,000, making Buffett's offer of Berkshire shares at $22,000 even more attractive. The extra $5m was the clincher. "Warren, if you do that, you've got a deal right now. It's all stock."[198]

Reassuring honesty

When the papers were ready for Bill and other family shareholders to sign, he noticed that Berkshire had erroneously put an extra four shares in the contract, adding about $100,000 to the price.

Bill phoned Berkshire HQ and spoke with Marc Hamburg, who said he'd let Buffett know in the morning. The next day the message came back: "Don't worry about it, Warren wants you to have it".[199] The effective date of the merger was 29 June, 1995.

After the deal

In terms of managerial decisions nothing really changed. The one exception was that Buffett held a veto over investments in new stores. Bill Child told *Utah Business* that Warren Buffett was a wonderful partner:

> "Rather than tell us how to run our business, he gives us a big vote of confidence, 100 percent support and total trust. We don't have anyone looking over our shoulder. He's interested in the long haul … If we were to sell every appliance and electronic product we have at a very low margin for the next four years to protect our market share, he would probably not say a thing. He's the perfect partner."[200]

Not on a Sunday

Now that R.C. Willey dominated the Utah furniture and electricals market it was natural for Bill to think of ploughing profits into other states. He'd been working on a plan to open a store in Las Vegas where Clark County alone was welcoming about 8,000 new residents each month. Henderson, in Clark County about 16 miles southeast of Las Vegas, had some excellent reasonably-priced large sites with good access.

After Child took Buffett on a helicopter tour of the area pointing out the rapid growth in households, he asked what Buffett thought of the prospects.

"We're not going to go," Buffett said.

Child was shocked. The plan was all worked out. A new store in Henderson could be more profitable than any store they had in Utah.

Buffett accepted that closing all stores on a Sunday made sense in Mormon country, but in most states Sunday was the biggest trading day for furniture – often one-quarter of the week's takings. Child could not compromise his principles and therefore proposed that any Henderson store would indeed close on Sundays.

Buffett respected Child's religious convictions, but it just didn't make financial sense to him to spend tens of millions on a new store if competitors then go and syphon off customers on Sundays. He told his friend, "We're not going to open on Sunday. But we're also not going to go into a market where we can't be successful."[201]

Child disagreed but accepted Buffett's perspective. He could see how difficult it might be for others to understand his vision.

One investment Buffett did agree to, however, was the construction, in 1997, of America's largest (860,000 sq ft) distribution centre in Salt Lake City, which offered an unrivalled capability to supply the Utah stores and customers.

Another tack

Westward expansion to Las Vegas was vetoed, but Child still saw potential elsewhere. He focused on the state to the north of Utah, Idaho. There, Boise was in need of a massive R.C. Willey store, he thought. It too was growing fast and was only 350 miles from the new distribution centre which could restock a new store overnight.

Buffett again said no. He was satisfied with the firm's performance in Utah. "We're doing okay", he said.

One morning, Bill was in the shower and decided that he wouldn't come out until he had thought of a way to convince Buffett to allow him to go ahead with the Boise store. Later that day he telephoned Buffett: "I'd like to talk to you about Boise, Idaho".

Buffett said curtly, "We've already talked about Boise."

"Warren, I'm going to make you a proposition you can't refuse. I will buy the land, and I will build the building, personally. And if we're not successful in six months, we'll walk. That guarantees that the company won't lose a dime".[202]

Berkshire could not lose, so Buffett said, "Okay. If the store can't do $30m in the first year, we'll walk. If the store does $30m, I'll lease it from you and pay you four percent of gross sales."

But Bill wasn't finished in his generosity. He then said that if it is really successful, he'll sell the store to Berkshire at what it cost him, with no interest added.

Buffett said, "Okay."

About two weeks later Buffett called and said that he had been thinking about the proposition and that he could not exploit his friend this way. "There's no upside for you. It's all downside."[203]

"Warren, first of all, I wouldn't have it any other way. Second, there is some upside. The upside is that if we are successful, you are going to let us go to Las Vegas",[204] replied Bill.

The store opened in August 1999 and was an instant success, with first week sales of $1m. A few months later Buffett wrote in his 1999 letter to shareholders about his scepticism of Bill's plan to take his no-Sunday policy to Boise and of Bill's "truly extraordinary proposition" which had cost $9m and could leave him with an empty building. He went on:

> "The store opened last August and immediately became a huge success. Bill thereupon turned over the property to us… And, get this: Bill refused to take a dime of interest on the capital he had tied up over the two years… You can understand why the opportunity to partner with people like Bill Child causes me to tap dance to work every morning."

Buffett was invited to cut the ribbon at the official opening of the Boise store. He told the crowd how sales had exceeded expectations by a long way and cheekily said that, after he discovered how well it was doing, it must have been his idea all along. "I'm really glad Bill didn't talk me out of it". First year sales were $50m.

Las Vegas, at last

In the glow of the Boise success Bill thought it a good time to speak with Warren about Las Vegas. "Warren, we've done it in Boise. Now you have to let us go to Las Vegas. And I'll make you the same deal as before."[205] Buffett said he could only take advantage of a guy once and that if he could do it in Las Vegas, "then you will really make a convert out of me."[206]

The store was opened in 2001. Sales after the soft opening indicated the store was going to be a huge success, so at the official ribbon-cutting Buffett announced they were to build another store in the greater Las Vegas area.

In his 2001 letter to shareholders Buffett declared that he was even more sceptical that the no-Sunday policy could work in Las Vegas than in Boise, but nevertheless gave Bill the go-ahead.

> "The result: This store outsells all others in the R.C. Willey chain, doing a volume of business that far exceeds the volume of any competitor and that is twice what I had anticipated. I cut the ribbon at the grand opening in October – this was after a 'soft' opening and a few weeks of exceptional sales – and, just as I did at Boise, I suggested to the crowd that the new store was my idea. It didn't work. Today, when I pontificate about retailing, Berkshire people just say, 'What does Bill think?' (I'm going to draw the line, however, if he suggests that we also close on Saturdays.)"

First year sales at Henderson were $86m.

How come R.C. Willey can outsell competitors which are open seven days a week? The answer must lie in value for money. But how do you get to the level of efficiency and commitment of associates to be able to give that value for money? There is something in the culture of the company, of values, of integrity and of caring. Buffett tried to express it: "Other people can buy the same furniture, the same land, build the same store – all these things can be duplicated. But they can't duplicate R.C. Willey."[207]

Four at home

Within Berkshire Hathaway, R.C. Willey was placed in the home furnishing segment alongside Nebraska Furniture Mart and, in 1997, Star Furniture of Houston. Jordan's Furniture of Massachusetts joined in 1999. In 2002, R.C. Willey were doing more than $400m in sales and the home furnishings group achieved $106m in pre-tax earnings.

Child spoke of the advantages being part of this group brings: "We exchange ideas. We meet together. We visit each other's stores. We are in constant communication. We don't buy together, but we do go on buying trips together to Asia."[208]

He also said his relationship with Buffett is a dream come true, a climax to a wonderful business career:

> "I love his philosophy, I love his integrity. I love the way he deals with people. Every conversation with him is uplifting, and I learn from him every time we talk … He has a way of motivating you. He trusts you so much that you just want to perform … I don't want to let Warren down, don't want to disappoint him."[209]

Yet more growth

In 2001, Bill Child retired as CEO. His current role, in 2021, is chairman of the board. At 89, he still goes into the office nearly every day, but he mostly spends his time managing his family affairs, including a Hawaiian resort called Koloa Landing (*USA Today* voted it as the most beautiful resort pool in all of America in 2020).

The last 20 years have seen continued growth for R.C. Willey. In 2003 yet another hugely successful store was opened in greater Las Vegas. This was followed in 2005 by one in Reno, Nevada, of which Buffett wrote, "Bill and Scott [Hymas, CEO] again asked for my advice. Initially, I was pretty puffed up about the fact that they were consulting me. But then it dawned on me that the opinion of someone who is always wrong has its own special utility to decisionmakers."[210] The pace of sales in Reno exceeded that of the Boise store.

Sacramento, California, was next in 2006, to be followed by a second Sacramento store in 2018. Utah got its largest furnishings store – 160,000 sq ft, 22 miles south of Salt Lake City – in 2014.

Oddly, throughout this building spree the number of employees only crept up from 2,486 in 2008 to 2,866 in 2018. Today, less than 2,500 associates work at R.C. Willey, but its turnover is $870m – over $350,000 per member of staff.

Bill, whose wife describes him as a workaholic, continues to work at R.C. Willey with fewer hours while stepping up his philanthropic work. He and Patricia's favourite areas for charities are education, hospitals, and homeless-youth centres. But we'll never know the full extent of his philanthropic work because it is a point of conscience and modesty for Bill not to speak of it. The couple have also been involved in many successful real estate projects.

For someone who has triumphed in the notoriously difficult furniture business, Child is remarkably humble about the formula to succeed. "It is not rocket science. If you try to be the best you can … and never be satisfied with where you're at, you're going to do well … You don't survive if you don't change."[211]

Learning points

1. **The strongest businesses tend to be those built brick by lean brick.** The decades of hard times and steady unspectacular growth for R.C. Willey gave it a stable base, allowing for safe moves into new areas and continued low-cost operations. Investors should be wary of fast-growing companies using extensive financial engineering or takeovers to grow.

2. **Do the right thing.** This applies not just to the way customers and associates are treated, but the way business partners are treated. Child and Buffett were both concerned that the other benefitted justly from the deals they made.

3. **Learn to trust some people completely.** Buffett could trust Child to act fairly toward investors and so gave him free rein on operations. This level of trust is highly motivating.

4. **Return on capital is the key.** The R.C. Willey economic franchise was strong in Utah, where it generated high rates of return on capital employed, but Buffett thought it would not be strong enough in Idaho to justify using millions of dollars.

5. **Learn from your mistakes.** It turned out that Buffett was wrong about the strength of the R.C. Willey name and business model in Idaho and Nevada. He freely admits his error – with an ironic joke or two – and now trusts the retail experts in Berkshire Hathaway even more.

Investment 7

FLIGHTSAFETY INTERNATIONAL

Summary of the deal

Deal	FlightSafety International
Time	1996
Price paid	$1.5bn
Quantity	100% of the equity
Sale price	Held today
Profit	Over $4bn of post-tax earnings received so far
Berkshire Hathaway in 1996	Share price: $30,200–37,950 Book value: $23,426m Per share book value: $19,011

Al Ueltschi fell out of an airplane in 1940 when he was 23 years old. One moment he was sitting comfortably, the next "the whole airplane was missing!"[212] The seat, with him strapped to it, had simply detached when the biplane was upside down. He was no longer an instructor pilot, "but rather a falling object heading straight for a patch of Ohio farmland".[213] It was very cold, but he knew he had to rip off his gloves to pull the ripcord on his parachute. The chute exploded through his legs, "so I guess I was upside down".[214] With only 150 feet to go, the canopy finally opened.

The episode was so jarring that the leg straps ripped his underwear. He landed in a briar patch, tearing more of his clothes. "Apart from some minor scratches and a severely bruised ego, I was fine".[215]

But the lesson in the importance of having a well-trained pilot who you could trust in all circumstances was truly learned. He had put his life in the hands of someone under his instruction. The student was trying a half snap roll. He kept failing and stalling the aircraft. The last attempt was so abrupt that Ueltschi's seat simply fell out of the biplane. In those days, most training took place in the air, rather than in simulators, which resulted in more deaths by accidents in training than in normal flying.

It was the same Al Ueltschi (pronounced Yule-chee) who 56 years later sold his pilot training business to Berkshire Hathaway for $1.5bn. He swapped his 37% holding for around $555m worth of Berkshire shares. The aviator who had flown solo at 16, continued to be in charge of the company into his 90s, by which time his shares were worth $2bn.

Much of that money has been used to provide sight-saving operations to millions of people in the developing world through the charity he established, Orbis. Today, FlightSafety International dominates the pilot training industry.

Lindbergh and Al Ueltschi's love of flying

Ueltschi was the youngest of seven born on a Kentucky farm in 1917. As he grew, he observed how his parents worked all day, seven days a week, for a meagre profit at the end of the year. He didn't want to be a farmer.

Alfred at 10 years old was enthralled when Charles Lindbergh flew the Atlantic, his ear glued to the family vacuum-tube RCA radio, "listening for every scratchy-sounding news report on the progress of his flight. When the bulletin came announcing that he had landed in Paris and was carried off the field on the shoulders of thousands of cheering Frenchmen, I was hooked."[216]

From then on there was no doubt in his mind that he was to be a pilot. (Running ahead of the story: Ueltschi and Lindbergh became friends and 35 years after the biplane mishap they ended up sharing a room at

Le Bourget, the place in Paris where Lindbergh had landed all those years before. The pair were in France to evaluate an airplane.)

The young Alfred quickly recognised that farming would not earn him the money needed for flying lessons, so he looked for something else. At 16, he opened a tiny hole-in-the-wall hamburger stand selling burgers and a Coke for 5 cents. He sold a lot. The only problem was that he wasn't making any profit. That was solved by doubling his prices. It wasn't long before he had two more stands run by school buddies. As profits flowed, they went into flying lessons at a grass-strip near Lexington.

Two years later, wanting to make flying his career, Ueltschi was desperate to buy an airplane. But that would cost thousands of dollars. Fortunately, one of his burger customers was the president of the Farmers Bank. Al asked for a loan of $3,500 and got it, using the hamburger stands as collateral.

He paced off a grass strip in a nearby farm and called it an airport. Leaflets were delivered across the area, advertising the Frankfort Flying Service. At first, the daily routine was burger-serving after school during the week and selling flying lessons at the weekend.

As if he wasn't busy enough, Ueltschi then enrolled at the University of Kentucky. He was a poor student though, unable to get his mind off planes. Literature, philosophy, history, etc., were no match for the excitement of flying. So he dropped out and sold his burger business to one of his brothers in order to concentrate on trying to make a living as a pilot. But the economy was still in the doldrums of the Great Depression.

He would do anything and everything to earn money. A short flight would cost $1 for an adult and 50 cents for a child. Acrobatic shows paid well but were dangerous: "folks came out to see if the fool kid would kill himself, and like a fool, on several occasions I almost obliged. Man, I scared myself … I'm amazed I survived."[217]

It was a financial struggle as well as hazardous. So when he was offered a steady job flying for Queen City Flying Service of Cincinnati, he jumped at it.

Pan Am

To fly big aircraft, he moved to Pan Am – his dream airline – in 1941. Back then, America had a raft of local and regional airlines, but only Pan Am was dedicated to scheduled services to other countries. Begun in 1928 with a service from Havana to Key West, by 1941 it had routes throughout Central and South America, the Pacific, New Zealand, the Philippines and China, and over to Ireland, Britain and Portugal.

Pan Am had the latest and most luxurious planes as well as the most experienced and respected flight crews in the world. Ueltschi became a general assignment pilot, working some time in the training department but also crewing flying boats and working on air ferries.

The air-ferry system delivered military planes to the Middle East via Africa. Following a request from President Roosevelt, in 60 days Pan Am created a new airline spanning 12,000 miles of ocean, jungle and desert. The route was Miami through the Caribbean and Brazil across to West Africa, then Central Africa to East Africa. No wonder Pan Am's pilots were regarded with a mixture of awe and reverence.

Juan Trippe, who founded Pan Am in 1928 when in his 20s, needed an executive plane to travel around America (regulators prevented Pan Am's planes from flying within the USA because it was so dominant internationally). Ueltschi was asked to go and pick up the plane from Colombia in 1943 and was then assigned to being Mr Trippe's personal pilot. He relished the prospect, regarding Trippe as "one of the greatest men I ever knew ... displaying tenacity, business savvy, canny politicking, penchant for publicity, and willingness to take huge risks."[218]

Ueltschi stayed as Trippe's pilot for 25 years and got to know him well. He was most impressed with his character, intelligence and insight: "he was a respectful and wise counsellor."[219]

His own business

In the late 1940s, many companies bought corporate airplanes to provide greater flexibility and save the time of their executives. Ueltschi knew most of the pilots working for the directors because they would frequently meet at airports all over the country. He noticed that some needed to update their flying skills.

The training at Pan Am was rigorous and never-ending, with pilots forever going back to the school to learn the latest system or navigation technique, or simply to refresh old knowledge. Pan Am's head of operations was a stickler for precision and professionalism. "And then we were tested to be sure we knew what we thought we knew. All of us understood that was what it took to be safe."[220] Ueltschi was often assigned to help out older Pan Am pilots with the transition to DC-6s and Constellations (newer aircraft).

In contrast, corporate pilots had usually ceased training years before, many after leaving the military. The lack of up-to-date knowledge was a problem because new high-performance aircraft were coming into the corporate fleets. These were much faster than the slow and low-flying boats and other light aircraft they were used to.

While major airlines were forced to keep up, through both internal pressure to be safe and government six-monthly proficiency tests, business aviation pilots were out on their own with no requirements to demonstrate competence.

Ueltschi thought about the problem for a long time, eventually concluding that there might be an opportunity to establish a business serving their needs, offering a training system as good as those provided at the major airlines.

He went to Trippe with the idea, who thought it excellent; it would improve aviation and it was a good business opportunity. Ueltschi also talked to Bernard Baruch, a leading financier, advisor to presidents and a friend, who was much more cautious: "You'd better be careful. You've got a good job at Pan Am, and you might lose everything."[221]

Ueltschi had to solve the problem of combining family security – by then he and his wife, Eileen, had four small children – with pursuing his dream.

His solution was to, first, take a $15,000 mortgage on their house and rent a 200-sq-ft office on the third floor of LaGuardia Airport for the new company, FlightSafety, in 1951. It had one paid employee, a secretary, who was to mostly type letters soliciting business. Ueltschi himself would be unpaid by the company for 17 years.

Second, he held onto his job at Pan Am. Trippe was okay with that, so long as he restricted his FlightSafety business to his off hours and days off.

For years there was little business because the older pilots generally couldn't see the need for training. "They already knew how to fly just fine, thank you, so why did they need advice from a bunch of outsiders?"[222]

Trippe was Ueltschi's greatest supporter, and he convinced many of his pals at the top of Fortune 500 companies that they really need to be flown around by pilots fully conversant with modern airplanes. Ueltschi recalls, "We hung in there, and one by one the customers came and, thankfully, so did their checks".[223]

Initially training was carried out by off-duty Pan Am instructor-pilots using the customer's own plane. Increasingly, on-the-ground trainers were used, rented at $10 per hour from Pan Am. Then, four second-hand trainers were purchased from TWA.

Leaps and bounds

State-of-the-art simulators were $150,000 each in 1955, which was way beyond the little company. Ueltschi came up with a brilliant finance plan: his customers would give him money. Companies such as Eastman Kodak, National Dairies and Coca-Cola were convinced to pay a total of $70,000 as advances for five years' worth of the best simulator training available. With those cheques in hand, Ueltschi had little difficulty obtaining the rest of the money.

Survival of the company then seemed possible, but profits were still meagre. In 1955, revenues were $177,096 and net profit $277.

The arrival of jet corporate aircraft (Gulfstreams, Learjets, etc.) in the early 1960s changed everything. The level of sophistication and speed was far and above what corporate pilots had been used to. And they cost a fortune – clearly it was best to have well-trained pilots to fly them, insurers as well as owners and pilots thought. It was downright dangerous at those speeds to make errors in training in the air; far better to make mistakes in a simulator.

FlightSafety engineers took real cockpits and married them with analogue computers and hydraulic-motion bases. Later the digital processor allowed better imitation handling, visuals, motion-instrument readouts and sound. In 1963, revenue topped $1m.

Another breakthrough was teaming up with private jet manufacturers. The first was the French firm Dassault which, in 1966, formed a joint venture with Pan Am called Pan Am Business Jets – hence the Ueltschi/Lindbergh trip to Le Bourget to evaluate the Falcon airplane.

It wasn't long before Ueltschi, still working as Trippe's personal pilot, persuaded him and the Business Jet team to include pilot and maintenance-technician training at FlightSafety as part of the purchase price of every Falcon.

The stock market

FlightSafety was pulling in the business but didn't have enough simulators. To pay for more, Ueltschi knew he would have to raise equity capital through a public stock offering.

So finally, after 17 years as an unpaid CEO, the 50-year-old resigned from Pan Am in 1968:

> "I felt it would be inappropriate for the CEO of a public company to be an employee of another company. Leaving Pan Am was probably both the hardest and the most exciting moment of my career … I loved that airline and my job, and I thought the world of Juan Trippe. Still, the prospect of leading my own company full-time thrilled me. And so the day finally arrived. After returning from a flight, I proudly carried Mr Trippe's luggage from the airplane, shook his hand and thanked him from the bottom of my heart for the wonderful career he'd given me. Then I crossed the ramp, climbed the stairs and became the full-time CEO of FlightSafety. It was only then, 17 years after I started the company, that I began collecting a paycheck from FlightSafety. I had to. I had just quit my regular job".[224]

That year revenue reached $5.6m.

Once the new simulators were in place more training deals packaged with aircraft sales followed, establishing FlightSafety training as the standard for Learjet, Gulfstream, Sabre, JetStar and Jet Commander among others.

Dedicated training centres were established near to the manufacturers' factories or service centres to allow pilots to train while their planes were built, and where they could interact with designers and engineers.

FlightSafety had the market to themselves. It was the only company with the trainers, equipment and experience to offer reassurance of corporate-jet-pilot competence.

Money generated was poured back into operations and facilities to ensure that FightSafety always offered state-of-the-art full-visual simulators, most of which they manufactured themselves. It wasn't long before they cost millions of dollars each. But the money kept on coming in to pay for them. Revenues soared past $9m in 1970, and $43m only eight years later.

Additional business streams were established. In 1973, MarineSafety for the instruction of merchant marine and surface Navy officers was created. Helicopter simulators were added in 1981, helping revenues grow to $110m in 1986. A coveted contract with the United States Air Force for the C-17 aircraft was won in 1989, followed by many other military contracts. In 1994, the cabin attendant training programme was begun.

By the time Warren Buffett became interested in buying it, FlightSafety operated 175 simulators for more than 50 different aircraft (including 747s), training more than 50,000 pilots and maintenance technicians a year at 36 learning centres. Revenue was over $325m.

The deal with Warren Buffett

Many large companies approached Ueltschi in the 1990s to ask whether he would consider selling the company. After all, he was already well into his 70s and needed to think about what might happen on his death, e.g., tax would have to be paid from his estate.

He could not bring himself to sell his creation, with its cadre of first-class trainers and technologists, many of whom were dear friends, to one of Wall Street corporate raiders. They might leverage it up, bring in their own inexperienced and clumsy managers, and/or sell it off piecemeal.

> "I've seen big companies when they buy little companies; they'll try to change everything. And I didn't want to do that. A lot of our workforce had been there for years, and I wanted to see that it could carry its mission of making aviation as safe as we can. These are good people."[225]

Ueltschi had not met Buffett, despite him sending his pilots for training at FlightSafety (Berkshire had bought an airplane for Buffett to move around the country, which he named 'the Indefensible').

In fact, the idea for a merger didn't come from either of them. Buffett's heroes of this story are Richard Sercer and his wife, Alma Murphy. Sercer was familiar with aviation and the market-commanding position of FlightSafety because he was an aviation consultant. He was also a shareholder in the company.

Murphy, an ophthalmology Harvard Medical School graduate, finally, in 1990, wore down her husband's reluctance to buy Berkshire Hathaway shares (they had seemed expensive to him in the 1980s). Thereafter they attended every annual general meeting and so knew Buffett's criteria for acquisition. They judged FlightSafety to be a perfect fit, and thought that Ueltschi would welcome a deal because it would give a good home to his business without disturbing the business model or leadership.

Making a pitch

Sercer had long had a good working relationship with FlightSafety's vice president of marketing, Jim Waugh, built on his work for corporate aviation clients. On 24 July, 1996, the two met. Sercer took along Buffett's 'owner manual', an updated version of which had been given to Berkshire shareholders the previous month (the original was written at the time of the Blue Chip merger in 1983).

In this document,[226] Buffett sets out the 13 principles by which Berkshire Hathaway will be managed, such as, "our attitude is partnership … we eat our own cooking ... [aim] to maximize Berkshire's average annual rate of gain in intrinsic business value on a per-share basis ... [and] use debt sparingly".

He also gave Waugh a copy of Berkshire's acquisition criteria, which includes some very attractive stances for managers who might be interested in selling a business. Things like: "Management in place (we can't supply it) ... We will not engage in unfriendly takeovers ... We can promise complete confidentiality and a very fast answer – customarily within five minutes – as to whether we're interested."

Waugh was keen on the idea, reasoning that something had to be done to secure the future of FlightSafety. The uncertainty surrounding what might happen after Ueltschi's death was on the minds of many of his employees. His four children and 12 grandchildren would probably have to sell shares so they could pay estate-tax liabilities, putting the control of the business in doubt. Would a Wall Street raider take it?

Sercer asked Waugh to discuss the possibility of a merger with Ueltschi, and in that discussion to emphasise that the only real change they would experience would be that owner earnings would flow to Berkshire for Buffett and Munger to deploy as they see fit, but that the investment needs of FlightSafety would come first.

Waugh thought the message would be more impactful if the person putting it to Ueltschi was Warren Buffett himself, so he requested that Sercer speak with Buffett and ask him to call Ueltschi direct and say, "Hey, Al, how about telling me about your business over lunch?"[227]

Sercer was not in the least bit confident that he could just pick up the phone and speak with Buffett who was by then getting vast amount of mail and calls daily. So, rather than contact Buffett directly, Sercer wrote to Bob Denham, CEO of Salomon, setting out his logic of the quality of fit and suggesting he explore the possibility of the merger (Sercer and Denham had chatted at Berkshire Hathaway annual meetings a couple of times).

The meeting

Denham, and then Buffett, clearly thought the idea was good because a meeting was arranged on 18 September in New York. Ueltschi recalls:

> "And when I met Warren, I could tell that I liked him. And we sat down in New York at a little table. And he had a hamburger and a Cherry Coke, and I had a hamburger and a Coke, and we put the deal together, the whole deal in a couple of hours or so. We shook hands, and he went back."[228]

Buffett says that in about 60 seconds he knew that Ueltschi was "exactly our kind of manager".[229] Ueltschi could take on faith Buffett's pledge that FlightSafety would remain an independent subsidiary, to continue its same course of business and to be run by the same people.

A few days after the meeting Buffett wrote a letter setting down exactly what he offered to do, which Ueltschi said "sounded reasonable to me."[230]

However, he met resistance from some of his shareholders, who complained that they should have more money. Ueltschi's riposte was "[if] anybody comes out with money – it's a public company – if they can beat the thing then let's have them". Nobody else stepped forward, and the deal was completed in December, two days before Christmas.

What was given?

Ueltschi insisted on his family's shares being swapped for shares in Berkshire Hathaway. But Buffett and Munger were reluctant to issue a large number of shares, so they structured the deal as a choice for FlightSafety shareholders to either take cash or shares in Berkshire, but the cash possibility was worth slightly more to discourage the take up of shares.

In the event, about 51% of FlightSafety's shares were exchanged for cash ($50 per FlightSafety share, a total of $769m), 41% for Berkshire A shares (17,728 of them, roughly $48 per FlightSafety share) and 8% exchanged for the recently created Berkshire B shares (112,655 B shares – there is a description of B shares in the chapter appendix)

When the public announcement was made Ueltschi told the press: "I personally consider Berkshire shares to be one of the finest investments that I could make and anticipate holding the shares indefinitely, I look forward to continuing to run FlightSafety as part of Berkshire, and working with Warren Buffett."[231]

Years later, the way Ueltschi looked at the deal was that he didn't sell his company but merely traded his stock for Berkshire stock. Laughing in a 2006 interview he added, "I still own it, I think … but I have these shares of stock, but they're Berkshire shares, and they're not FlightSafety's."[232]

Noting Ueltschi's age Buffett joked about the fact many of his key people were way past the normal retirement threshold in his 1996 letter:

> "An observer might conclude from our hiring practices that Charlie and I were traumatized early in life by an Equal Employment Opportunity Commission bulletin on age discrimination. The real explanation, however, is self-interest: It's difficult to teach a new dog old tricks. The many Berkshire managers who are past 70 hit home runs today at the same pace that long ago gave them reputations as young slugging sensations. Therefore, to get a job with us, just employ the tactic of the 76-year-old who persuaded a dazzling beauty of 25 to marry him. 'How did you ever get her to accept?' asked his envious contemporaries. The comeback: 'I told her I was 86.'"

Richard Sercer and Alma Murphy received a standing ovation at the 1996 Berkshire annual meeting.

Investing is not complex, nor is it easy

In the context of recently paying $1.5bn for FlightSafety, Warren Buffett, in his 1996 letter to shareholders, emphasised that intelligent investing is not complex. FlightSafety's technology might be complex, but the evaluation of the business is relatively straightforward. It was the dominant supplier of flight training outside of governments and major airlines. It had the best trainers and an excellent team of managers. It had a deep moat that is dangerous for potential rivals to try and cross because it has the reputation, the technical knowhow and the facilities – a combination hard to replicate.

While intelligent investing is not complex, it is far from easy. Not everyone has the focus, inclination or the business knowledge to be able to evaluate matters such as strategic positioning, or the competence and integrity of leaders.

Many would rather focus on squiggles on a chart, guess the mood of the stock market or get a feel for the next big thing (is it lithium, online payment firms or bitcoin this month?) than look at businesses. To invest successfully you don't need beta, option-pricing theory, modern-portfolio-theory or familiarity with emerging markets.

Buffett tells us that "what an investor needs is the ability to correctly evaluate selected businesses."[233] The word 'selected' is very important. You cannot be an expert on every company, or even many businesses.

But that doesn't stop you from being an intelligent investor. "You only have to be able to evaluate companies within your circle of competence. The size of that circle is not very important; knowing its boundaries, however, is vital."[234]

You need to learn two things:

1. How to value a business.
2. How to think about market prices.

Once these are under your belt, you'll be able "to purchase, at a rational price, a part interest in an easily-understandable business whose earnings are virtually certain to be materially higher five, ten and twenty years from now."[235]

Even with these tools, and even if you worked ten hours a day at it, you would find only a few companies a year that meet these standards, "so when you see one that qualifies, you should buy a meaningful amount of stock."[236]

And when you find one, you will expect to hold it for many years: "If you aren't willing to own a stock for ten years, don't even think about owning it for ten minutes."[237]

Buffett's approach is to construct a portfolio of companies whose earnings will rise over the years, and not to trade in and out, nor worry about market index levels.

A tip to simplify portfolio construction to manageable proportions – favour low-change industries

Buffett and Munger made life easier for themselves by investing in businesses and industries unlikely to experience major change. "The reason for that is simple: we are searching for operations that we believe are virtually certain to possess enormous competitive strength ten or twenty years from now. A fast-changing industry environment may offer the chance for huge wins, but it precludes the certainty we seek."[238]

This advice does not mean searching out areas where there will be no change at all. That wouldn't work because all businesses are subject to some change. But it does mean looking for areas where the fundamental economics (pricing-power relationships) are unlikely to alter.

Buffett highlights the example of See's Candy, where change has clearly come. The range of candy has changed, as has the machinery used in production and some of the methods of distribution.

But people today still buy from See's Candy for the same reasons they did in 1972, when Berkshire bought the company, and these reasons are not likely to change over the next 50 years (in California there is long established devotion to See's Candy – no Californian would want to give their girlfriend, wife or mother a lower quality candy).

Another example: Coca-Cola.

Coca-Cola is continually looking to improve the way it carries out its operations to gain efficiencies – new technology will help, new advertising methods on the internet will help – but the fundamentals of the business do not change. Those fundamentals give Coca-Cola its "competitive dominance and stunning economics,"[239] and include the 'share of mind' (people automatically think of Coca-Cola when looking for a drink), the brand name and the highly developed distribution system.

Don't cut off successful investments

If you've bought at a good price (i.e., with a margin of safety) a stake in a business with excellent economics and able, honest managers, you don't want to be chopping and changing thereafter. Certainly monitor whether the economics and managers continue to be excellent and be prepared to sell if they deteriorate. But why sell out if there is every prospect of earnings growing at a good clip in future?

In that case, it's certainly not a good idea to rebalance a portfolio by selling those shares that have risen a lot and now constitute a high proportion of the overall fund. It is fine to have a few shares representing a large share of your portfolio.

> Such an investor "would get a similar result if he followed a policy of purchasing an interest in, say, 20% of the future earnings of a number of outstanding college basketball stars. A handful of these would go on to achieve NBA stardom, and the investor's take from them would soon dominate his royalty stream. To suggest that this investor should sell off portions of his most successful investments simply because they have come to dominate his portfolio is akin to suggesting that the Bulls trade Michael Jordan because he has become so important to the team."[240]

After the deal

In the year before Berkshire bought it for $1.5bn, FlightSafety International produced $111m in pre-tax earnings. Buffett was correct in thinking that its strong market position would lead to a significant rise in profits. By 2007, pre-tax earnings were $270m. Then the company could have been sold on to someone else at much more than Berkshire paid.

But Buffett had made a solemn commitment to Ueltschi and his staff that Berkshire would never sell. Also, a sale wouldn't make sense when the economic franchise was even stronger in 2007 than it was in 1996, and the managers even better.

Pre-tax profits over the first 13 years of ownership amounted to about $2.5bn. By 2009, annual profits were over $300m and rising. Berkshire gained another $3.5bn or so of pre-tax profits over the next decade. Even after tax is deducted that is over 233% of what was paid for the company in that decade alone. And still Berkshire gets to own it, receiving, year in, year out, the hundreds of millions of dollars of cash it generates.

Carry on carrying on

In terms of managing the business, Ueltschi said that nothing changed after 1996 and that is just the way he wanted it. He said:

> "Warren Buffett … he's not the type of guy that would try to break something up. Some of these big companies they buy the company then there is big stuff they want to change: they put their name on it, they want to change everything. All the people that worked there for years, that built this thing up – and they're in there because it's their life's blood and they believe it – they lose all their enthusiasm because there's somebody from the big office comes in and tells them how to run it. And these people know how to run it. I've got some of the finest people in the world working at FlightSafety and they all are dedicated, they're loyal, respectful and they're honest and they do everything to take care of the customer."[241]

Buffett once asked a group of Columbia University students, "do you think Al Ueltschi, who owns $1 billion in Berkshire stock, is going to want to keep running his business if I'm over his shoulder making decisions?"[242]

There were other benefits for Ueltschi to being in the Berkshire fold, including avoiding Wall Street analysts constantly asking how much money FlightSafety was going to make next quarter and why it didn't make more last quarter. "Now we run the company for the long term without worrying about the next quarter. That's one of the best things about working with Warren."[243]

Ueltschi pointed to Buffett's amazing leadership ability, saying the letters of the word represent the qualities he possesses:

L is for loyalty

E for enthusiasm

A for attitude

D for discipline

E for example – you have to set a good example

R is for respect

S for scholarliness

H for honesty

I for integrity

P for pride[244]

What motivated a man in his 80s, who was already a billionaire, to carry on working? "I try to make [Buffett] proud, and I try to make every shareholder proud. I feel obligated to do that. I don't want to run a company that you read bad things about in the newspaper."[245]

An old hand takes the joystick

In 2003, Bruce Whitman, who had been Ueltschi right-hand man, or co-pilot, since 1961, took over the role of president and CEO. But as Buffett said in his 2004 letter: "Al's not going anywhere; I won't let him".

When he was 88, Ueltschi said of his role:

> "I still run the company, don't worry about that. We got a team there. If people work as a team, they're all working together, working for a mission. They all know what they are doing and I'm very proud of them. And I want to see this continue on."[246]

The mission was to continually make aviation safer: "The most important thing any human being has is life, in order for this industry to grow we must do everything possible to prevent people from being killed."[247]

A few years earlier, Charlie Munger was approached by a tycoon friend who had taken a course at FlightSafety and failed. The tycoon asked Munger to intervene to change the decision. Ueltschi's reply to Munger was: "Tell your pal he belongs in the back of the plane, not the cockpit."[248]

Bruce Whitman had exactly the same commitment to rigour and integrity, something Buffett commends: "Bruce shares Al's conviction that flying an aircraft is a privilege to be extended only to people who regularly receive the highest quality of training and are undeniably competent."[249] Buffett exhibited the same level of trust in Whitman as he did in Ueltschi:

> "Warren lets you run your business as though it was your own and spend money as though it was yours. And he's a terrific supporter. He's a cheerleader, but he's available if you need him. He doesn't require budgets. He doesn't require business plans."[250]

It is a capital-intensive business, yes. But it's still great

Warren Buffett prefers to make outstanding rates of return on capital in businesses that do not require much of a capital base, such as See's Candy or Scott Fetzer. FlightSafety needs to invest $19m or more in one simulator. When you have over 300 simulators and need to replace them regularly with more advanced models, then you have a large amount of money being ploughed back into the business. For example, in 2000 alone $248m was invested in simulators.

But this does not make it a bad business in which to invest. It may not be sensational, but it can produce high rates of return. Its durable competitive advantage, due to its best-in-class reputation, means that customers will pay high fees for each hour of training.

As Buffett says, "Going to any other flight-training provider than the best is like taking the low bid on a surgical procedure."[251] This gives it good business economics, and is therefore able to factor in high operating profit margins.

Some illustrative numbers

On its purchase date, 23 December, 1996, FlightSafety had $570m in fixed assets. With those it generated $111m of pre-tax operating earnings.

Between then and the end of 2007, Buffett says depreciation charges cumulated to $923m (written off, reducing profits each year) but capital expenditure was much larger, as simulators capable of imitating a wide range of new airplanes were acquired, totalling $1,635m.

In 2007, fixed assets were $1,079m, an enormous total investment by any standard. However, its market power allowed FlightSafety to make pre-tax operating earnings of $270m that year.

Thus, profits had risen by $159m between 1996 and 2007, while incremental investment was $509m ($1,079m − $570m = $509m). Buffett commented on those numbers: "Consequently, if measured only by economic returns, FlightSafety is an excellent but not extraordinary business. Its put-up-more-to-earn-more experience is that faced by most corporations."[252]

Buffett accepts that he cannot always find businesses with the extraordinary economics of See's Candy, and so is quite content to put money to use earning excellent operating returns, rather than stratospheric returns, in fields such as electricity generation and railroads as well as aviator training.

Giving until the end

In the 1970s, Juan Trippe asked a favour of Ueltschi, who was more than willing to do what he could to repay all the kindnesses received from his mentor. The favour was simply to have lunch with Trippe's daughter, Betsy, and a friend of hers, Dr. David Paton. It seemed modest enough, but that meeting was the start of something big.

Dr. Paton was the head of the ophthalmology department at Baylor College of Medicine in Texas. He had a dream to use the technology and knowledge held in the rich world to help the poorest be free of eye disease.

There are hundreds, if not thousands, of eye specialists in western hospitals and clinics eager to help but unable to reach those most in need. Paton had come up with a plan: put the eye specialists in an airplane and fly it to where the patients are and where local medical professionals could be mentored by the world's best.

At the lunch he and Betsy quizzed Ueltschi first on whether it would be possible to put a hospital inside an airplane. "I told them I wasn't sure, but if the airplane was big enough, it seemed like it could work."[253]

That led to the second question: Where do you go to get such an airplane? And they added for good measure, "for a discount of approximately 100 percent". Ueltschi wasn't sure but thought there might be a manufacturer or an airline that would donate one. And there and then, Ueltschi volunteered to get an airplane for free and to oversee the modifications to make it a Flying Eye Hospital. (He later took on the chairmanship of the continuing effort to keep it airborne.)

He called every airline and manufacturer he knew. Eventually, United Airlines offered an old DC-8 parked in the Las Vegas desert. It dripped hydraulic fluid and leaked fuel but was fixable. Then the search began for microscopes, fuel, operating room equipment, etc.

The charity established after that lunch is called Orbis International. Its DC-8 lasted around ten years flying to some of the most impoverished places on earth carrying volunteer doctors and other medical staff and restoring the eyesight of thousands of children and adults. It was replaced in 1994 with a DC-10 and, in 2008, United Airlines and FedEx donated a replacement for that one. The fourth generation Flying Eye Hospital, a DC-10 donated by FedEx, was unveiled in 2016 complete with back-up generator, water-treatment plant, 46-seat classroom, sterilization room and operating room.

The most important work for Orbis' volunteers is to help local medical professionals learn new skills and promote good eye care. Ueltschi never forgot watching a little Russian girl climbing the stairs and entering the examining room, shy and hesitant. Her left eye stared hard to the right, and the right was focused on the far left, caused by a congenital muscular disorder.

"The Orbis doctors went to work, performing delicate surgery to correct the muscular aberration. The following day the child returned to have her bandages removed. When she raised her eyelids, her left and right eyes stared straight and true into the eyes of the doctors who had operated on her. The joy in her face and the tears of happiness that followed from her, her doctors, me, and everyone else is a moment that will live with me always."[254]

Today, hundreds of the best ophthalmologists in the world donate their time to teach doctors, ophthalmologists, nurses and biomedical engineers in the developing world on board the Flying Eye Hospital, but mostly in hospitals on land. Orbis now has long-term country programmes in Bangladesh, China, Ethiopia, India and Vietnam and offers internet-based professional mentoring, real-time consultations and eye-care techniques.

A life well lived

Throughout his career Al Ueltschi's motto remained: the best safety device in any aircraft is a well-trained pilot. Indeed, the thing that he was most proud of was not the wealth he had accumulated nor his rising from a Kentucky farm boy to high social status, but the thousands of lives he and his colleagues had saved.

> "I am proud of this company, of its people and what they do. At FlightSafety we believe we've helped our customers in their quest for safe, reliable transportation. In doing that, we've saved lives as a matter of course. Knowing that makes it fun to go to work every day and helps me sleep like a baby at night."[255]

Al Ueltschi died in October 2012 having lived a full, productive and generous life. And Berkshire Hathaway shareholders can enjoy fat profits from safety training for many years to come.

Learning points

1. **Most of the entrepreneurs brought into the Berkshire fold concentrate on one segment of one industry.** They continuously innovate, continuously improve the offering to customers, incessantly peer into the future to predict technology and social change in that field. This contrasts with the type of entrepreneur who nurtures a business for a while and then moves onto the next, then the next.

2. **Respected brands plus high barriers to entry provide a deep and dangerous moat.** FlightSafety is the largest non-airline non-government training organisation in the world. It has an excellent reputation, top-quality trainers, high-capital-cost simulators which it manufactures itself and a wide breadth of operation (types of aircraft, location of training centres, etc.). These are difficult factors for potential rivals to emulate.

3. **A driving non-monetary passion such as to improve flight safety around the globe can lead to both that goal being achieved as well as a lot of money.** This "obliquity"[256] phenomenon is common in business life, e.g., James Dyson's determination to solve engineering problems in vacuum cleaners, Boeing engineers obsessed with creating the marvel of the 1960's 747 Jumbo or all those scientists working on the inoculative power of mRNA.

4. **Patience is needed in business.** Most businesses take many years/decades to establish firm foundations in terms of market-beating collaborative teams, defused intrinsic knowledge, efficient managerial systems, high reputation, and warm relationships with customers and suppliers. Some things just can't be rushed.

5. **Even capital-intensive businesses can be good investments.** If operating margins on good turnover are high enough then excellent returns on capital can be enjoyed.

6. **Merger deals are about people.** Psychology and personal commitments are far more important than the hard numbers. If you can't trust the leader of the firm you're buying, you will not get a good deal. If you lose the goodwill of employees, returns will be much worse than anticipated.

7. **Intelligent investing is not complex.** But it does require focus on the true investing-related elements, such as business economics, rather than speculative-related elements, such as stock-market movements. You must have an interest in business, the ability to judge managerial character and an independence of mind regarding market prices. You must be so choosy that you will find few firms with a satisfactory margin of safety within your circle of competence; and when you do, buy meaningful quantities, and hold for years or decades. Don't sell out of your Michael Jordan's to rebalance the portfolio – continue to hold a disproportionate amount of the best.

Appendix: Berkshire Hathaway Class B Shares

May 1996 was a landmark month for Berkshire Hathaway: it created and sold 517,500 B shares,[257] which had only one-thirtieth the economic interest in Berkshire as one original class 'A' share. The sale generated $565m for Berkshire.

But it wasn't the need to raise money that prompted the sale. Rather, it was the threat of soon-to-be-launched unit trusts, which intended to market themselves as Berkshire lookalikes. With one A share costing over $30,000, many Buffett enthusiasts couldn't afford to buy, and Wall Streeters stepped in by proposing to buy Berkshire A shares through unit trusts which then sold 'units' to small investors. Each unit would then represent a fraction of an A share.

So many novice small investors were attracted to putting a few hundred or a few thousand dollars into these planned unit trusts that Buffett feared a speculative bubble in Berkshire stock. Unit trusts are 'open ended', which meant that as demand rose more units would be created, sucking in more money which is then used to buy more A shares "indiscriminately" – as Buffett put it – thus pushing up the price artificially.

Buffett said in his 1996 letter that, "For at least a time, the price jump would have been self-validating, in that it would have pulled new waves of naive and impressionable investors into the trusts and set off still more buying of Berkshire shares."[258]

Such a speculative bubble might have benefitted a few old shareholders choosing to exit at that time, "since they could have profited at the expense of the buyers entering with false hopes".[259] But those shareholders (Buffett's 'partners') remaining would eventually suffer in two ways. First, when reality set in and prices fell back to earth, Berkshire would have hundreds of thousands of unhappy, indirect owners through unit trusts. Second, Berkshire would have a stained reputation.

Had the unit trusts launched with heavy marketing, unit holders would have been duped into believing that Berkshire's performance between 1965 and 1996 was representative of their likely future returns. This was despite Buffett repeatedly stating in public that his record was definitely unrepeatable.

Purchasers of B shares, on the other hand, would only do so after hearing of Buffett's warnings about past performance not being a good guide to likely future returns.

Furthermore, unit holders would have been required to pay high fees and commissions to hold an interest in Berkshire. If they bought B shares instead, there would be low transaction and ongoing costs. And they would have a direct relationship with the company.

Buffett and Munger tried to direct the B shares to those investors with a long-term perspective to fit in with their investing ethos. This seemed to work, as evidenced by the fact that many of the 40,000 who bought in that sale still hold and attended Berkshire's annual general meetings each spring.

Investment 8

DAIRY QUEEN

Summary of the deal

Deal	Dairy Queen
Time	1998
Price paid	$587.8m
Quantity	100% of the equity
Sale price	Held today
Profit	Not released
Berkshire Hathaway in 1998	Share price: $47,000–80,900 Book value: $57,403m Per share book value: $37,801

In the late 1990s the stock market was booming. Berkshire Hathaway's shares were jumping more than most. The A shares rose from $47,000 at the beginning of 1998 to $68,300 at the end, after briefly touching $80,900 in June. That was impressive enough. But the change over the nine years since the start of the decade, when they were $8,625, was a quite remarkable eight-fold increase.

Figure 8.1: Berkshire Hathaway A shares $ (1990–1998)

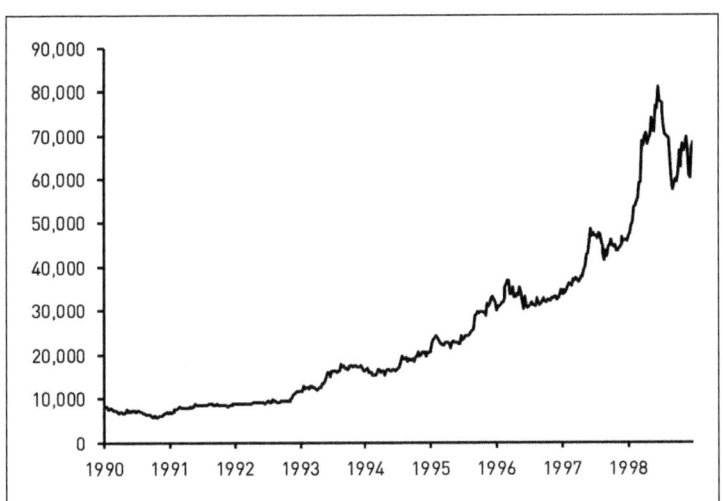

Intrinsic value is not the same as book value, but they generally move in the same direction

But it isn't jumps in stock market prices that Buffett measures himself by. Rather, he focuses on increases in intrinsic value. A very rough-and-ready proxy for annual changes in intrinsic value is movement in net worth (book value). In just the 12 months of 1998, Berkshire's balance sheet net-worth gain was $25.9bn, which translates to a per-A-share book value rise of 48.3%.

Over the 34 years since Buffett had taken a substantial stake in that down-at-heel textile maker, Berkshire Hathaway, its per-share book value had grown from $19 in 1964 to $37,801, a rate of 24.7% compounded annually.

Even this underestimates the achievement because in 1998 "intrinsic value … far exceeds book value."[260] In other words, the balance sheet net-asset figure does not adequately capture the value of the discounted owner earnings expected to accrue to Berkshire from its collection of excellent economic franchises and high-class businesses in future years.

"Gains in book value are, of course, not the bottom line at Berkshire. What truly counts are gains in per-share intrinsic business value. Ordinarily, though, the two measures tend to move roughly in tandem."[261]

While Buffett remained focused on intrinsic value, he found himself surrounded by people caught up in the psychology of a stock-market mania, later called the dot-com bubble, when shares were pushed up by punters hoping for increasing numbers of eyeballs looking at a Silicon Valley company's website.

Despite the great gains in Berkshire's share price as it was swept along with the naïve excitement, Buffett never lost sight of the real origins of value – that is, the soberly-assessed likely cash to flow to shareholders in the long run.

Don't preen yourself if a general market rise lifts you up

In his 1997 letter to shareholders, Buffett pointed out the error in thinking you, as an investor, had done well when in reality all that had happened was the market was on a tear.

When, in 1997, Berkshire's A shares went up by 35.6% and per-share book value went up by 34.1%, Buffett said it was tempting to declare "victory and move on." But he reminded himself and his followers that "any" investor can achieve large returns when shares generally soar. He wrote, "In a bull market, one must avoid the error of the preening duck that quacks boastfully after a torrential rainstorm, thinking that its paddling skills have caused it to rise in the world. A right-thinking duck would instead compare its position after the downpour to that of the other ducks on the pond."[262] That year the S&P 500 index (with dividends included) rose by 33.4%, a number similar to Berkshire's gain.

Aware of his need to constantly reinforce key principles and to learn from experience – good and bad – Buffett is always honestly self-critical. In assessing his 'duck rating' he declared that, even though he paddled furiously, the passive ducks, who had simply invested in the S&P, rose almost as fast as Berkshire shareholders. His appraisal of his 1997 performance was "Quack".

Buffett shouldn't be so hard on himself. There was a key mitigating factor for Berkshire's merely average performance, which is that the S&P, unlike Berkshire, does not have to bear capital gains tax or tax on interest or dividends.

What do value investors do when markets have been lifted high?

Buffett, in the late 1990s, faced a dilemma common to all investors from time to time (perhaps with smaller sums): he had money to invest, billions in cash or near cash, but "prices were high for both businesses and stocks".[263] What to do?

First, he was not interested in selling companies such as See's Candies or stakes in world-beating companies such as Coca-Cola or the Washington Post, saying he was delighted with what Berkshire owned. Beside which he had made commitments to the company leaders that he would not sell them on.

Second, he did not act on the basis of a prediction of a market fall: "we have absolutely no view on that matter".[264]

That left the great difficulty of a buying at a time when Berkshire would "get relatively little in prospective earnings when we commit fresh money".[265]

Let the balls go by

Such times call for extreme discipline. Buffett used a baseball metaphor to explain the level of self-control required:

> "We try to exert a Ted Williams kind of discipline. In his book *The Science of Hitting*, Ted explains that he carved the strike zone into 77 cells, each the size of a baseball. Swinging only at balls in his 'best' cell, he knew, would allow him to bat .400; reaching for balls in his 'worst' spot, the low outside corner of the strike zone, would reduce him to .230. In other words, waiting for the fat pitch would mean a trip to the Hall of Fame; swinging indiscriminately would mean a ticket to the minors."[266]

In this period Buffett was seeing business pitches, but most just weren't in the strike zone at all. The few that were headed for the 'lower outside corner' were not all that attractive. Swinging at these would lead to Berkshire being locked into low returns.

Unlike a baseball player, investors can't be called out if they resist three pitches that are at the extremes of the strike zone. They can let ball after ball fly by. For Berkshire, this means the cash flowing from its operating businesses, insurance float and dividends from minority stakes in American giants like Disney would just pile up or be put into Treasury bills.

But, as Buffett says, "just standing there, day after day, with my bat on my shoulder is not my idea of fun", even if it is the right thing to do.

Your time will come

To cheer yourself up at moments like these it is important to bear in mind that the time will come – maybe soon – when there is again a plethora of fat pitches, just as there was for Buffett in the 1970s and 1980s, and then again after the dot-com crash (2000–2002) and the financial crisis of 2009. These are the bonanza periods, because low prices mean the long-term investor can lock in future cash flows cheaply while ignoring short-term market worries and fluctuations.

Don't go with a cheery consensus

When shares were cheap in the summer of 1979, Buffett wrote a much-quoted article for *Forbes* entitled, 'You pay a very high price in the stock market for a cheery consensus.'[267] In it he castigated pension-fund managers for making "investment decisions with their eyes firmly fixed on the rearview mirror … this generals-fighting-the-last-war approach has proven costly in the past and will likely prove equally costly this time around."

Equities were then selling at low prices relative to earnings and potential earnings, and were thus likely to produce good long-term returns. But fund managers, having felt the fear of loss in the downswings of the recent past, tended to shun them, preferring to stick to, supposedly, safe bonds. Buffett wrote in *Forbes* in 1979 that "the enthusiasm of professionals for stocks varies proportionately with the recent pleasure derived from ownership."

Buffett pointed out the similarity with 1972, when the companies in the Dow Jones were, on average, earning a healthy 11% on their book value. Perversely, *after* the Dow had risen from 607 to 1020 (68%) the pension funds piled into shares. He wrote: "The more investment managers paid for stocks, the better they felt about them".

After it had declined through 1973 and most of 1974 to 690, the Dow yielded 14% on book value. "[S]uch bargain prices produced panic rather than purchases", with only 21% of newly available investible funds going into equities and the proportion of pension-plan portfolios devoted to equities declined by 20 percentage points compared with when the Dow was flying high at over 1,000 (from 74% to 54%).

It was during the 1974 market slump that Buffett declared he felt "like an oversexed man in a harem. This is the time to start investing."[268] It was only months later that one of the greatest ever Dow rallies began, taking it to over 1,000.

Again in 1976, with the market up to around 1,000, funds piled in. But when the Dow fell in 1978, making stocks reasonably priced, only 9% of net new funds was invested in equities that year.

This pattern of inverse fondness for equities relative to cheapness could, Buffett conjectures, be a simple Pavlovian response. Fund managers had experienced much investment pain in the previous decade and did not want to "return to the scene of the accident".[269]

Buffett's devotion to rationality meant that he could leave to one side the ups and downs in the financial markets and instead focus on business performances.

He found that in 1978–9 many companies were performing well at an operational level. It was apparent that stocks had underperformed the underlying businesses – the market was trading at around book value per share and earnings were an attractive 13% of book value. "Such underperformance cannot prevail indefinitely, any more than could the earlier overperformance of stocks versus business that lured pension money into equities at high prices."[270]

Why do they do it?

One perennial excuse given for not investing in equities when prices are low is "we are living through a time of uncertainty". Fund managers say to themselves and their sponsors, "wouldn't it be better to wait until things cleared up a bit?" It's a very human response. Buffett's counter is direct:

> "Before reaching for that crutch, face up to two unpleasant facts: The future is never clear; you pay a very high price in the stock market for a cheery consensus. Uncertainty actually is the friend of the buyer of long-term values … Those now awaiting a 'better time' for equity investing are highly likely to maintain that posture until well into the next bull market."[271]

History rhymes

Again, in the late 1990s Buffett observed a cheery consensus. While the late 1970s consensus of scepticism, disappointment and pessimism concerning equities offered braver long-term focused investors an opportunity to pick up excellent companies at truly attractive levels, the cheery consensus of the late 1990s was on the other side: it was far too positive.

True, businesses were then earning good money from operations, but stock-market prices had risen so much that they "materially eroded the 'margin of safety' that Ben Graham identified as the cornerstone of intelligent investing".[272]

It was in this pumped-up environment that Buffett contemplated buying Dairy Queen.

Would you buy this? At this price?

The Dairy Queen of 1997, at first glance, didn't seem much of a bargain. It had pedestrian profit growth and the cost of taking it over would mean paying a price-to-earnings ratio of 17.4. Before presenting the profit data, I'll briefly describe the business.

Investment 8. Dairy Queen

Dairy Queen was, and is, a franchisor company with, in 1997, over 5,700 franchised stores selling fast food – the posher description is quick-service restaurant, or QSR – plus 34 wholly or jointly-owned outlets. Its origins, and primary emphasis, was selling soft ice cream, but by 1997 it had extended its reach to savoury food, such as hamburgers and hot dogs, and to beverages. Some stores only offered ice cream, and then only seasonally, while others offered a wide range of hot and cold foods year-round. Most stores were in the US and Canada, but they did stretch to 24 other countries.

Its 420 Orange Julius-branded outlets sold blended fruit drinks and snacks, and the 60 Karmelkorn stores featured popcorn and other treats. It also franchised Golden Skillet rights outside of the US, with 21 stores selling fried chicken and side dishes.

Income sources

IDQ, or International Dairy Queen Inc. to give its full title, saw its role as supporting its franchisees, who were often running a single store as a family enterprise – although there were many multi-million-dollar chains of franchisees operating dozens of restaurants. The support it gave came in the form of brand promotion, with a heavy emphasis on advertising through TV, radio and newspapers. Franchisees paid 3–6% of gross sales to the advertising and sales-promotion funds.

IDQ also undertook product development, market testing, training and advisor services (product preparation, business and financial management, marketing) and enforced quality-control standards to ensure uniformity. The franchise service fee was levied at either 4% or 6% of gross retail sales, depending on the type of store.

To ensure high quality, stores were generally required to use only approved products. Thus, IDQ received revenue by selling the 'Dairy Queen mix', concentrates and other approved foods to franchisees. Equipment, such as refrigeration units, containers and paper goods, were also purchased through Dairy Queen.

Strategically positioned

Going all the way back to the 1940s there had been a deliberate strategy of locating most stores in smaller towns or suburbs of larger cities where competition was lighter. The Dairy Queen store was often the only meeting place for miles around and so it became a focal point, a place wrapped up in American folklore of small-town life, a place with memories of teenage liaisons or after-football meals. Its Blizzards and Dilly Bars were legendary, associated forever in the mind with long hot summers and lazy holidays.

Table 8.1: Dairy Queen; selected financial data 1987–1996

Year ending November 30	Revenue ($m)	Income after taxes ($m)	Earnings per share ($)	Total stockholders' equity, beginning of year ($m)
1996	412	34	1.52	148
1995	372	33	1.43	131
1994	341	31	1.30	117
1993	311	30	1.19	103
1992	297	29	1.12	97
1991	289	28	1.05	83
1990	283	27	0.97	76
1989	255	23	0.83	58
1988	243	20	0.70	43
1987	211	15	0.51	

Source: International Dairy Queen Inc. 1996 annual report

For each Dairy Queen share, Berkshire paid $27 cash or $26 of Berkshire A or B shares – an average of about $26.45, a total of $587.8m (45% of Dairy Queen's shareholders opted for cash).

The price-to-earnings ratio using the most recent full-year earnings was $26.45/$1.52 = 17.4. Inverting that, we obtain an earnings yield of 5.7%. To give perspective, the safest long-term investment around at the end of 1997/beginning of 1998, that of lending to the US government by buying ten-year bonds, produced a greater yield of 5.8%. Dairy Queen was far from risk-free, but at least it had the potential to increase earnings.

The equity market as a whole was in full bull phase and had pushed the price-to-earnings ratio on the S&P 500 on 31 December, 1997 to 24.8,[273] giving an earnings yield of only 4% on the typical US share. So, relative to the equity market, 17.4 didn't seem so bad. The problem with measuring price levels relative to the market is that you can get carried away during bubbles.

A more anchored measure is Benjamin Graham's cyclically-adjusted price-to-earnings (CAPE) ratio, which uses average earnings per share over ten years. For Dairy Queen in late 1997, this was $26.45/$1.06 = 25, significantly above the long-term average for US shares at 15.05 (CAPE ratios calculated for 1881–1997 using data supplied by Professor Robert Shiller at Yale).[274]

So Dairy Queen wasn't cheap when looking at earnings. But nor was it cheap relative to net assets – the amount Berkshire paid was five times net assets (total shareholders' equity).

Given the generous price relative to earnings and assets, what did Dairy Queen have going for it that attracted Warren Buffett?

First, high returns on capital

Dairy Queen had a relatively asset-light business. Most of the capital expenditure to build and maintain thousands of restaurants was borne by the franchisees. The franchisor, IDQ, had little in the way of property, for example. Its main US office amounted to only 114,000 sq ft, and 27,000 sq ft of that was surplus and so leased to third parties. It owned only a handful of other buildings: a mix-manufacturing site in Georgia, a small warehouse, a small Canadian office building/warehouse, 11 regional offices (which only had 15,918 sq ft between them), six offices in Minnesota, and six stores.

IDQ had some money tied up in plant, machinery and vehicles, and, of course, in inventories of food and other goods ready to be shipped to the stores. But even with all that thrown into the pot, net assets amounted to only $148m. (Net tangible assets did not differ from total net assets of $148m because the balance sheet did not carry any intangibles.)

A business capable of producing an operating income of $55m on net assets of $148m, as Dairy Queen did in 1996, looks like an exceptionally good one, because it means the managers generated a return of 37% on the capital they had at their disposal at the beginning of the year.

And 1996 was not an outlier. In fact, 37% was the *lowest* return for nine years – see table 8.2. As further evidence of good money being made for shareholders, we can look at the net cash flow from operations. As the fifth column of table 8.2 shows, these were high numbers relative to the amount shareholders had in the business. Even after deducting the money used to invest in the business, such as on new machines, vehicles, etc. (sixth column), we see a business generating large amounts of cash.

Table 8.2: Dairy Queen return on net assets (total shareholders' equity) 1988–1996

Year ending Nov 30	Operating income ($m)	Total Stockholders' Equity, beginning of year ($m)	Operating Income divided by Total Stockholders' Equity	Net cash from operating activities ($m)	Cash used in investing activities ($m)
1996	55	148	37%	47	18
1995	53	131	40%	22	2
1994	50	117	43%	34	5
1993	48	103	46%	35	17
1992	48	97	49%	26	4
1991	45	83	54%		
1990	44	76	58%		
1989	39	58	67%		
1988	35	43	81%		
1987	29				

Sources: Dairy Queen International annual reports

Stock-market investors knew that IDQ made high returns on capital. For example, when the merger proposal was announced in October 1997, Stephen Yacktman of Yacktman Asset Management in Chicago – which owned almost a million IDQ's shares – declared Buffett was getting a good deal. "It's right up his alley," said Mr Yacktman, pointing to the constant flow of income from franchisees and low overhead costs because it owns so few stores. So long as a store stays in business, he added, IDQ "is pretty much guaranteed a revenue stream."[275]

But the price paid by Berkshire was $587.8m. Now, okay, operating income and net cash generated from operating were around the $50m mark. But, after deducting interest, taxes and depreciation, we observe the money generated for shareholders that they could actually take away without disturbing the unit volume of the business or the quality of its strategic position falls to around the $29–34m area.

Still good, but is that really worth $587.8m? There must have been an expectation by Buffett and Munger that earnings power could be lifted. The secret to that lay in the next two factors.

Second, strong economics with outstanding management

Shortly after completing the purchase, Buffett wrote in his 1997 letter that IDQ had "excellent economics" and was run by "outstanding people". Its rich cash flow came from a series of virtual monopolies in many towns, counties and villages, where local governments put out the welcome mat for their treasured Dairy Queen.

While it was not the absolute best fast-food brand around, it was a good solid brand in niche markets in the heartlands of America. It was a business Buffett could understand, by which he meant, relatively simple and likely to be unchanging in its fundamentals as time passes.

When Buffett was interviewed on *Nightline* (a TV show), on 2 March, 1999, from a Dairy Queen in Omaha he said:

> "It was a business that I could understand. Now, there's all kinds of businesses I can't understand, and I try not to buy into those because ... why should I expect to make money on something I can't understand? So I'm not in any high tech businesses, for example. But I understand, you know, an Ultimate Hamburger

or, you know, a Peanut Buster or a Dilly Bar and I can handle that. And I like the people that run it. I like the economics of the business. It's a good business."[276]

A Berkshire shareholder pithily expressed the stability of such a business: "since you can't download calories from cyberspace, it'll be difficult for Captains of Technology to eat much into Dairy Queen's profits."[277]

There was a share-of-mind advantage: in many places when people thought of ice cream they thought of Dairy Queen. It had 60 years of history of family treats and meetings with friends, and bucket loads of nostalgia, all of which engendered loyalty to both the brand and to the people who owned the franchises as the faces of Dairy Queen in their communities. The brand got into customers' blood from a young age. It was much more of a place to hang out than, say, Taco Bell or Subway.

Remarkably, it had become a symbol of small-town American life, referenced in literature such as *Walter Benjamin at the Dairy Queen: Reflections at Sixty and Beyond* by Larry McMurtry, *Dairy Queen Days* by Robert Inman and *Chevrolet Summers, Dairy Queen Nights* by Rob Greene.

All these factors suggested that as the American and Canadian populations grew and as society became wealthier, more Dilly Bars would be sold and profits would rise. Also, there was potential to push the brand abroad.

Third, earnings had been held down and were due for a bounce

It was thought that profit growth had been constrained in the 1990s by the tension between IDQ and many of its franchisees. This came to a head when about one-third of disgruntled franchisees sued IDQ. There was a general feeling that the company had little sense of direction or an answer to rivals such as McDonalds coming and taking customers in their small towns.

But the legal issue was the claim that IDQ was over-controlling the sources of supply for product and charging too much for what it was supplying, ice-cream mix, etc., and franchisees wanted to gain the legal freedom to find alternative suppliers. The ill feeling first exploded in 1994, but the lawsuit dragged on for years.

While the public spat continued, behind-the-scenes relations were on the mend by the late 1990s under the leadership of John Mooty. He and his management team reached out to the franchisees. They developed new products and marketing concepts to compete with hot-food rivals. They were also more transparent about IDQ's finances and lowered margins on products supplied to franchisees.

Mooty also invested in marketing and sought to evolve the group to remain relevant to consumers. They introduced the ice-cream-and-hot-food formula under the branding 'Grill & Chill', which expanded the hot food side from standard fare like burgers, fries and hot dogs to a variety of sandwiches, salads and chicken items. The 5-buck lunch (meal items with a dessert) was a great hit.

The changes seemed to energise the franchisees even while the court case dragged on. And that was settled amicably in 2000 with an order for IDQ to commit to contributing $5m annually over the six years 2000–2005 to the franchise system's national-sales-promotion programs, plus $6m to IDQ's Operators' Cooperative to provide for continued availability of alternative food products and other supplies to franchisees.

The judgement was seen by both sides as fair, with IDQ focusing on the benefit of the extra promotional spending to raising the Dairy Queen brand. The person in whose name the complaint had been brought, Hugh Collins, was conciliatory afterwards, saying "it was imperative that we conclude this litigation and resolve our differences. The areas of agreement between the 'Dairy Queen' franchisees and IDQ far outweigh our points of difference. We can now put this dispute behind us and concentrate on the many advantages of being part of the 'Dairy Queen' system."[278]

Long-time franchisee Mike McKinnon, with five Grill & Chills in the Olympia, Washington, area added:

> "typically when you get disputes between franchisors and franchisees, they have to do with the products coming through the back door, [but that] we've really seen things improve … If you're litigating against your franchisor, it's pretty hard to work

collaboratively. IDQ has done a good job of lowering the price on products it sells to its franchisees."[279]

When, in late 1997, Buffett was discussing his deal to buy IDQ with managers and shareholders, he was able to detect the degree to which the relationship between franchisees and franchisor was rapidly improving – he was also able to talk to his friends who owned his local Dairy Queen franchise. He could see that franchisees were truly excited by the new formats being offered to customers and the relatively warm relationships with the franchisor. Therefore, he had good reason to believe that the profits of 1996 would be exceeded.

Fourth, Buffett loves the product

Warren Buffett has loved Dairy Queen for a long time. As a boy he took a young lady to Dairy Queen. John Gainor, who became CEO of IDQ, recounts Buffett telling him that the lady had a "great experience" and that Buffett "said that if he ever had the opportunity, he would buy the business. So he did, in 1998".[280]

In May 2019, Bill Gates and Warren Buffett had a little fun serving customers in an Omaha Dairy Queen. Gates posted a video of their escapades on his GatesNotes blog titled 'Grilling and Chilling with Warren'. Bill and Warren finally sat down after their exertions, and Gates asks Warren, "How long ago did you buy Dairy Queen and what was it that made it look good?"

Buffett replied, "I've known Dairy Queen all my life. Dairy Queen actually started in the 1930s and when they were contemplating selling, he actually thought of Berkshire. Who better than some guy that loves the product, and we made a deal and we lived happily ever after."

Bill Gates greatly values his friendship with Buffett. In the blog he says, "Every time I get to see Warren, I'm struck by his surprising, insightful, 'upside-down' view of the world. He thinks differently—about almost everything. For starters, he credits his amazing success to something anyone could do. 'I just sit in my office and read all day.' he explained."

The lead up to the deal

John F. 'Grandpa' McCullough and his son Alex experimented in a basement with the texture and temperature of ice cream in the 1930s, eventually coming up with semi-frozen and soft ice cream. They named it after Grandpa's cow, which he referred to as the queen of the dairy business. The secret to good soft ice cream is to pump in air during the freezing process to make it light. Also, if it is served at a higher temperature than hard ice cream it doesn't freeze the tastebuds, allowing a fuller flavour.

In 1938, one of the customers for their traditional hard ice cream, Sherb Noble from Kankakee, Illinois, put on an all-you-can-eat-for-ten-cents day to test demand for soft ice cream. It was a hit, with 1,600 servings in two hours.

It took a while to sort out the freezer technology to dispense the ice cream in a consistent manner. They solved that with the help of Harry Oltz, who developed a machine to keep a constant temperature. The rights to use the machines and the ice-cream formula were valuable and could be used as the basis of a franchise-type business. By 1940 they were ready to open the first Dairy Queen store jointly with Noble in Joliet, Illinois. Within 30 months there were eight stores.

In 1943 they made a deal with Harry Axene whereby he would hold the rights to sell the ice cream in certain states for a fee. Axene resold sales territories in return for initial fees plus a royalty cut of ice cream sales. By 1947 the business had grown to 100 stores. The deals with Harry Axene weren't true franchise arrangements because there was no central coordination, with each store owner running them according to their own methods. Still, the Dairy Queen name spread rapidly across the USA and Canada to over 2,600 stores by 1955.

In 1962 the McCullough family sold their interest to a group of DQ store owners for $1.5m. The new team set about creating a more ordered system through proper franchising, marketing and purchasing coordination, operating procedures and quality-control standards. Thus, in a strange twist, a bunch of franchisees created the franchisor.

In 1970, a group of Minnesota businessmen including Rudy Luther and John Mooty were approached by Dairy Queen with a view to purchase their car-rental business (they believed in the then-popular conglomerate approach to strategy). That deal didn't come off but, after the car business was sold to another firm, the Minnesota group were persuaded to buy a majority stake in Dairy Queen for $5m after it had run into financial difficulties.

The new controllers pumped in millions more to increase efficiency and standards. Dairy Queen joined the Nasdaq in 1977. Under John Mooty's leadership, it rose to be the fifth largest fast-food business in America.

In the summer of 1997, 15%-shareholder Rudy Luther died. The family needed to raise money to pay estate taxes and so approached Warren Buffett to buy some shares. Buffett had previously shown an interest in purchasing the entire firm, and again expressed that desire, but said he would not be willing to buy in a minority stake. Mooty and the leading shareholders concluded that it was a good time to sell the business and so were willing to begin negotiations with Buffett.

A quick bid

A year before Rudy Luther died, Dick Kiphart of William Blair & Co., an investment bank, introduced Buffett to John Mooty and Mike Sullivan, IDQ's CEO. Buffett "had been impressed with both men".[281] Thus, the groundwork had been prepared even though a deal was not forthcoming in 1996.

But in autumn 1997 Kiphart picked up the phone and spoke with Buffett in Omaha, telling him that a deal would be both possible and wise for Berkshire Hathaway. A day later, Buffett sent in his bid.

Selling shareholders were to be offered the option of choosing either cash or Berkshire shares having a slightly lower immediate value. "By tilting the consideration as we did, we encouraged holders to opt for cash, the type of payment we by far prefer. Even then, only 45% of IDQ shares elected cash."[282]

In the 21 October announcement, Mooty said:

"Our family will vote our entire 35% of the voting shares of Dairy Queen in favor of the merger and will elect to receive Berkshire

Hathaway common stock for all the Dairy Queen shares owned by us. We are not interested in trading our Dairy Queen shares for any other securities. I personally consider Berkshire shares to be one to the finest investments that our family could make and we anticipate holding the shares indefinitely."

Buffett responded in the same statement with, "Dairy Queen is a business that I like, run by an outstanding management team. Dairy Queen will be a great addition to the Berkshire family." Helped by the fact that Dairy Queen's officers and directors controlled 50.9% of the voting shares, the deal sailed through for a completion on 7 January, 1998.

The next month Buffett joked in his 1997 letter that, "Charlie and I bring a modicum of product expertise to this transaction: He has been patronizing the Dairy Queens in Cass Lake and Bemidji, Minnesota, for decades, and I have been a regular in Omaha. We have put our money where our mouth is."

In an interview for Lawrence Cunningham's 2014 book,[283] Mooty said that the deal closed "possibly at a price below financial value" because Berkshire offered something else of value to three constituents – shareholders, employees, and franchisees.

1. **Shareholders:** those who took Berkshire Hathaway stock became shareholders in an exceptionally well-run diversified company auguring a large increase in share price over the next decade.
2. **Management:** autonomy was the normal mode of operating within the Berkshire empire and IDQ's team could see dozens of examples of Buffett and Munger encouraging independence and freedom to operate.
3. **Franchisees:** they needed stability, permanence and commitment to continuously building the brand and the customer offering. Buffett and Munger clearly saw the need to invest in key parts of the business for decades to come.

After the deal

Berkshire Hathaway has not revealed any information on the financial performance of Dairy Queen other than for the first two years of ownership. In 1998 Berkshire benefitted from $35m of Dairy Queen's earnings after tax on revenue of $420m (up slightly from $412m in 1996). Capital expenditure was relatively low, at $10m (depreciation and amortisation was $7m), so the company was throwing off over $30m of cash for Buffett to invest elsewhere.

Again in 1999, $35m after-tax profit was generated. But this time revenue rose by $40m to $460m. Under Buffett's watchful eye capital expenditures actually fell to a mere $9m (depreciation and amortisation amounted to $4m), so, again, around $30m of profits was available to Buffett for deployment.

There was a degree of bullishness about the potential to open hundreds more stores in the first couple of years. Indeed, outlets rose from 6,244 in 1998 to 6,400 in 1999 – see figure 8.2. After that, however, there appeared to be a cull of stores, rather than an expansion, as the overall number fell over the decade to about 5,700 in 2008.

It seems brand names do not always travel well. While Americans and Canadians are familiar with Dairy Queen, Chill & Grill, Blizzards and Dilly Bars, most Europeans, for example, have never developed an affection for the products. They have their own. It's notable that there are no Dairy Queens in my country, the UK. IDQ are aware of a lack of brand recognition in Britain and so do not even try to offer franchise opportunities to entrepreneurs here.

Figure 8.2: Total number of Dairy Queen, Orange Julius and Karmelkorn stores (1996–2020)

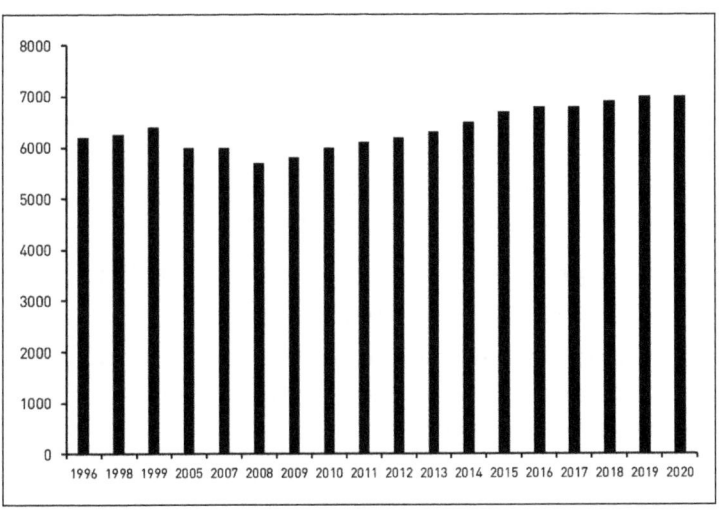

Dairy Queen is similar to See's Candies in having a strong strategic position, due to the high regard in which the product and brands are held by consumers in certain areas. With See's Candies, that is very limited – mostly to California and nearby. Fully aware of an absence of brand loyalty beyond the historic market, Buffett has restrained expansion to only where it has, or is likely to quickly develop, a competitive advantage and thus pricing power.

Having said that, there are now Dairy Queen stores in 27 countries other than the US and Canada, and the number of stores in the last decade has grown steadily to over 7,000, so about 100 locations were found each year where the team thought the formula would work.

In overseas markets Dairy Queen may not benefit from American small-town nostalgia, but it does have Warren Buffett as an ace marketer. When, for example, Buffett was on hand to formally open a new DQ store in Shanghai over 250 media outlets turned out to interview him, resulting in a massive amount of free publicity. There are now over 800 Dairy Queens in China. Now that would have impressed Grandpa McCullough.

Learning points

1. **Focus on gains in intrinsic value of your portfolio, not stock market prices.** Intrinsic value is the total of discounted future-owner earnings.

2. **Don't be a preening duck.** Don't quack boastfully after a torrential rainstorm, thinking that your paddling skills have caused you to rise in the world. Compare price changes in your portfolio with the general market. Be honestly self-critical.

3. **When share prices are high do not sell on a prediction of a market value hoping to buy cheaper later.**

4. **As in baseball, investors do not have to swing at every ball.** Indeed, investors can let hundreds of 'balls' go by when prices are too high relative to firms' prospects.

5. **Don't go with a cheery consensus.** Think independently and rationally about the current gap between intrinsic value and market price. Occasionally the market consensus is excessively optimistic, resulting in price rising far above intrinsic value. On other occasions the consensus view is far too pessimistic and bargains abound.

6. **The future is never clear.** If investors waited until the fog of uncertainty is lifted, they would never invest. Uncertainty is the friend of the buyer of long-term value.

7. **Look beyond recent profit numbers when estimating earnings power and intrinsic value.** Buffett paid a high trailing price-to-earnings ratio of 17.4 for IDQ because he saw in the qualitative factors potential for profit growth. Namely, the business model meant franchisees took the burden of most capital expenditure, resulting in high returns on capital for the franchisor; excellent economics and good management with many of the DQ stores dominating local markets; business fundamentals not subject to rapid change in the future; a high share of mind; and, disputes and mistakes holding back historical profits were being resolved.

Investment 9

NETJETS

Summary of the deal

Deal	NetJets
Time	1998
Price paid	$725m
Quantity	100% of the equity
Sale price	Held today
Profit	Losses for 11 years, then profits
Berkshire Hathaway in 1998	Share price: $47,000–80,900 Book value: $57,403m Per share book value: $37,801

When asked about the influence of the French Revolution, the late Chinese premier Zhou Enlai is reputed to have said: 'Too early to say'. It's much the same with Warren Buffett's August 1998 investment in NetJets, at $725m. For the next 11 years it made an aggregate loss of $157m.

By 2010, the investment was certainly looking like a dud. But then the turnaround began, resulting in annual profits regularly north of $200m. If this pattern continues, Berkshire should end up with a decent amount of money from NetJets. But it was an awfully long time coming, and during that time billions of Berkshire's cash or debt guarantees were taken from other investment prospects to expand NetJets.

It is no great surprise that Buffett declared in his 2011 letter that, "A few years ago NetJets was my number one worry: Its costs were far out of line with revenues, and cash was hemorrhaging. Without Berkshire's support, NetJets would have gone broke."

The opportunity cost of this investment in the first years of the twentieth century was considerable. Future Buffett historians may conclude that although the money put in has been recovered it was a poor investment choice. But we'll have to wait and see – maybe it'll start producing $1bn of cash year after year for Buffett to invest elsewhere. It certainly overwhelmingly dominates its niche market of fractional aircraft ownership, so there is potential there – *if* the niche grows and *if* price competition is restrained. A couple of big 'ifs'.

The business model

Before the NetJets model was invented, if you were a time-poor executive or wealthy person wanting to fly you had three choices. First, you could book like everybody else on a scheduled flight. Even with first-class treatment there are obvious downsides, such as being limited in destinations and timing. Also, the hub-and-spoke system can be a trial of endurance, even without flight delays.

Second, you could buy your own private jet. But this becomes expensive, especially if the depreciating asset spends most of the time in hanger. And it is a lot of hassle to maintain, insure, staff etc. Also, most private planes cannot fly intercontinental. As a rule of thumb, buying your own plane is not worth it unless you are going to be in the air around 400 hours per year.

The third possibility is to charter a private plane trip by trip to take you where you want to go with minimal fuss. The downsides here are the higher cost per mile and the limited availability of planes in the right place.

Richard Santulli, a former mathematics academic and Goldman Sachs alumni, thought of a better way for people who did not need a plane every day, which he called fractional ownership. With this you buy a portion – say one-quarter or one-eighth – of a jet. You are then entitled to 200 or 100 flying hours per year.

In addition to the up-front cost of purchase, which could be a million or two, you pay a monthly management fee to cover things like pilot salaries and training, insurance and hanger space ($5,000–20,000 per month for a smallish plane (seven seater)). You also pay extra for each hour flown to cover fuel, maintenance, landing fees, cleaning and catering ($1,300 and upwards per hour)).

NetJets makes sure that your plane, or one equally as good, is available at any one of thousands of airports when you want it (just give them at least four to six hours' notice depending on aircraft type).

Santulli thought that if Netjets got big enough, with hundreds of planes, there would be blanket coverage of a continent, so customers could rely on the guarantee of plane availability even at busy times – such as Thanksgiving – without the hassle and expense of owning their own plane. And these planes could fly to smaller, more convenient airports than scheduled planes.

The final element of the formula was that after five years the fraction owner can ask NetJets to repurchase it at a fair-market price, usually about 80% of the original list price.

Before Richard Santulli bought the company

Business aviation in the 1960s was in its infancy, and the few aircraft around were company-owned or privately-held aircraft. A group of retired second-world-war Air Force generals saw a gap in the market: private jet flying for those who couldn't justify buying their own plane.

In 1964, they formed Executive Jet Aviation (EJA) as the world's first business-aviation charter company. The president of the company was Brigadier General Paul W. Tibbets Jr., who 19 years before piloted the Enola Gay over Hiroshima. Also on the board was the actor and second world war pilot Colonel James Stewart, who had purchased an equity stake. (In the war, Stewart set aside acting to fight, leading squadrons on

20 combat missions over Germany, and winning, among other medals, two Distinguished Flying Crosses and the Croix de Guerre.)

They set up a base in centrally located Columbus, Ohio, and went out and bought ten of the newly launched Lear Jet 23s, regarded as the 'Ferrari of the skies'.

Things went well for a few years, but then the oil crisis of the mid-1970s reduced the number of executives willing to pay to fly privately. EJA continued to struggle and by 1984 General Tibbets and the board were ready to sell the business. Tibbets had met Rich Santulli six months before and thought he might be interested, so he asked a banker to call Santulli.

Rich Santulli buys EJA

Richard T. Santulli, born in 1944 to a working-class Brooklyn family, worked his way to Brooklyn Polytechnic Institute. After gaining two master's degrees (maths and operations research), he became a mathematics faculty member while working on a PhD.

He liked being a teacher but felt, after the birth of a son in 1967, that he should "get a real job".[284] He joined Shell Oil and rose to become head of an operations research group. Loyal to Brooklyn, he refused to move to Houston when Shell's bosses decided to up-sticks. Not previously knowing the name Goldman Sachs, he applied for a position there to help with a project to apply computer-based modelling to investment banking, a novel concept at the time.

In 1972 he moved across to Goldman Sachs' lease-financing section. It wasn't long before he was the head of this very profitable department while still in his mid-30s. Then suddenly, in 1979, he tendered his resignation:

> "The next year was my partner year, and I certainly would have been a partner. And that's exactly the reason that I left. I loved the company, and I knew that if I became a partner at Goldman, it would be basically a commitment for life. And at that point in my life, I wasn't prepared for a lifelong commitment ... I wanted

to see if I could do it without the Goldman name. And the only way to find that out was to start my own business."[285]

When Goldman's co-head John Whiteman learned that Santulli was leaving, he said to his partners: "If he does start something, make sure we invest in it."[286]

Santulli set up RTS Capital Services to focus on putting together leasing deals for helicopters, an area that the big banks neglected because it was so small compared with fixed-wing leasing. Thus, competition was limited, coming only from a handful of regional banks, "and they had no expertise at all in something as complicated as lease financing".[287] Five year later he had built the largest helicopter leasing business in the world.

By the time Santulli discovered it, EJA was on its last legs. He had a terrible introduction in 1983. Santulli had been on a guys' skiing jaunt in Vail, Colorado – one of those where you wear tatty clothes and don't bother to shave. The day before leaving, a client called to say he was flying back in his Lear jet, did he and his three friends want a lift back to New York? "Sure."

After a couple of hours, the plane descended to ostensibly refuel, which was odd as a Lear jet is perfectly capable of getting to New York without refuelling. Even odder was that on that Sunday at Columbus airport was a besuited General Tibbets ready to greet them. The client said, "Rich, if you have a minute, I would like you to talk to these people at Executive Jet. I am thinking of buying the company and I want you to finance it for me."[288]

They walked into the boardroom and there were eight men dressed in suits and ties who had gathered on the understanding that Santulli was there to talk about buying the company. He was 'really pissed' at being snookered into this situation without warning. Apologising, he explained what had happened, and that he had no interest in the business and didn't even know who they were. He got back in the plane and left.

Six months later Santulli took a call from a banker calling on behalf of General Tibbets. The deceiving client was no longer on the scene and now the General wanted to talk about the possibility of Santulli buying EJA.

It was losing money but at least, Santulli thought, it would be a nice side business for his leasing operation, a place to dump planes coming off lease programs. So RTS Capital Services bought it in 1984.

The building of fractional ownership

Now that Santulli owned an airplane company, he thought he ought to buy himself a private jet – it seemed only fitting – and EJA could look after it for him. But being a mathematician, he sat down and worked through the numbers on outright ownership. Taking into account the limited hours he'd actually be flying – less than 50 per year – it just didn't make any sense at all. He'd be better off chartering a plane each time he needed one.

But then he thought of a better option: buy a plane with a group of friends. Three friends joined Santulli to discuss the plan. It made good financial sense to share the one plane; they could all see that and were willing. But then the trouble started. One said that if they got a plane then he would insist on having it every Tuesday and Thursday. Another said he wanted it when he needed it, which might well be a Tuesday or Thursday. Deadlock.

After the failed meeting Santulli pondered the problem: shared ownership combined with guaranteed access when you wanted your airplane. If he could crack that he would have it made.

An intellectual challenge

It was a mathematical puzzle. The key input needed to solve it was to use the extensive database containing every trip EJA had taken over the previous 20 years (these military types kept good records). Looking at flying patterns, he found a high degree of predictability in terms of origin, destination, day of the week, time of day, mechanical breakdowns, etc.

It took nearly six months to figure it out, but the solution turned out to be for every 20 planes sold in fractions, NetJets had to buy for itself five and one-quarter planes to put in its corporate fleet to fill gaps where two or more co-owners wanted to use their plane at the same time. NetJets could then supply a substitute plane of the same or better specification at only a few hours' notice. This would allow a 98% availability.[289] NetJets could charter planes for the remaining 2% of occasions.

NetJets would take care of everything from maintenance to pilot training. All the client had to do was tell the customer service people where they wanted to go when.

Takeoff

EJA launched the NetJets programme in 1986. Initially, targeted potential clients were sceptical, thinking there were bound to be numerous occasions when they needed a plane but none were available. Santulli simply told them it was all worked out and NetJets could indeed guarantee availability. If they still didn't believe it worked then after six months they would be entitled to all their money back.

Santulli says he realised that unless NetJets were "absolutely perfect for the first 10, 15, or 20 customers, the whole deal was going to blow."[290] To make sure it didn't blow he bought eight Cessnas. These were not to be sold on to clients, but were the back-up planes for the 25 he expected to sell in fractions of one-sixteenth (50 hours of flight time), one-eighth, one-quarter, and one-half (400 hours). Thus, if the selling effort was successful, the fleet would amount to 33 planes.

Turbulence

But it took time. Only four planes were sold in the first year. And it didn't pick up – only four were sold in the second, and four in the third. Then the 1989 recession struck, and no fractions were sold.

Santulli lost $35–40m because he had personally guaranteed the debt and there were high fixed costs – such as pilots – even for a plane for which only one-sixteenth had been sold. He thought it was the end, bankruptcy loomed. To cap it all, competitors were entering the market thus limiting price rises.

But the recession had another effect: corporations looked carefully at their costs of flying and questioned whether they really needed to continue to own 100% of a plane. Selling a jet would raise millions to see them through hard times. If they needed to make only a few journeys each year, then fractional ownership was the perfect solution.

Santulli knew that the way to ultimate success was to be the biggest and the best, with the largest fleet, greatest geographical coverage and variety of planes. This meant buying hundreds of millions of dollars' worth of planes. The money had to come from somewhere.

A lifeline was thrown by Goldman Sachs buying a 25% equity stake in 1995. The fleet grew as the model was increasingly understood by those in the upper echelons. Even those corporations with their own jet saw advantages in using NetJets planes to supplement what their own jet could do.

Acceptability was greatly enhanced by the signing up of famous people, from Arnold Schwarzenegger to Tiger Woods. A network effect took hold: growth in client plane numbers meant lower costs per hour and greater coverage, and thus greater benefit to being a member of the largest group, the NetJet family of clients. The rich and famous started queuing up to join the lists for hot new planes.

Santulli kept the brand exclusive by refusing to 'commoditise' the business by offering, say, a one-thirty-second share or by buying anything less attractive than the pricier Hawkers, Falcons and Gulfstreams. Its positioning was deliberately up-market. Not only does this appeal to elite customers, but the extra spending on aircraft quality and safety training is reassuring. As Buffett says, "if you were hiring a brain surgeon, would you ask 'who's the cheapest?'"[291]

By the late 1990s, EJA was by far the largest fractional jet operator in the US, with more than 1,000 customers, over 600 pilots and 163 aircraft – 23 of which were core owned or leased by EJA itself. And it was growing fast: in 1997 alone it was the customer for 31% of all corporate jets ordered in the world.

The NetJets team were targeting growth in Europe, which it entered in 1996, to build critical mass there as well as in North America. Clients could fly a US-based aircraft to Europe and then use the NetJets Europe aircraft within the continent, and the European-based clients could do the reverse. Plans were being drawn up for a Middle Eastern programme set for launch in 1999.

A change in share ownership

Goldman Sachs in 1998 wanted to realise a return on its 25% stake, or at least obtain a market value and trading venue for its shares, and so pressed Santulli to float the business on a stock market. Santulli was hesitant because he believed stock-market investors would run scared of the volatility and poor profits while NetJets was in its fast-growth phase.

If he could sell it to investors at all, the price was likely to be low, he thought. "I could never take this company public. Shareholders wouldn't be able to stomach the ups and downs of this business", he explained to journalist Stephen Pope.[292] And Santulli did not want "a 28-year-old analyst" telling him how to run his business.[293]

But maybe there was someone he knew who recognised the strength of its market position and its potential, and would be willing to pay a decent price while leaving him to grow the business?

Selling Buffett a fraction

In 1995, Frank Rooney at H. H. Brown (investment four in this volume) had been extolling the virtues of his NetJets membership and suggested to Buffett that he meet Richard Santulli to investigate signing up.

Buffett said, "It took Rich about 15 minutes to sell me a quarter (200 hours annually) of a Hawker 1000."[294] Warren and his wife Susan went to look at a plane at Teterboro, New Jersey, "and Rich was there in a Hawker 1000, and my wife fell in love on the spot," Buffett recalled in an interview with Warren Berger, who then cheekily asked: "with Santulli or the plane?" Buffett laughed, "Believe me, I don't ever want to give her a choice between me and Rich. She would probably leave me in a minute."[295]

In the following three years the Buffett family flew 900 hours on 300 trips. They loved the service, finding it friendly, efficient and safe. Buffett liked it so much that he enthusiastically took part in a testimonial advertisement long before he knew there was a possibility of buying the company. But he did say to Santulli that if he ever did want to sell then please give him a call.

A short discussion and then a deal

That call came in May 1998, by which time revenues were close to $1bn, up from $100m in 1995. Santulli wanted Buffett's advice on him caving-in to Goldman Sachs' insistence that his company be taken public. Buffett's response: "Well, what if I buy the company?"[296]

The deal was made in less than three weeks with minimal examination of accounts. More important to Buffett than detailed due diligence is the character of the person selling shares to him. The key question he asks on every deal is whether the seller "would take the money and go sit on a beach or stay and run the company".[297] Santulli easily convinced Buffett that he would remain the driving force behind the firm. "I still think of it as my company," Santulli told *Forbes* shortly after the merger.

Buffett has another question he always asks: Is this service worth the money to people? Regarding NetJets he concluded, "the answer in my book is yes – and the proof is, nobody that tries it ever quits."[298]

We've only just begun

Santulli wasn't like other company owners who looked to cash out of a company that had already demonstrated its full potential. No, he saw NetJets as only at the beginning of its most exciting period of growth. It therefore needed an owner with deep pockets who could support very rapid expansion without interfering in operations. NetJets had to stay well ahead of rivals and become so powerful that would-be rivals were scared off before even trying to enter the market.

He thought big, ordering 220 more planes with orders for another 60 in the pipeline, all told, costing nearly $4bn. He wanted to dramatically increase the service in Europe as well as North America, which would not only mean expending a considerable amount but most likely result in short-term losses. "Warren Buffett is a long-term player. He's not worried about the next three months or six months" Santulli told the *Columbus Dispatch* in August 1998.[299] Buffett and Santulli were as one on the vision of fast growth and market dominance in the long run.

Berkshire Hathaway agreed to pay $725m, with $350m of that in cash and the remainder in Berkshire shares, for all the shares in EJA. The merger closed on 7 August, 1998, with Santulli receiving more than half the proceeds: $250m in cash and 3,437 Berkshire A shares.[300]

Santulli later divulged that his Goldman Sachs friends were disappointed about the price, believing that they would have received more for their 25% holding from an IPO. But he explained in an interview with Lawrence Cunningham that he wanted the company to go to Berkshire because "along with the money, he valued Berkshire's culture of autonomy and permanence",[301] motives we have seen time and again in Buffett's deals.

Buffett publicly told Santulli that he was a managerial artist, with the vision to know what should be on his mural when no one else did. All Buffett had to do was bring Santulli some paint and a few brushes, and otherwise stay out of the way.

> "In addition to being a terrific executive, Rich is fun. Like most of our managers, he has no economic need whatsoever to work. Rich spends his time at EJA because it's his baby — and he wants to see how far he can take it. We both already know the answer, both literally and figuratively: to the ends of the earth."[302]

Why did he buy it?

Buffett had many reasons to think NetJets a good buy.

As market leader with over half of the industry, NetJets had a competitive advantage because "our customers gain because we have an armada of planes positioned throughout the country at all times, a blanketing that allows us to provide unmatched service. Meanwhile, we gain from the blanketing because it reduces dead-head costs."[303,304] And it had the potential to achieve the same customer service dominance in other continents.

NetJets' independence from plane manufacturers gave it a competitive advantage because it could offer a variety of craft, whereas its principal competitors were tied to one or other of the manufacturers and so offered only planes from their stables. NetJets procured "products from Boeing, Gulfstream, Falcon, Cessna, and Raytheon … In effect, NetJets is like a physician who can recommend whatever medicine best fits the needs of each patient; our competitors, in contrast, are producers of a 'house' brand that they must prescribe for one and all."[305]

Rich Santulli was a brilliant entrepreneur and manager and would have an information and experience edge in this industry.

Another competitive advantage: clients in need of a range of aircraft for a variety of types of trips could buy a few fractions in different-sized craft at a total cost less than buying and operating one wholly-owned aircraft. "For example, a client might own one-sixteenths of three different jets (each giving it 50 hours of flying time), which in total give it a virtual fleet, obtained for a small fraction of the cost of a single plane."[306]

Being a client of the largest fractional airplane operator with the most comprehensive coverage was attractive to large corporations that already had one or two aircraft of their own. "Some of America's largest companies use NetJets as a supplement to their own fleet. This saves them big money in both meeting peak requirements and in flying missions that would require their wholly-owned planes to log a disproportionate amount of dead-head hours."[307] So again, the dominant player has an edge.

Eventually, clients picked up the bill for the high capital cost of most planes, which reduced the amount of Berkshire capital tied up. But that still left a substantial amount of money committed to, first, the core fleet and, second, to planes bought from manufacturers but where fractions remain unsold.

Berkshire's AAA credit rating could cut the cost of borrowing for NetJets and ease the path to much higher borrowing and therefore rapid expansion.

Growth, but at a price

With Berkshire behind them the managers at Netjets really went for growth. Within two years revenue had more than doubled and customers held $2bn worth of planes. As early as 1998 Buffett asked Santulli, "Who's the competition in Europe?" to which he replied "No one." Then Buffett pointedly said, "What do you need to make it stay that way?"[308] Money flowed from Berkshire to achieve the ambition of dominating fractional ownership in both the USA and Europe.

With the task of building critical mass in Europe well underway in 1999, Buffett wrote that he intended to support NetJets' expansion all round the world. "Doing that will be expensive — very expensive — but we will spend what it takes. Scale is vital to both us and our customers: The company with the most planes in the air worldwide will be able to offer its customers the best service. 'Buy a fraction, get a fleet' has real meaning at EJA."[309]

The accelerator pedal was pushed even harder in 2000, with $4.2bn new planes on order. NetJets' managers would have signed up for even more, but they were already taking about 8% of all business jets manufactured in the world and the makers could not keep up.

The fast-talking salesman

Buffett became NetJets' number one salesman. From the off there was a fully fitted out cabin on display at the May Berkshire annual meeting (in 1998 it was a 737 Boeing Business Jet complete with bedroom, two showers, 14-hour range and 19 passenger seats). The scores of billionaires and hundreds of millionaires enjoying the Berkshire weekend events each year are prime targets for the NetJets sales teams. And Buffett started a tradition of always giving the company a mention in his annual letter.

In 1999 he persuaded two of Berkshire's outside directors to buy fractions. Then he announced a breakthrough: "And now, brace yourself. Last year, EJA passed the ultimate test: Charlie signed up. No other endorsement could speak more eloquently to the value of the EJA service."[310] Munger, renowned for being careful with money, used to fly coach class, even when wealthy, so jumping to private-jet travel was quite something.

Buffett was bold enough to include in his letter a free-phone number: "Give us a call at 1-800-848-6436 and ask for our 'white paper' on fractional ownership".[311] The May 1999 meeting had initiated the sale of at least eight fractions. To promote NetJets, Buffett would speak at dinners or business forums in places like Hollywood or London. And there was a famous advertisement with Bill Gates and Warren Buffett lounging on a jet enjoying a joke. Priceless publicity.

Go for it

In October 2000, Santulli spoke of Buffett's attitude to growing the company: "One of the nicest things about being part of Berkshire is that if I said to Warren, 'I'm going to go buy $1bn worth of planes,' he would say, 'Why are you asking me? Go do it.'"[312] Aircraft were bought at scale – with large discounts on list prices – and fractions sold; in 2001, customers took delivery of more than 50 new jets – 7% of world output.

But rapid growth was coming at a cost to profitability, as the operating costs in the infant European market ran ahead of revenues and chasing after growth in the US raised operating costs there. In 2001, the chickens came home to roost. While revenues rose over 20%, the business made a loss, despite an uplift of interest in private jet flying after the 9/11 attack on the Twin Towers.

By then NetJets looked after 300 planes in the US alone. But rivals' shares, when added together, accounted for almost half the market, and they were determined to remain price competitive, which left little room for profits. Buffett wrote that he expected "for a few years" only "modest profits".[313]

Despite this gloomy prospect, Buffett insisted that the strategy was correct:

> "Maintaining a premier level of safety, security and service was always expensive … No matter how much the cost, we will continue to be the industry leader in all three respects. An uncompromising insistence on delivering only the best to his customers is embedded in the DNA of Rich Santulli … I'm delighted with his fanaticism on these matters for both the company's sake and my family's".[314]

But the debt was rising. Berkshire Hathaway had borrowed well over $1bn to support NetJets.

In 2002, EJA changed its name to its most valuable brand name, NetJets, as revenues reached a new record. But still losses were made. Buffett held onto his optimism:

> "The bald fact is that airplanes are costly to operate. Over time, this economic reality should work to our advantage, given that for a great many companies, private aircraft are an essential business tool. And for most of these companies, NetJets makes compelling sense as either a primary or supplementary supplier of the aircraft they need. Many businesses could save millions of dollars annually by flying with us [and] increase their operational capabilities by using us. A fractional ownership of a single NetJets plane allows a client to have several planes in the air simultaneously."[315]

The next year there was a real plunge, with a loss of $41m. Most of the loss, $32m, was attributable to falling prices of used aircraft. NetJets was obliged to buy back fractions from withdrawing owners at prevailing prices, but before it could sell them on, the market fell. This type of risk comes back to haunt NetJets managers, especially when recession strikes.

Even though Europe was still spilling red ink, Buffett was chirpy:

> "Overwhelmingly, our owners love the NetJets experience. Once a customer has tried us, going back to commercial aviation is like going back to holding hands. NetJets will become a very big business over time and will be one in which we are preeminent in both customer satisfaction and profits. Rich will see to that."[316]

Buffett backed up that optimism by permitting orders for new jets to rise above $6bn, as fractional client contracts rose to 3,877 compared with approximately 1,200 in August 1998.

With relief, Buffett was able to report to his shareholders a modest profit in 2004. While the US market was profitable the European market, though gaining momentum, was "far more expensive than I anticipated",[317] wrote Buffett.

Nevertheless, he added that Berkshire must keep investing in the European market, not least to keep its American customers happy:

"Our U.S. owners already want a quality service wherever they travel and their wish for flight hours abroad is certain to grow dramatically in the decades ahead. Last year, U.S. owners made 2,003 flights in Europe, up 22% from the previous year and 137% from 2000. Just as important, our European owners made 1,067 flights in the U.S., up 65% from 2003 and 239% from 2000."[318]

But then it all went the wrong way again in 2005, with the US operation dipping far into the red, on top of the drag on profits in Europe. Still, Buffett and Santulli pushed on with expansion with the outstanding orders for planes exceeding $10bn, a total of over 400 aircraft.

Expansion had paid off on the revenue side – which in 2006 was six times the level of 1998 – so hundreds of clients had been won over. And, at last, Europe was profitable after suffering a cumulative pre-tax loss there of $212m to December 2006. The US operation had a good year too, resulting in NetJets pre-tax profits of $143m.

Then operating 487 planes in the US and 135 in Europe in 2007, Santulli wanted to grow much bigger still so he had another 541 on order. He and Buffett were encouraged by seeing increased profits in 2007 compared with 2006. Maybe this is a trend, the breakthrough they had been looking for? Profits were even better in 2008, with $213m of pre-tax earnings.

But then it all went horribly wrong

The Great Recession hit. With a whopping $1.9bn of debt outstanding, NetJets made a "staggering"[319] loss of $711m in 2009, which wiped out all the profits made since Berkshire had acquired NetJets 11 years before (aggregate pre-tax loss $157m). In that year revenues declined by $1,465m, or 32%, due to a 77% decline in aircraft sales and a 19% fall in hours flown, which lowered flight-operation revenues.

But the biggest problem was being left holding an enormous quantity of used planes at a time of tumbling market values. As a result, NetJets was forced to record 'asset write downs and other downsizing costs' of $676m. The attraction to fractional owners of being able to sell back to NetJets at a fair-market price came back to bite NetJets.

The financial crisis had induced bankers and other executives to go on an economy drive, and it was poor PR to be seen climbing into a corporate jet, especially when on your way to Congress to ask for a bailout – yes, some were that crass.

In 2009, owners sold fractions at an unprecedented rate. NetJets would buy, but then found a few months later prices had declined even more with no buyer in sight. Some were held on the books at 40% less than what NetJets had paid.

Will it survive?

Buffett's 2009 letter included a *mea culpa*: "It's clear that I failed you in letting NetJets descend into this condition". His solution was to call in a Berkshire executive known for taking tough decisions, especially cutting back costs and staffing, David Sokol, who Buffett described as "the enormously talented builder and operator of MidAmerican Energy".

Sokol became CEO of NetJets in August 2009 when Santulli resigned. In Buffett's 2009 letter Santulli was briefly mentioned as the 'previous CEO', as a stickler for safety and service, and the 'father' of fractional ownership, but no detailed explanation of Santulli's resignation was given. Was he pushed after a period of massive losses?

But note, while he had resigned as CEO he had agreed to stay on for a year as a consultant, so that didn't sound like a 'don't darken the door again' type of resignation.

On the other hand, there were rumours that Santulli had been resistant to downsizing the business and the redundancies that would entail. "Sources tell us he was forced out for failing to move aggressively enough to stem financial losses at the fractional-ownership giant. Others say he fell out of favor after rejecting calls to let go of senior managers who'd worked alongside him for years",[320] wrote Stephen Pope in *Business Jet Traveler*.

Aviation International News' Chad Trautvetter caught a whiff of the gossip: "The speculation about whether or not the company founder left of his own volition was rampant in the immediate aftermath of the announcement, and several sources told *AIN* at the time that NetJets' finances might have been a factor."[321]

The speculative fever was not helped by Santulli's use of the time-honoured phrase used in resignation statements, the one usually received with scepticism, "to spend more time with my young family and pursue other interests".

But there were plenty of people who were willing to take Santulli at his word. He had a passion for thoroughbred horses, three children and three dogs. So there were plenty of other aspects to his life which he had been sacrificing to some degree while struggling to turn NetJets to profits.

Buffett seemed regretful and friendly in his August 2009 release:

> "It is with reluctance that I accept Richard's decision to step down. Richard Santulli is synonymous with the fractional jet ownership industry and his vision and energy has made NetJets the leader that it is today. All of Richard's friends at Berkshire Hathaway wish Richard well in this transition."

In December 2009, Santulli became chairman of Loan Value Group (a mortgage market company) and in August 2010 he launched Milestone Aviation Group, a helicopter and business-jet leasing company. He also further developed philanthropic activities, focusing on individuals with developmental disabilities; supporting public education for underserved youth; military personnel suffering the effects of a traumatic brain injury and post-traumatic stress, and the Andre Agassi Foundation for Education. He vowed "everything I have will be given away while I am alive, minus enough for my wife to live."[322]

Can the business be saved?

There was much comment around the question of whether the fractional business model was broken. Had it become too expensive relative to the alternative facing an executive of simply chartering a plane as needed? Were there too many planes chasing too few clients?

Michael Riegel of AviationIQ, an advisory firm, declared in 2009 the fractional business model to be failing, "there are a lot of irate consumers monitoring what's going on,"[323] noting that the decline in net annual sales of fractions had been a trend since 2002. This meant that the precipitous loss of customers in 2009 could not be dismissed as a mere blip due to the recession.

He thought clients were not being treated well, being presented with rising hourly fees (ahead of inflation), and the amount received for used fractions had dropped lower than anyone expected.

> "The cost of being an owner is far higher than before. A lot of owners are saying it's become too expensive and they don't want to keep doing this. The industry has dug itself into a hole."[324]

Other commentators, while acknowledging the problems, thought they were solvable, saying 'adjustment' would be needed rather than the death of the industry. Consultant Brian Foley said he thought demand for fractions might have been overestimated, that the main players had talked up the market to the point of excess capacity, that the "core demand wasn't there".[325]

NetJets and its rivals needed to learn how to operate efficiently in a mature, not a growing, industry. Foley predicted "a big shakeup coming … Fractionals will survive, but there will be fewer players, which is better for those remaining. They have to find a way to remain profitable while in the mature stage."[326]

Profits at last

Dave Sokol took rapid action. Within a week he had reshaped the managerial structure, including appointing a new head for NetJets North America and a new chief operating officer. He also announced that NetJets' headquarters would be relocated from Woodbridge, N.J., to Columbus, Ohio, where the company's flight operations were based.

Buffett seems to have accepted Foley's argument, writing in his 2009 letter that NetJets owns "more planes than is required for its present level of operations". Aircraft orders were cancelled and by Spring 2010 Sokol had lowered debt to $1.4bn. Within two years, 1,700 employees were laid off (from 7,945). Sokol had plans to dispose of 'selected aircraft' but refused to do so in a fire-sale way, rather waiting until prices were reasonable. The fleet went from 629 planes to under 500 over three years.

He said the tough decisions were necessary:

> "When you have a major economic shift such as in the fall of 2008, you have to reinvent yourself. Five years from now, I'll wager all of us will look back at 2008 and say it was the best thing that ever happened to the aviation industry because it's forcing innovation that wasn't going to happen."[327]

Stephen Pope's verdict, writing in *The Business Jet Traveler*, was that:

> "the prognosis for the company is good, I think. The fractional-ownership business model has matured and adapting for the next growth cycle will require fresh thinking … the company's core customer base is still out there. They don't want to go back to charter. They want to be able to pick up the phone, arrive at the airport four hours later and climb aboard a meticulously maintained airplane crewed by well-trained, by-the-book pilots. The trick will be finding the right balance to make the numbers work again."[328]

The remarkably quick turnaround pleased Buffett greatly and in Spring 2010 he wrote (in his 2009 letter) that the plans already implemented would lead to rightsizing. Furthermore, NetJets was on course to make a profit in 2010.

Unfortunately, David Sokol's time at NetJets was limited. Indeed, his time at Berkshire Hathaway was cut short by a regrettable incident early in 2011. He bought shares in Lubrizol before proposing to Buffett that Berkshire Hathaway buy the company. He purchased them because he thought the company to be outstanding and an excellent investment, but he was also asking Lubrizol's CEO if he might be interested in being bought by Berkshire.

Sokol didn't know for sure that Buffett would buy Lubrizol when he invested his $10m. He had told Buffett that he owned stock in Lubrizol but "It was a passing remark and I did not ask him about the date of his purchase or the extent of his holdings", wrote Buffett.[329]

Carol Loomis of *Fortune Magazine* wrote, "the facts about Sokol's buying – combined with the lift in Lubrizol's stock that accompanied Buffett's decision to indeed buy – put Sokol into disrepute for what some onlookers thought might be insider trading."[330]

Buffett was careful to publicly note that Sokol's actions were not unlawful, even though he made $3m profit, which was a fraction of his annual remuneration.

Sokol resigned on the 28 March to, as he put it, "utilise the time remaining in my career to invest my family's resources".[331] He had submitted two similarly worded resignations in previous years, but Buffett had persuaded him to stay on. In the March announcement Buffett wrote that he had not asked for his resignation and it came as a surprise to him, but he did not set out to ask him to stay in post this time.

In April, a Berkshire audit-committee report concluded that its policy of precluding share-buying by its managers in companies Berkshire was considering acquiring had been violated. Also, its policy of not using confidential information for personal use had not been followed, and Berkshire's reputation had been damaged.

A few days later, at the annual meeting, Buffett said he regretted that he hadn't expressed a greater rebuke to Sokol. He corrected that by describing Sokol's actions as "inexcusable and inexplicable". Sokol was later told by the Securities and Exchange Commission that he would not face enforcement actions. He continued to maintain his innocence in the matter.

Consistently profitable

The turnaround within a year was remarkable. NetJets in 2010 reported $207m pre-tax profits on revenues, 7% ahead of 2009. Buffett hailed "Berkshire's only major business problem" becoming a "solidly profitable operation".[332] Market share was five times that of the nearest rival and customer satisfaction was hitting new highs.

The next year earnings rose by a tenth, helped by a 10% reduction in fleet size which lowered maintenance costs. Jordan Hansell took over as chairman and CEO in April 2011, two years after being recruited as chief administrative officer and general counsel. He started to build a footprint in Asia, partnering with some local firms.

Earnings were static in 2012 but moved ahead by 7% in 2013, followed by another steady rise in 2014.

There was a slip-up in profit progression in 2015, when the company paid lump-sum amounts to pilots following the resolution of a bitter dispute. NetJets pilots had even picketed in front of Berkshire Hathaway shareholders filing into the spring 2014 Berkshire meeting in Omaha. They were angry about reduced pay and increased healthcare costs. The union president reported that 98% of the pilots voted "no confidence" in Hansell. Lawsuits flew.

In June 2015 Hansell left, to be replaced by Adam Johnson, a NetJets man since 1996. He had resigned from the company only a month before and was just about to take a new role with another company.

Also returning to his role as president and COO was Bill Noe, a former pilot, who had departed NetJets two months before after 22 years with the company. The union leader was 'cautiously optimistic' that the new leadership would rebuild strained relationships. He seems to have been right because profits moved higher in 2016, 2017, 2018 and 2019.

It is interesting to note that since the crisis of 2009 the lesson of not outrunning growth in the core market has resulted in the directors limiting fleet expansion. Indeed, the number of planes in 2020 – 629 – was the same as in 2008 (having dipped below 500 between 2011–13).

NetJets has truly become a mature company with a focus on profits, rather than a start-up looking for rapid growth, fearful it would not be big enough to dominate its industry.

Profits of well over $200m per year for over a decade suggest that it is strong enough to attract the clientele it desires, those willing to pay a mutually-agreeable price to jet around the world at four hours' notice – something that was but a dream back in 1986, when Rich Santulli was struggling to get his maths equations to show a profitable path.

As to whether Buffett should have paid $725m for NetJets; well, we'll have to wait and see.

Learning points

1. **An investor needs to be very patient sometimes.** Buffett continued with his belief in the strategy of entrenching market dominance – deepening the moat – despite years of losses.

2. **Some market segments are just too small to permit large profits, even if the dominant firm has several competitive advantages.** After Buffett paid $725m and then millions more in annual losses, he discovered the market for fractional ownership was much more limited than first thought. Once recognised, the company cut its cloth accordingly, resulting in a flow of (unspectacular) profits.

3. **Benjamin Graham emphasised proven facts such as past evidence of profits or solid net-current-asset value, but Buffett's investment in NetJets moved him significantly away from this principle.** He concentrated on hope of what might become of NetJets many years in the future if enough money was pumped into it. Is this really value investing?

Investment 10

GENERAL RE

Summary of the deal

Deal	General Re
Time	1998
Price paid	$22bn
Quantity	100% of the equity
Sale price	Held today
Profit	Losses for 5 years, then underwriting profits. Plus daily use of $15–23.7bn float for investments
Berkshire Hathaway in 1998	Share price: $47,000–80,900 Book value: $57,403m Per share book value: $37,801

Insurance is at the heart of Berkshire Hathaway. The first significant act after Warren Buffett took control of Berkshire was the 1967 purchase of National Indemnity for $8.6m. There are two main attractions to holding a well-run insurance company within the Berkshire fold. First, it might, although most insurance firms don't, make a profit on underwriting. That is, what it pays out on claims together with its operating costs (wages, etc.) is less than it takes in premiums.

Second, the delay between policyholders handing over premiums and insurance claims being paid leads to a 'float' of money being held in the company. When Buffett took control of National Indemnity it had a float of $17.3m. That was a considerable sum of money for Buffett to invest; after all, Berkshire Hathaway then had less than $30m net assets. His skill would lead to large returns on money under his command.

Technically, accountants treat float as a liability for Berkshire because it is set to one day be paid out in claims. In truth, float is a tremendous asset in the right hands.

Experiencing the excitement of making money from the float while achieving profitable underwriting (in most years) in the 1970s, Buffett was determined to build the insurance side of the business. To National Indemnity, he added an array of other companies, the most significant of which was GEICO. By 1998, the insurance side had a float of over $7bn and was generating annual premiums totalling over $5bn.

Then Buffett went for a giant leap by trebling the size of Berkshire's float from $7bn to $22.8bn by buying market-leading General Re. It was paid for, not with cash, but by the issue of A and B shares,[333] amounting to approximately 272,200 Class A equivalent shares in Berkshire. This raised its issued share capital by 21.8% and doubled the number of Berkshire shareholders to about 250,000.

Another way of looking at it is, after the deal, former General Re shareholders owned over one-fifth of the economic worth of See's Candies, FlightSafety, NFM and the other wholly-owned businesses, as well as over one-fifth of Berkshire's marketable securities, such as its 8.1% holding of Coca Cola (worth $13.4bn) and its 11.3% holding in American Express (worth $8.4bn).

Also, by issuing new shares in Berkshire Hathaway, Warren Buffett's share of the economic benefit from the enterprises owned by the group went down from 43% to 34% (but he and his wife Susan between them held 38.4% of the voting rights through their A-share holdings).

But what did Berkshire receive in return?

Buffett thought he was getting a conservatively-run insurance company that either made underwriting profits or small losses here and there. And he was getting a $15bn float, greatly increasing his firepower. On acquisition, he almost immediately reduced General Re's investment office from 150 to one person, himself, to direct that float.

But the company came with a whole heap of trouble. It took Buffett and Munger years to sort out the problems, which ranged from under-pricing of insurance and poor provisioning for likely insurance claims, to a massive number of derivative deals (over 23,000 contracts involving 884 counterparties). General Re bled money after Berkshire purchased it. In the first five years it lost $7.9bn on underwriting.

By the end of 2001, after the terrorist attack on the Twin Towers in New York, things got so bad that Buffett said General Re would have gone bust had it not been for the deep pockets of Berkshire to bail it out. At that point many, including Buffett, thought the purchase a mistake.

But later it was to become what Buffett called a treasure. The story of its fall and rise is instructive to anybody interested in investing in insurance companies, not least the importance of having managers with the right cautious mindset for creating float at low cost through taking on underwriting business with a rational profit-focused determination.

The insurance business

To understand the significance of the General Re acquisition we need to go right back to basics both in terms of where Berkshire's insurance business came from, and in how the insurance industry works.

Building on National Indemnity

Following the purchase of National Indemnity and its sister company National Fire and Marine Insurance, Buffett took a close interest in their underwriting. And he assumed complete control over the investment of its float. At this stage, National Indemnity concentrated on property and casualty insurance, particularly for vehicles. (There is more on National Indemnity in volume one, investment 11.)

From the start, Buffett set underwriting profitability as the company's primary goal. This meant sacrificing revenue if the premium charged was unlikely to be greater than the payout to the insured and operating expenses. To encourage employees not to go for top-line growth, he said that even if customer numbers fell by two-thirds for a year or two they would all keep their jobs. He once gave a talk to students at Notre Dame in which he said that when insurance prices are unattractive, "we have a lot of people doing crossword puzzles". The company would wait it out until insurance rates picked up again. Then employees would be fully occupied.

Things were looking good, with underwriting profits reported in 1967, 1968 and 1969 generating float without a cost attached. At first, float was increased only gradually to $23.4m in 1969. In that year, Berkshire started a reinsurance business under the leadership of George Young.

Reinsurers lessen exposure to risk of primary insurers by transferring some risk to themselves in return for a premium. Thus, a reinsurer might take half of the exposure to a Californian earthquake from a primary local Californian insurer, or might agree to cover losses above a certain amount, say, the Californian insurer took the first $10m loss, anything above that would be paid out by the reinsurer.

Also, reinsurers often accept reinsurance business from other reinsurers, as risk is offloaded onto bigger or more diverse shoulders (this is often called retrocession). The almost-instantly profitable reinsurance business grew rapidly.

In 1970 Berkshire expanded in another direction, with the formation of Cornhusker Insurance,[334] a 'homestate' business. Homestate insurance is property and casualty insurance provided locally (covering home, auto, workers compensation for healthcare and work-time lost).

Cornhusker, a nickname for Nebraska, was followed by Lakeland Fire and Casualty Company in Minnesota during 1971, Texas United Insurance in 1972, and the Insurance Company of Iowa in 1973. In 1976, Kerkling Reinsurance Corporation (later renamed Central Fire and Casualty Company to better reflect its focus on homestate insurance rather than reinsurance)[335] was bought, and in late 1977 Kansas Fire and Casualty Company[336] was purchased.

Each of these companies had its own local underwriting and management presence in their respective territories, but Buffett took a close interest in underwriting and, of course, controlled their floats.

More geographically wide-ranging insurance companies were also added. Home and Automobile Insurance Company, located in Chicago, writing about $7.5m in premium volume was bought in 1971, and in 1977 Cypress Insurance Company of San Francisco, a writer for workers compensation insurance, was welcomed to the group.

The main contributors to the rise in float in the first decade were the original National Indemnity primary insurance and its reinsurance arm, but the other insurance businesses made useful contributions. Between 1967 and 1977, insurance premium volume grew from $22m to $151m and the float from $17.3m to $139m.

Table 10.1: Profit and float of Berkshire Hathaway Insurance businesses 1967–1981

	Underwriting loss ($m)	Average float ($m)	Approximate cost of funds (Ratio of loss to float) (%)	Year-end yield on long-term govt. bonds (%)
1967	profit	17.3	less than zero	5.50
1968	profit	19.9	less than zero	5.90
1969	profit	23.4	less than zero	6.79
1970	0.37	32.4	1.14	6.25
1971	profit	52.5	less than zero	5.81
1972	profit	69.5	less than zero	5.82
1973	profit	73.3	less than zero	7.27
1974	7.36	79.1	9.30	8.13
1975	11.35	87.6	12.96	8.03
1976	profit	102.6	less than zero	7.30
1977	profit	139.0	less than zero	7.97
1978	profit	190.4	less than zero	8.93

	Underwriting loss ($m)	Average float ($m)	Approximate cost of funds (Ratio of loss to float) (%)	Year-end yield on long-term govt. bonds (%)
1979	profit	227.3	less than zero	10.08
1980	profit	237.0	less than zero	11.94
1981	profit	228.4	less than zero	13.61

Source: Warren Buffett's 1997 Letter to Berkshire Hathaway shareholders

The insurance float was invested in a mix of bonds and equities, including some of Buffett's best picks, such as the Washington Post (1974), GEICO (1976) and ABC (1978).

Interest and dividend income quickly flowed to Berkshire from the float. For example, in 1977 alone that income amounted to $12.3m. In addition, a realised capital gain of $6.9m was made that year, and there was a cumulative $74m of unrealised capital gain.

Another type of insurance market was entered in 1979: surety reinsurance. Surety reinsurance is where the insurer guarantees to a creditor, e.g., a bank lending money or building contractor expecting to be paid later, that it will receive the amount due even if the debtor defaults. Berkshire took fees for reinsuring the primary surety insurers.

Testing years

Until 1982 Buffett assumed personal responsibility for insurance business strategy, senior appointments, and monitoring. As the business grew, he realised the need to take more of a back seat, freeing time to concentrate on investments. He looked around for a talented manager to take over as head of all Berkshire insurance operations, and found such a talent in Mike Goldberg, a former McKinsey & Company consultant.[337]

Self-deprecatingly, Buffett said in his 1982 letter that "planning, recruitment, and monitoring all have shown significant improvement since Mike replaced me in this role." The following year, Buffett was again hard on himself:

> "in aggregate, the companies we operate and whose underwriting results reflect the consequences of decisions that were my responsibility a few years ago, had absolutely terrible results. Fortunately, GEICO, whose policies I do not influence, simply shot the lights out. The inference you draw from this summary is the correct one. I made some serious mistakes a few years ago."

Perhaps it wasn't self-deprecation. The chickens of the late 1970s and early 1980s were coming home to roost in the mid-1980s. Those chickens were some poor underwriting decisions which went unrecognised for some time but had to be acknowledged eventually.

In 1983, for every $100 taken in premiums, Berkshire recorded an expense of $121 for claims and operating costs. In other words, the 'combined ratio' was 121 (a combined ratio is the total cost of underwriting divided by the total earning premiums).

Buffett said that it would "be nice" if the underwriting shortcomings could be placed at the doorstep of Mike Goldberg, but that insurance has a long lead time before the effects of decisions are seen: "so the roots of the 1983 results are operating and personnel decisions made two or more years back when I had direct managerial responsibility for the insurance group."[338]

Insurers often have great difficulty estimating claims for a 12-month period. The lack of clarity and the dependence on judgement opens the door to over-optimism. The extent of many insurance claims, or even their existence, is not known for many years because there are four parts to insurance loss expenses in any one year:

1. Losses that occurred and were paid during the year;
2. Estimates for losses that occurred and were reported to the insurer during the year, but which have yet to be settled;
3. Estimates of ultimate dollar costs for losses that occurred during the year but of which the insurer is unaware; and
4. The net effect of revisions this year of similar estimates for (2) and (3) made in past years.[339]

Revisions under two and three may occur many years down the line, which adds to the cost line of that later year, distorting the profitability of underwriting then. Take an injury from a car accident. The true extent of medical or time-off-work costs may not be known for some time. If, say, an unexpected additional $100,000 is paid out five years later then the amount is charged to underwriting profits in the year it is settled.

Even well-intentioned CEOs and their accountants conscientiously aiming at conservative estimates often make mistakes. In the mid-1980s Buffett had to admit to such: "At Berkshire, we have added what we thought were appropriate supplemental reserves but in recent years they have not been adequate."[340] In 1984, for example, of the overall $45.4m underwriting loss, $27.6m was a loss on 1984's business, but $17.8m was a correction for the loss amount recorded for 1983.

Errors in this period were largely caused by underestimating the tendency of juries and courts, influenced by publicity on high-profile cases, to continuously push up payouts for injuries in accidents and other events regardless "of the factual situation and the past precedents for establishment of liability",[341] according to an annoyed Buffett.

Berkshire also erred in the reinsurance area. Much of this being down to client primary insurance firms making errors – "their mistakes have become our mistakes",[342] wrote Buffett.

Buffett ruefully likened the painful experience of having to make surprisingly large payments on business he thought was finished years before to that of the man travelling abroad who received a phone call from his sister informing him that their father had just died. He couldn't get home but asked his sister to make the funeral arrangements and send the bill to him. When he got home, he found a bill for a few thousand dollars and promptly paid it. But then the following month another bill came for $15, and he paid that. Other months followed with demands for $15, so eventually he called his sister to ask what was going on. "Oh", she said. "I forgot to tell you. We buried Dad in a rented suit."[343]

At least Buffett could laugh about it.

Shafts of light

Even in the mid-1980s there were a couple of bright spots. Buffett pointed in particular to an area he hoped would become increasingly active: reinsurance. Here, premium rates held up better than in, say, auto insurance where buyers look for lowest cost. This was because there were few players with the renown of Berkshire.

As Buffett expressed it: "The buyer's overriding concern should be the seller's long-term creditworthiness,"[344] and Berkshire was by then a broadly-based business with a fortress-like balance sheet and impressive profit history. It had creditworthiness in spades. "In such transactions our premier financial strength should make us the number one choice of both claimants and insurers who must rely on the reinsurer's promises for a great many years to come."[345]

A fast-developing area of reinsurance for Berkshire was then 'structured settlement', where the claimant, say for a life-changing injury, receives monthly payments for life rather than a lump sum that they might squander. To sell such insurance, there must be no question about the stability of the insurer for decades ahead. "No other insurer we know of – even those with much larger gross assets – has our financial strength."[346] This category of business was attractive for Berkshire both in the pricing of premiums (few competitors pushing down prices) and for generating float that will hang around for years.

Berkshire's capital position, being able to withstand both a prolonged depressed financial market and exceptionally poor underwriting results occurring at the same time, led to their unrivalled ability to keep promises made. This also attracted other, weaker insurance companies to buy insurance from Berkshire against claims on their 'expired business'.

Under expired-business policies, Berkshire would be on the hook for claims should, say, a former insured employee of a client company (say a construction company) of a primary insurer develop problems from working with asbestos decades before. By purchasing this reinsurance, the weaker insurance company could more or less forget about that long-tail risk. Technically, it transfers loss reserves in return for a one-off fee to Berkshire.

Berkshire's strength made it more willing than most competitors to accept substantial risks onto its own books. In contrast, most competitors laid off large risks through reinsurance arrangements. So, a rival to Berkshire might take a $25m exposure on, say, a directors-and-officers policy (D&O insurance pays out the cost of compensation claims made against a business' directors and key managers for alleged wrongful acts). But this primary insurer would keep just $1m of exposure on its own books by purchasing $24m of reinsurance.

A problem with this business model arises if the reinsurers have had a string of unpleasant surprises. They then tend to withdraw from the market and eventually the primary insurer has nowhere to turn for reinsurance. The $25m exposure is too great for the primary insurer to take onto its balance sheet, so they simply stop writing such policies, leaving Berkshire to take the business.

> "We have the underwriting capability whereas others do not. If we believe the price to be right, we are willing to write a net line larger than that of any but the largest insurers. For instance, we are perfectly willing to risk losing $10 million of our own money on a single event, as long as we believe that the price is right and that the risk of loss is not significantly correlated with other risks we are insuring. Very few insurers are willing to risk half that much on single events."[347]

There was an event in 1985 that illustrated the insurance industry's supply and demand imbalance. Berkshire advertised in an insurance trade journal that it was willing to write large risks, that is, only those offering a premium of over $1m. So desperate were they that in a short time over 600 insurance brokers and others responded. Clearly, there was a dearth of competitors willing to do the same.

With so many potential clients, Berkshire could afford to be choosy. It ended up only accepting premiums totalling $50m from this exercise. A delighted Buffett wrote shortly after that experience: "today, our insurance subsidiaries continue to be sought out by brokers searching for large net capacity".[348]

Table 10.2: Underwriting losses of Berkshire Hathaway Insurance Group 1982–1995

	Underwriting loss ($m)	Average float ($m)	Approximate cost of funds (Ratio of loss to float) (%)	Year-end yield on long-term govt. bonds (%)
1982	21.56	220.6	9.77	10.64
1983	33.87	231.3	14.64	11.84
1984	48.06	253.2	18.98	11.58
1985	44.23	390.2	11.34	9.34
1986	55.84	797.5	7.00	7.60
1987	55.43	1,266.7	4.38	8.95
1988	11.08	1,497.7	0.74	9.00
1989	24.40	1,541.3	1.58	7.97
1990	26.65	1,637.3	1.63	8.24
1991	119.59	1,895.0	6.31	7.40
1992	108.96	2,290.4	4.76	7.39
1993	profit	2,624.7	less than zero	6.35
1994	profit	3,056.6	less than zero	7.88
1995	profit	3,607.2	less than zero	5.95

Source: Warren Buffett's 1997 Letter to Berkshire Hathaway shareholders

Ajit Jain enters the scene

Mike Goldberg was encouraged to expand the reinsurance business and so hired a team of what Buffett called "young managers with excellent potential."[349] One such manager was Ajit Jain, who joined in 1986. He was later, according to Buffett, to become more important to Berkshire than himself. Over the nearly four decades since he joined, Jain has produced more revenue and profit for Berkshire than any other manager – he has been tipped as Buffett's successor.

When, in 2001, shareholders were worried about Buffett's health, he wrote in his 2000 letter: "it is impossible to overstate how valuable Ajit is to Berkshire. Don't worry about my health; worry about his." Even 15 years after being hired, Jain worked with only 18 employees who were bringing in $2.4bn in annual premiums. He was very frugal, often going for months without a secretary.

Ajit (pronounced Á-gheet) Jain was born in Calcutta in 1951 and educated at the Indian Institute of Technology in Kharagpur, graduating with a BTech in mechanical engineering. This was followed by a stint at IBM in India and a Harvard MBA, after which he joined McKinsey & Company. When his former boss, Mike Goldberg, called from Omaha, he jumped at the chance. Modest to a fault he said: "When I joined Berkshire I didn't know how to spell insurance, or reinsurance, but I was hired to do a job in the reinsurance operations of National Indemnity".[350]

Jain joined at a time of excitement because Berkshire, being one of the few companies with capital, was being "bombarded with deals and phone calls from people wanting insurance. Being new, I didn't understand most of it, but, every now and then, I would see something where I would look at the numbers and say 'This looks interesting.'"[351] He learned fast and within six months was asked to take over all the reinsurance operations.

An iron discipline approach

In the years preceding 1985, Berkshire was the slowest-growing large US insurer. In fact, it shrank. It wasn't that it withdrew from the market. Indeed, it was the industry's most steadfast provider, but it would only quote premiums that "we believe to be adequate",[352] said Buffett. There are times, such as the lead up to 1985, when other insurers slash prices to bargain levels to maintain volume. Naturally, clients leave Berkshire and go to them during these times.

Then the cycle turns – as rivals run out of capital or become frightened by the losses generated by low premiums, they exit the market. Customers then flood back to Berkshire.

"Our firmness on prices works no hardship on … our employees: we don't engage in layoffs when we experience a cyclical slowdown at one of our generally-profitable insurance operations. This no-layoff practice is in our self-interest. Employees who fear that large layoffs will accompany sizable reductions in premium volume will understandably produce scads of business through thick and thin (mostly thin)."[353]

This policy produced huge swings in volume of primary-insurance business. For example, monthly volume of $5m premiums in the final quarter of 1984 jumped to about $35m in the first quarter of 1986. A similar discipline, and therefore volume variability, pervaded the reinsurance business.

The target of achieving profitability on underwriting, i.e., a combined ratio under one, is a harsh one. Most insurers are content to make small losses on underwriting which they make up for by investing the float. Even Buffett does not require a profit on underwriting, preferring the metric which compares the percentage underwriting loss on float with the rate of interest available on risk-free investments – see tables 10.1 and 10.2.

He is comparing what he calls the 'cost of float' with a rough proxy of what Berkshire would obtain if it invested all its float in long-term government bonds. Another way of looking at it is that the long-term government bond rate is a rough proxy (although slightly lower) interest rate that Berkshire Hathaway would otherwise have to pay to borrow that much money to invest.

If the float costs less than this then underwriting losses make sense. For example, in 1987 Berkshire's combined ratio was 105, which Buffett described as 'excellent'. So despite receiving in premiums about 5% less than what it is due to pay out in claims and operating expenses, Buffett praises his managers. This is because the loss on underwriting was merely 4.38% of the average float that year of $1,267m. This rate was less than half the interest rate on government bonds, at 8.95%. Buffett could have placed all $1,267m in government bonds and come away with a good income.

But Buffett being Buffett went for higher returns by investing in a mixture of bonds and equities, mostly Capital Cities/ABC, GEICO and the Washington Post shares. These three holdings had a total market value of over $2bn at the end 1987 compared with their purchase cost of under $0.6bn – the float was generating impressive unrealised capital gains.

By 1990, Berkshire had a net worth of about $6bn. This gave a strong base from which to expand operations in a sector of insurance with extreme ups and downs called catastrophe coverage (CAT covers). Here, a primary insurer might sign up hundreds of clients to coverage against loss from a single event, such as a tornado or hurricane. It might decide to retain, say, $10m of the risk and pay reinsurers to take 95% of any loss above $10m. Reinsurers would ask premiums of between 3% and 15% of the amount of protection.

Berkshire had two advantages that allowed it to, when the premiums were right, accept more reinsurance risk on its own account than any other company. First, its high net worth, with low debt and high profits from subsidiaries operating in diverse sectors. Second, unlike rivals, Buffett and Munger were unconcerned about quarterly or annual earnings volatility, "just as long as the decisions leading to those earnings (or losses) were reached intelligently."[354] An oft repeated phrase around Berkshire is that Charlie and Warren always prefer a lumpy 15% return to a smooth 12%.

This attitude allowed it to be bold. For example, in 1989, many insurers and reinsurers were low on capital and licking wounds after Hurricane Hugo and an earthquake in California. And while many withdrew from the market or raised prices, Berkshire advertised in insurance trade journals offering to write up to $250m of catastrophe coverage. If a catastrophe resulting in $250m of payouts ($165m after tax) did occur, that would wipe out normal quarterly earnings for Berkshire. This would bother directors of rival insurers who looked to smooth earnings to satisfy Wall Street analysts, but it didn't bother Buffett.

So he, Goldberg and Jain stole a march on other firms.

> "This posture is one few insurance managements will assume. Typically, they are willing to write scads of business on terms that

almost guarantee them mediocre returns on equity. But they do not want to expose themselves to an embarrassing single-quarter loss, even if the managerial strategy that causes the loss promises, over time, to produce superior results. I can understand their thinking: What is best for their owners is not necessarily best for the managers. Fortunately Charlie and I have both total job security and financial interests that are identical with those of our shareholders. We are willing to *look* foolish as long as we don't feel we have *acted* foolishly."[355]

Measuring insurance performance

Float comes in different qualities. Insurance against hail damage to crops over a few days or weeks does not produce much float at all because premiums are paid shortly before the threat and claims are paid shortly afterwards. This means that a combined ratio of 100 is of no value to the insurer because it offers no chance to produce profit from investing float.

In contrast, doctors, lawyers and accountants buying malpractice insurance generate a large amount of float compared with the annual premium – lodges of claims are often long after the alleged bad behaviour, and even after that payouts might only occur after lengthy litigation.

With this type of long-tail business, a combined ratio of 115 or more can be profitable because the income and capital gain on the float over a number of years can mount up.

The snag with long-tail insurance is that outcomes are far less predictable than short-term insurance, and it might be that the combined ratio ends up at 200 or 300, a disastrous loss for most insurance companies. Clearly long-tail insurers need to be very careful in selecting the risks they accept and be diversified so that if a mistake is made in one area they have resilience in many others.

Because of the different qualities of float, Buffett suggests we measure insurance performance using the metric 'loss/float ratio' over a period of years to gain a rough indication of the cost of funds generated by insurance operations.

Examination of tables 10.1 and 10.2 gives us some idea of Berkshire's loss/float ratio, but only if we avoid looking at single years and instead focus on groups of years – say three or four.

Clearly, with so many out-and-out profitable underwriting years, Berkshire had a very low cost of float – with the possible exception of 1983–5. Indeed, it had an underwriting *profit*/float ratio for the first two decades taken as a whole.

> "All in all, the insurance business has treated us very well. We have expanded our float at a cost that on the average is reasonable, and we have further prospered because we have earned good returns on these low-cost funds … By any measure, however, the business is worth far more than its carrying value. Furthermore, despite the problems this operation periodically hands us, it is the one – among all the fine businesses we own – that has the greatest potential."[356]

Growth

The 1990s were a period of rapid growth for both the traditional insurance business and for reinsurance, which by then was producing the bulk of Berkshire's float. Berkshire's net worth was expanding fast and so it had the capacity to assume risk on a scale few other companies could.

Ajit Jain, even while rejecting 98% of the business offered, pushed the business forward. A big area of growth was super-catastrophe insurance, or 'super-cat' business. Under these policies, Jain would accept premiums from primary insurers to cover risk for major events such as hurricanes, but the payouts would only be activated if two conditions were met.

First, the primary insurer or reinsurer client must suffer a loss of a given amount from the event, say, $20m. Second, industry-wide insured losses from the catastrophe must exceed some minimum level, which was usually $5bn. These policies might have additional features. For example, some super-cat policies were not activated until a second or third catastrophe occurs in the period. Other policies may be restricted to specific types of events, such as an earthquake.

Buffett was so fascinated by the reinsurance business that he and Jain would chat on the phone each evening (around 9 or 10 pm). This is what Jain said about his relationship with Buffett:

> "He's smart, he's quick, he's decisive, and he's supportive. I can take a deal that I've spent ten days trying to analyse and give it to him, and in five minutes he's two steps ahead of me. And he'll give you an answer; he won't send you back to the drawing board and say, 'Do these three other things and then come and talk to me' … [He] is a boss who not only understands the business, but could teach it to me and everyone else in the business. He's just a unique individual. To have a boss like Warren is even better than having no boss at all."[357]

Jain says that Buffett has been involved in every piece of business he has done. He appreciates Buffett's ability to simplify the thinking process by looking at deals in terms of their fundamental economics, as opposed to getting lost in detail. "He has discouraged me from getting too close to the line when it's a close call. He's taught me this whole notion of doing first-class business in a first-class way."[358] Buffett says he calls Jain for enjoyment as much as anything else.

Buffett has nothing but praise for Jain, for example, "our ability to choose between good and bad proposals reflects a management strength that matches our financial strength: Ajit Jain, who runs our reinsurance operation, is simply the best in this business."[359]

By 1993, Berkshire's net worth was ten to 20 times larger than that of its main competitors in the super-cat reinsurance business, meaning that these rivals were forced to offer far smaller limits to clients than Berkshire. No one else in the world was able to take, say, $400m of risk from a Californian insurer for earthquake cover like Berkshire accepted in 1994.

Berkshire was so big that each of the four largest reinsurers in the world bought significant amounts of reinsurance coverage from it. "Better than anyone else, these giants understand that the test of a reinsurer is its ability and willingness to pay losses under trying circumstances, not its readiness to accept premiums when things look rosy."[360] explained Buffett.

Berkshire also branched out into some unusual types of insurance. For example, in 1995, Ajit Jain insured the life of Mike Tyson; Lloyd's of London against more than 225 of its 'names' dying during the year; and the launch and subsequent year of orbit of two Chinese satellites. You can see why Buffett enjoyed his evening conversations with Jain to find out what interesting deals had been made that day.

Meanwhile, National Indemnity's traditional primary business was having a very profitable time. Over the three years 1994–6 it had an average combined ratio of 83, so Berkshire was being paid by policyholders to hold float for investment. The homestate segment had a similarly impressive three combined ratio of 83.2.

Buying GEICO

For 19 years Berkshire had enjoyed dividends flowing from its 51% stake in GEICO when it bought the remaining shares in 1996 for $2.3bn. GEICO was an exceptionally well-run primary insurer with a focus on auto policies (volume two, investment one). Its two key managers continued to run the business: Tony Nicely managed underwriting (until 2019) and Lou Simpson invested their float (until 2010). The acquisition of GEICO immediately increased Berkshire's total float by nearly $3bn.

In the lead up to the 1998 purchase of General Re, Berkshire's insurance operations were firing on all cylinders – see table 10.3. GEICO achieved an underwriting profit in 1997 of 8.1% of premiums (underwriting profit of $281m on revenue of $3,482m), an outstanding result for the auto-insurance segment.

But even that was trumped by the 32.9% 1997 underwriting profit on National Indemnity's traditional business (it had a three-year average underwriting profit of 24.3%). The homestate operation produced 14.1% profit (15.1% average over three years) and Berkshire's workers' compensation business turned in a three-year record of a positive 1.5%. Aggregating these operations with Central States Indemnity and Kansas Bankers Surety, in the Berkshire Hathaway Direct Insurance Group we see an underwriting gain of $53m on a revenue of $321m.

Berkshire Hathaway Reinsurance Group made a small underwriting profit, which was more than satisfactory given that it generated nearly $1bn in premiums, helping to keep its float topped up to around $4bn.

Table 10.3: Underwriting profits of Berkshire Hathaway Insurance Business (including GEICO) 1996-97

	Underwriting loss ($m)	Average float ($m)	Approximate cost of funds (Ratio of loss to float) (%)	Year-end yield on long-term govt. bonds (%)
1996	profit	6,702.0	less than zero	6.64
1997	profit	7,093.1	less than zero	5.92

General Re in 1998

General Re is primarily a reinsurance company with a focus on property and casualty risks based in Stamford, Connecticut, the same town where Ajit Jain had his HQ. Indeed, Berkshire and General Re had done a lot of business together over the years. General Re was among the top three global reinsurance companies based on net premium written and capital. It operated in 61 cities in 31 countries, providing coverage in over 150 countries and employing 3,869 people.

It had four divisions, but almost half of its revenue came from the North American property/casualty business and a third from international property/casualty – see table 10.4. Life and health insurance was a large business – with $1.3bn of revenue – but in the context of the huge General Re, this constituted only 15% of the total. The financial services division had $301m of revenue.

Table 10.4: Revenue and operating earnings for the four divisions of General Re

Division	Revenues ($bn)	% of total revenue	% of pre-tax earnings
North American property/casualty reinsurance	4.0	48%	63%
International property/casualty reinsurance	2.7	33%	23%
Global life/health reinsurance	1.3	15%	6%
Financial services	0.3	4%	8%

North American property/casualty reinsurance

Operating in the USA and Canada, this division predominately wrote excess reinsurance (indemnifies the primary insurer for that proportion of the loss that exceeds an agreed amount). Casualty accounted for 57% of revenue, with property another 30%. The rest was specialty (unusual coverage such as high-risk behaviour like skydiving) and surplus lines (high limit and hard-to-place risks).

International property/casualty reinsurance

In 1994, General Re became much more international with the acquisition of 75% of Germany's Cologne Re, expanding its operations to 29 countries and providing cover in over 150 (by the end of 1998 the stake was 82% of Cologne Re). The majority of business was reinsurance treaties (covers all or a portion of a specified class of risks ceded by the primary insurer), but some was facultative (underwriting individual risks). Property accounted for 61% of premiums and casualty approximately 39%.

Global life/health reinsurance

This division covers risks for primary insurers in the areas of life insurance for individuals or groups, individual and group health, and long-term care.

Financial services

This division dealt in derivatives offering a full line of interest rate, currency and equity swaps and options. Mostly located in the USA, UK, Japan, Hong Kong and Canada, it also acted as an insurance broker, investment manager and real estate manager.

The key figures for General Re

Everything about the General Re numbers – see table 10.5 – say growth. Over the 11 years leading up to Berkshire buying it, revenue and profits had more than doubled. It was profitable in every year and looked set to breach the billion-dollar mark.

Table 10.5: General Re selected financial data 1987–1997

	Revenue ($bn)	After-tax income excluding realised gains or losses ($m)	Earnings per share ($)	Investment holdings ($bn)	Investment income after tax ($m)	Common stockholders' equity ($bn)
1997	8.3	965	12.04	24.6	969	8.2
1996	8.3	877	11.00	23.2	909	7.3
1995	7.2	788	9.92	21.1	787	6.6
1994	3.8	621	7.97	17.2	622	4.9
1993	3.6	604	8.28	12.0	619	4.8
1992	3.4	465	7.55	11.0	620	4.2
1991	3.2	563	7.46	10.5	618	3.9
1990	3.0	566	6.89	9.3	581	3.3
1989	2.7	559	6.52	8.8	558	3.1
1988	2.7	518	5.04	7.8	494	2.7
1987	3.1	458	5.04	7.0	435	2.6

Source: General Re Report and accounts 1997

Judging by tables 10.6 and 10.7, General Re was producing float at near-zero cost, with combined ratios generally falling near to 100, which was much better than the average for insurance companies in the 1990s (mostly above 105). In rough terms, about 30% of premium income was spent on operations and 70–75% paid out on claims.

Table 10.6: General Re's North American operations combined ratio 1987–1997

	Loss ratio (%)	Expense ratio (%)	Combined ratio (loss + expense) (%)	Year-end yield on long term govt. bonds (%)
1997	68.4	30.8	99.2	5.92
1996	69.0	30.1	99.1	6.64
1995	67.3	32.3	99.6	5.95
1994	71.4	30.5	101.9	7.88
1993	70.0	31.1	101.1	6.35
1992	78.8	29.9	108.7	7.39
1991	72.0	29.3	101.3	7.40
1990	67.5	31.5	99.0	8.24
1989	69.7	28.3	98.0	7.97
1988	70.7	28.8	99.5	9.00
1987	74.5	24.7	99.2	8.95

Source: General Re Report and accounts 1997

Table 10.7: General Re's international property/casualty operations combined ratio 1987–1997

	Loss ratio (%)	Expense ratio (%)	Combined ratio (loss + expense) (%)	Year-end yield on long term govt. bonds (%)
1997	72.1%	30.3%	102.4%	5.92%
1996	73.2%	28.9%	102.1%	6.64%
1995	77.0%	25.8%	102.8%	5.95%
1994	69.2%	29.4%	98.6%	7.88%
1993	75.1%	30.9%	106.0%	6.35%
1992	80.2%	32.8%	113.0%	7.39%
1991	75.8%	35.2%	111.0%	7.40%
1990	71.5%	37.5%	109.0%	8.24%
1989	62.4%	33.4%	95.8%	7.97%
1988	64.4%	31.3%	95.7%	9.00%
1987	64.2%	31.9%	96.1%	8.95%

Source: General Re Report and accounts 1997

For the three years 1995–97, the global health and life division produced positive net-underwriting income and investment income of between $40m and $73m. The financial services division reported splendid income before taxes and realised gains/losses of over $100m in each of the three years.

So the accounts seemed to show General Re was firing on all four cylinders, making almost $1bn in profits. It held $14.9bn of float when Berkshire bought it, which was available at apparently no cost because underwriting pricing was so good.

Synergies

But would you pay $22bn for this? It seems a high price-to-earnings ratio, and shareholders' equity (net assets) was just over $8bn, so the price-to-book ratio was 2.7 times. Buffett must have anticipated some synergies that would considerably enhance profits. Shortly after agreeing to buy, he outlined his thinking in six steps:

1. They can teach us

In his 1998 letter, Buffett wrote that Berkshire can add absolutely nothing to the skills of General Re's and Cologne Re's managers, "on the contrary, there is a lot that they can teach us". He expected General Re's distribution force, technical facilities and management to allow it to enter "every facet of the industry",[361] drawing on Berkshire's financial strength.

2. Greater ability to absorb underwriting earnings volatility

General Re, like many insurance companies, was held back from accepting many offers of business because the directors feared Wall Streeters would be critical and downgrade its shares should the managers have a bad year or two. To avoid reporting quarterly losses, they would either decline risky but attractive business or lay off (buy reinsurance for) a substantial proportion. The directors were very keen to maintain General Re's AAA credit rating, which could be jeopardised by wide swings in earnings.

Berkshire, on the other hand, happily accepts volatility, just so long as there is an expectation of good profits over time. Buffett wrote:

> "As part of Berkshire, this constraint will disappear, which will enhance both General Re's long-term profitability and its ability to write more business. Furthermore, General Re will be free to reduce its reliance on the retrocessional market over time, and thereby have substantial additional funds available for investment."[362]

3. Abundance of capital

Berkshire's deep pockets meant that General Re's directors could "follow whatever asset strategy makes the most sense, unconstrained by the effect on the capital of the company of a sharp market decline. Periodically, this flexibility has proven of enormous advantage to Berkshire's insurance subsidiaries."[363]

4. International expansion

Buffett expected most market growth to come outside of America and General Re already had the managers, systems and reputation in dozens of countries. "General Re has substantial opportunities to develop its global reinsurance franchise. As part of Berkshire, General Re will be able to make investments to grow its international business as quickly as it sees fit."

5. Buffett's expertise on investing float

While General Re's float was $14.9bn, the gross amount of investments before deducting liabilities was more than $24bn. Buffett had his eye on this from the start. In the deal announcement (19 June, 1998) he stated, "The merger will bring more than $80,000 of investments to Berkshire for each Class A or Class A-equivalent share issued. That's beneficial, being nearly double the existing level, or, put another way, the merger brings more than $24 billion of additional investments to Berkshire."

On acquisition General Re's common equities comprised only $4.7bn of the portfolio, less than one-fifth. Until that point it had taken a very conservative approach, placing around three-quarters of funds in bonds. This resulted in low returns compared with Buffett's investments or those of Lou Simpson over at GEICO.

6. Tax advantage

"General Re will gain tax flexibility as a result of the merger. In managing insurance investments, it is a distinct advantage to know that large amounts of taxable income will consistently recur. Most insurance companies are in no position to make this assumption. Any Berkshire insurance subsidiary can fashion its investment strategy without worry as to the presence of taxable income in the future due to Berkshire's large and diverse streams of taxable income."[364]

The deal

The connections between Berkshire and General Re go back a long way. In 1976, for example, General Re helped resuscitate GEICO from near-death by taking some risk exposure off its books – see investment one of the second volume. General Re was also a regular customer for Berkshire Hathaway Reinsurance, when it laid off reinsurance risk.

Buffett first met Ron Ferguson, then president of General Re (later CEO and chairman) in February 1985, at a New York dinner arranged by John Steggles, a former General Re man. They sat down together with Jack Byrne of GEICO and General Re's chairman, Frank Munson.

By then General Re was receiving a lot of work from the fast-growing GEICO, and Buffett was getting increasingly engrossed in reinsurance, so it seemed natural that the senior people at the three companies should get to know each other. Steggles remembers that "Warren arrived considerably late"[365] having been in a meeting with 20 others which overran to thrash out a deal for Capital Cities to buy ABC-TV.

Ferguson first approached Buffett to discuss a joint venture in summer 1997. Later Buffett suggested, instead of a JV, a full combining of the companies to create what he called the "premier reservoir of financial strength in the insurance industry for time immemorial."[366] At first the talks were pretty informal, but they became more pointed in May 1998.

All shares deal

Under the deal announced in June 1998, General Re shareholders had the option of accepting either 0.0035 Class A Berkshire shares or 0.105 Class B shares. Making the payment in shares allowed General Re shareholders to avoid taxation on their capital gains (they remained 'unrealised'). It took until December for the Internal Revenue Service to agree that the deal could be tax free, so it didn't close until 21 December, 1998.

Back in June, Berkshire shares had been riding high – above $80,000 each – and so the deal priced a General-Re share at approximately $276.50, a 29% premium to where they had been trading on the stock exchange, making the total consideration for the transaction approximately $22bn.

Ron Ferguson told the *Wall Street Journal* that uniting under Berkshire offered an "extraordinary financial canvas" on which his managerial team could paint. He called Buffett "the kind of owner we want to have."[367]

The investment portfolio intrigued journalists, who observed that Buffett would be faced with almost $5bn in equities and a very large collection of bonds, adding, in all, 25.2% to Berkshire's investments. He told them he hadn't any particular plans for those funds – note this was the time of the raging bull market of the dot-com era – but "I operate on the theory that there will be times when we will be able to effectively deploy the capital … there will be times when we're hunting elephants".[368]

Buffett assumed responsibility for General Re's portfolio (though not for Cologne Re's) and immediately sold all 250 equities it held, incurring a tax bill of $935m, viewing this as a price worth paying to have a clean sweep. He wrote that the action, "reflects a basic principle that Charlie and I employ in business and investing: We don't back into decisions."[369]

Another immediate action was to replace General Re's stock option plan, which had rewarded executives for pushing up the share price. Buffett and Munger preferred a cash reward system that "tied the incentive compensation of General Re's managers to their operating achievements".[370] Targets were set, and performance pay related to float growth and cost of float.

On the underwriting side, Buffett left well alone, stating from the outset that General Re will "operate independently" of Berkshire's other insurance and reinsurance operations – a clear indication of his admiration of Ferguson and his team.

The strategic ambition was set out in Berkshire's 1998 annual report:

> "For many decades, General Re's name has stood for quality, integrity and professionalism in reinsurance – and under Ron Ferguson's leadership, this reputation has been burnished still

more. Berkshire can add absolutely nothing to the skills of General Re's and Cologne Re's managers ... We will simply ask the company to exercise the discipline of the past while increasing the proportion of its business that is retained, expanding its product line, and widening its geographical coverage – making these moves in recognition of Berkshire's financial strength and tolerance for wide swings in earnings. As we've long said, we prefer a lumpy 15% return to a smooth 12%. Over time, Ron and his team will maximize General Re's new potential."

But this faith in Ron Ferguson and his team was to be sorely tested in the years that followed.

The first five years

Once inside Berkshire, General Re's executives were encouraged to feel free, released of previous constraints limiting growth. The renewed push lifted annual premiums from $6bn to $8.7bn within two years – see figure 10.1. Buffett wanted them to continue "increasing the proportion of its business that is retained [rather than passed on to other reinsurers], expanding its product line, and widening its geographical coverage".[371]

General Re's float was building up nicely, as were the floats of Ajit Jain's operations at Berkshire Hathaway Reinsurance, GEICO and Berkshire Hathaway Primary Insurance – see figure 10.2.

Buffett sounded a little worried with the "huge" underwriting loss at General Re when he reported Berkshire's results for 1999, a total of $1.18bn, the worst in 15 years – see figure 10.3 – but he thought it "aberrational".[372]

In contrast, GEICO reported an underwriting profit of $24m, thus supplying float for Buffett to use at better-than-zero cost. Primary insurance also produced a profit, at $22m, so again Berkshire was paid for holding and investing other people's money. The 1999 underwriting loss at BH Reinsurance of $251m sounds a lot, but it was only 4% of its float compared with the US government 10-year bond rate of 6.7%, and so was a relatively cheap float for Buffett to employ. General Re's float cost, on the other hand, was 7.8% of float in 1999.

Figure 10.1: Premiums earned by Berkshire's four insurance groups $m (1998–2002)

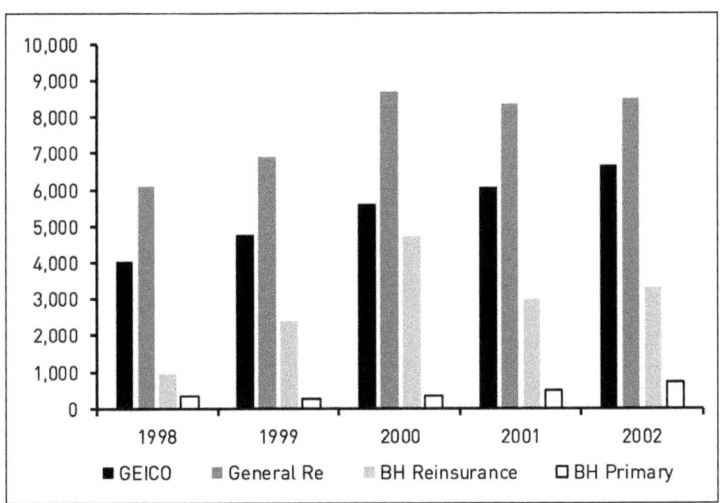

Source: Berkshire Hathaway annual reports

Figure 10.2: Float held by Berkshire's four insurance groups at year ends $m (1998–2002)

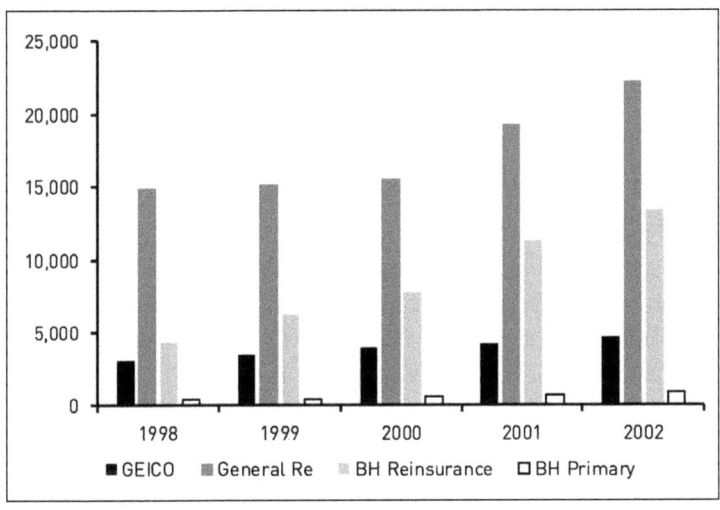

Source: Berkshire Hathaway annual reports

Figure 10.3: Underwriting profits/losses by Berkshire's four insurance groups $m (1998–2002)

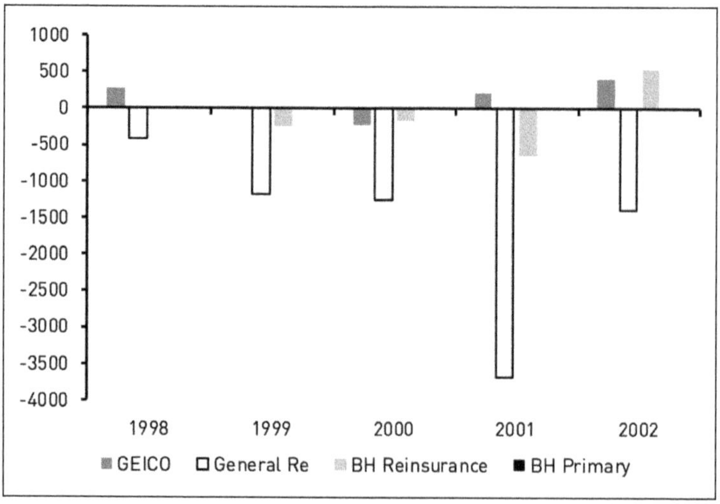

[Bar chart showing underwriting profits/losses in $m for GEICO, General Re, BH Reinsurance, and BH Primary from 1998 to 2002, with values ranging from approximately +500 to -4000]

Source: Berkshire Hathaway annual reports

Although seeing worrying signs at General Re and writing in his 1999 letter that its business was "extremely underpriced, both domestically and internationally", Buffett maintained that General Re had "the distribution, the underwriting skills, the culture, and – with Berkshire's backing – the financial clout to become the world's most profitable reinsurance company. Getting there will take time, energy and discipline, but we have no doubt that Ron Ferguson and his crew can make it happen."[373]

It was during this period that Buffett started talking about Joe Brandon and Tad Montross as "a talented supporting cast"[374] standing alongside Ferguson. Buffett was convinced that they were taking the right tough decisions, "and Charlie and I applaud them for that."[375]

By the time Buffett reported 2000's results, he really was unhappy with what he was seeing. The overall underwriting loss across all Berkshire insurance operations that year was $1.6bn, giving a float cost of 6%, when government long-bond interest rates were slightly less than that. The worst result came from General Re, with a float cost of 8.1%, but, again, Buffett said he expected things to improve thereafter due to "corrections in pricing"[376] of policies.

But this wasn't to be. Admittedly, the whole insurance industry had to cope with the massive hit of the Twin Towers attack in 2001, but nevertheless General Re's underwriting loss of $3.67bn was outstanding. It was 19% of float at a time when the government bond rate was 5%. BH Reinsurance also made a loss, but at $647m, it was a more modest 5.7% of the float. GEICO and BH Primary both made profits.

In his letter written February 2002, Buffett blamed himself for allowing General Re to take on business without a safeguard he knew was important, "and on September 11th, this error caught up with us". He was referring to a failure to implement fully his three key principles on underwriting discipline:

1. Accept only those risks that you are able to properly evaluate (stay within your circle of competence) and that carry the expectancy of profit. Such an expectation should remain after you have evaluated all relevant factors including remote loss scenarios. You ignore market-share considerations and are sanguine about losing business to competitors that are offering foolish prices or policy conditions.

2. Limit the business you accept in a manner that guarantees you will suffer no aggregation of losses from a single event or from related events that will threaten solvency. Ceaselessly search for possible correlation among seemingly unrelated risks.

3. Avoid business involving moral risk: No matter what the rate, trying to write good contracts with bad people doesn't work. While most policyholders and clients are honorable and ethical, doing business with the few exceptions is usually expensive, sometimes extraordinarily so.[377]

Buffett wrote that in setting prices and evaluating aggregate risk, he and the team at General Re had either overlooked or dismissed the possibility of large-scale terrorism losses. "That was a relevant underwriting factor, and we ignored it".[378]

He was starting to regret earlier positive statements about the quality of underwriting discipline at General Re: "I was wrong" he wrote in February 2002. As well as breaking the three rules, the managers had not reserved correctly – that is, had been too optimistic on likely future claims – and therefore severely miscalculated the cost of the insurance sold. "Not knowing your costs will cause problems in any business. In long-tail reinsurance, where years of unawareness will promote and prolong severe underpricing, ignorance of true costs is dynamite."[379]

The managers were psychologically locked into the industry institutional imperative of taking share from competitors. This may be satisfying in the short run, but if premiums are set too low market share might be gained but profits in the long run are lost. "No must be an important part of any underwriter's vocabulary",[380] advises Buffett.

Ron Ferguson was replaced by Joe Brandon as CEO in September 2001 and Tad Montross became president. Buffett was newly optimistic: "At the risk of sounding Pollyannaish, I now assure you that underwriting discipline is being restored at General Re … with appropriate urgency … General Re should be a huge asset for Berkshire. I predict that Joe and Tad will make it so."[381]

This time Buffett's optimism proved well founded. Underwriting discipline was restored in 2002. General Re still reported a hefty underwriting loss at $1.4bn (6.3% of float) but almost all of this was a legacy of previous years' underwriting and the business actually written during 2002 was nearly zero-cost. "I'm delighted to report that under Joe Brandon's leadership, and with yeoman assistance by Tad Montross, enormous progress has been made … freshly endowed with increased authority and eager to rapidly correct the errors of the past. They knew what to do – and they did it."[382]

But it is sad to reflect that, in all, General Re's underwriting losses in this five-year period were nearly $8bn – almost equivalent to its net-asset value when Berkshire bought it.

Meanwhile, Ajit Jain and his tiny team at BH Reinsurance had raised premium income from under $1bn in 1998 to over $3bn in 2002. More significantly, underwriting losses averaged only $0.1bn on float that grew from $4.3bn to $13.4bn.

Trouble with derivatives

The underwriting issues were a knotty enough problem for Buffett and Munger to sort out, but there was something else which really upset them. They had inherited General Re's massive collection of derivative positions, whose value related to movements in underlyings adding up to $1trn. Both viewed view them as "time bombs, both for the parties that deal in them and the economic system".[383]

At first they tried to sell the derivative operation but failed. Instead, they started the laborious process of closing it down. But, "like Hell, both [reinsurance and derivative businesses] are easy to enter and almost impossible to exit. In either industry, once you write a contract – which may require a large payment decades later – you are usually stuck with it."[384]

Another commonality of reinsurance and derivatives is that in both managers can be led to report wildly overstated earnings because they are based on estimates of the value of positions which may not be settled for many years. The judgements required give plenty of latitude for rose-tinted views or even conscious bias.

> "Those who trade derivatives are usually paid (in whole or part) on 'earnings' calculated by mark-to-market accounting. But often there is no real market and 'mark-to-model' is utilized. This substitution can bring on large-scale mischief. As a general rule, contracts involving multiple reference items and distant settlement dates increase the opportunities for counterparties to use fanciful assumptions … the two parties to the contract might well use differing models allowing both to show substantial profits for many years. In extreme cases, mark-to-model degenerates into what I would call mark-to-myth."[385]

In a phrase that was to go around the world, Buffett condemned derivatives as "financial weapons of mass destruction"[386] for the economy as a whole. This was despite admitting that Berkshire occasionally engaged in large-scale derivative transactions to facilitate some investment strategies.

At the start of the derivative close-down strategy in early 2002, the group had 23,218 outstanding contracts with 884 counterparties. As an indication of how difficult it is to escape from some of these deals, two years later it still had 7,580 tickets outstanding with 453 counterparties. Buffett sighed, "As the country song laments, 'How can I miss you if you won't go away?'"[387]

General Re's derivatives business made pre-tax losses of $173m in 2002 and $99m in 2003, and then carried on making losses. In total, by the end of 2006, $409m was lost, by which time the number of live contracts had dwindled to 197.

> "Long ago, Mark Twain said: 'A man who tries to carry a cat home by its tail will learn a lesson that can be learned in no other way.' If Twain were around now, he might try winding up a derivatives business. After a few days, he would opt for cats."[388]

In a prescient passage written two years before the financial crisis, precipitated by derivatives on sub-prime mortgages, Buffett said that Berkshire was the canary in this business coal mine "and should sing a song of warning as we expire."[389] He said that one of the reasons he regularly wrote about the Berkshire problems in this area was the hope that "our experiences may prove instructive for managers, auditors and regulators."[390]

He noted that there was a mushrooming in the number and value of derivative contracts outstanding in the world, many times what it was only seven years before.

Another prescient comment:

> "Imagine, if you will, one or more firms (troubles often spread) with positions that are many multiples of ours attempting to liquidate in chaotic markets and under extreme, and well-publicized, pressures. This is a scenario to which much attention should be given now rather than after the fact."[391]

Abundant underwriting profits

Brandon and Montross really had turned around General Re. In 13 of the next 14 years it reported an underwriting profit – see figure 10.6. It did so on a decreasing level of business: premiums fell from $8.25bn in 2003 to only $5.64bn in 2016 – see figure 10.4. In 2017 the data for General

Investment 10. General Re

Re was subsumed within the Berkshire Hathaway Reinsurance Group, when Ajit Jain was put in charge of all insurance activities in early 2018.

The lower revenue also pushed down float from $23.65bn in 2003 to $17.70bn in 2016 – see figure 10.5. It seems that Joe, Tad and the rest of the team at General Re really were dedicated to Buffett's philosophy of focusing only on profitable business, even if that meant saying no to business, pithily summarised by Buffett as "size simply doesn't count".[392]

Figure 10.4: Premiums earned by Berkshire's four insurance groups $m (2003–2020)

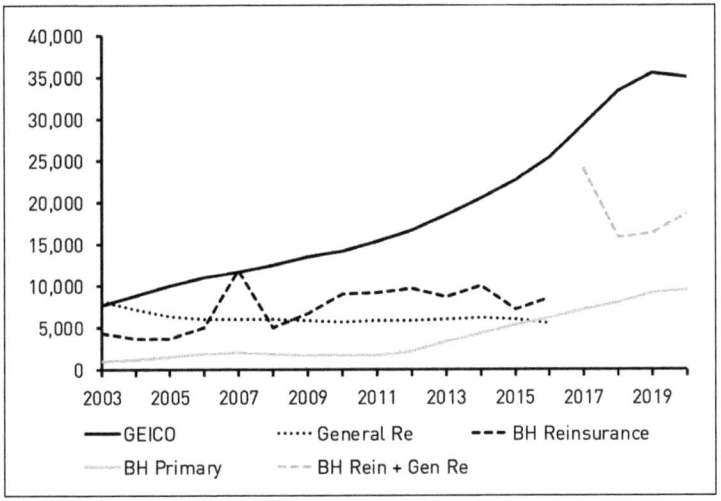

Source: Berkshire Hathaway annual reports

Figure 10.5: Float held by Berkshire's four insurance groups at year ends $m (2003–2016)

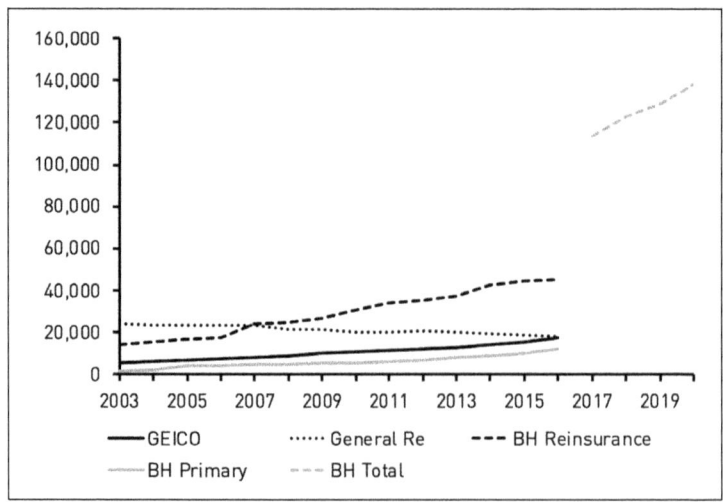

Source: Berkshire Hathaway annual reports

Figure 10.6: Underwriting profits/losses by Berkshire's four insurance groups $m (2003–2020)

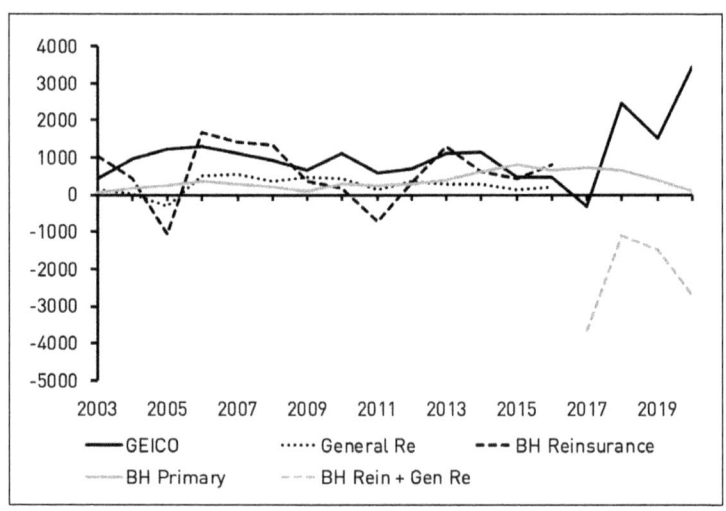

Source: Berkshire Hathaway annual reports

While General Re held back its volume growth to become a 'jewel' in Berkshire's crown on account of its zero-cost float, Ajit Jain's BH Reinsurance was powering ahead both in volume and profitability. Its handful of people pushed up revenue to beyond that of General Re in 2007 (General Re then had 2,647 employees, it now has under 2,000). BH Reinsurance premiums grew from $4.43bn in 2003 to $8.50bn in 2016, and it was profitable in every year except two, sometimes massively so. And Buffett enjoyed investing its rapidly growing float, which reached over $45bn.

Arguably, GEICO was even better. It more than trebled its float to over $17bn, while quadrupling premium volume and producing underwriting profits of over $1bn in many years. What a business: Berkshire was paid a billion or so in a year for holding other people's money, and those funds could be invested in Coca Cola and the like to generate dividends and capital gains.

The original BH Primary insurance business was small by comparison, but nevertheless was impressive in terms of its growth of premiums – $1bn in 2003 and nearly $10bn in 2020. And its float went from $1.3bn in 2003 to $11.65bn in 2020. But most impressive of all was the completely unblemished record of underwriting profits. In many years it made profits of 8% or 10% on float.

In 2008, Joe Brandon stepped down from his duties at General Re and Tad Montross became CEO. Buffett was very much aware of his contribution to saving the company: "Charlie and I are grateful to Joe for righting the ship and are certain that, with Tad, General Re's future is in the best of hands."[393]

Also that year, General Re finally attained 100% ownership of Cologne Re. Tad retired in 2016 after 39 years at the company. In his 2016 letter Buffett wrote, "Tad was a class act in every way and we owe him a ton of thanks". His replacement was Kara Raiguel, who had worked with Ajit Jain for 16 years.

A foolish purchase?

General Re eventually became a greatly-prized part of the Berkshire family. But questions remain. Would $22bn be the price offered if Buffett and Munger had known in 1998 that executives had been mispricing insurance for some years, thus inflating the profit record? Almost certainly not.

Should the consideration have been newly minted Berkshire Hathaway shares? Definitely not. The value of these shares is now well in excess of $100bn. Buffett, in 2016, publicly kicked himself for using stock:

> "I followed the GEICO purchase by foolishly using Berkshire stock – a boatload of stock – to buy General Reinsurance in late 1998 … It was … a terrible mistake on my part to issue 272,200 shares of Berkshire in buying General Re, an act that increased our outstanding shares by a whopping 21.8%. My error caused Berkshire shareholders to give far more than they received (a practice that – despite the Biblical endorsement – is far from blessed when you are buying businesses)."[394]

But it worked out well for two reasons. First, because Buffett and Munger identified able managers whose philosophical approach to running an insurance company, i.e., for profit, chimed with theirs.

Second, they exercised extreme patience as the losses mounted up over five years. Their long-time horizon, holding a business 'forever', meant that they could see light at the end of even a long tunnel. They knew that the value of a company is the discounted cash flow it generates for shareholders over a lifetime. The discounted value of the first five years of cash is but a fraction of that total present-value calculation.

Learning points

1. **There are two key contributory factors in underwriting profitability: saying no frequently and being financially strong.** Insurance in largely a commoditised business, meaning low-premium prices, drives demand. But it is possible to build-in differentiation, and thus underwriting profitability, by (a) being prepared to sacrifice volume to focus on profit – volume can be

allowed to rise when competitors are not running after that type of business – and (b) being exceptionally strong financially so that your promises to meet claims many years from now are more valued by customers than those of competitors.

2. **Judge the quality of the people making the judgements.** Insurance accounts are drawn up using much judgement/guesswork rather than hard facts. Be sure that the leaders, therefore, are people whose judgement is both trustworthy and conservatively biased, rather than inclined to short-term boosterism.

3. **Measure insurance underwriting performance using the metric loss/float ratio measured over groups of years.** Single years are subject to distortion due to poor clarity on claims.

4. **Float is a liability in the eyes of accountants but an asset in the hands of the right managers.** Buffett's investment skill with float turbo-charged Berkshire's growth.

5. **Insurance-company profits can be greatly improved if the holding company has exceptionally strong finances, allowing greater weighting toward equity investments.** Having vast amounts of capital in Berkshire's insurance companies coupled with the huge cash flow from its other businesses means that the insurance float can safely be invested in an equity-heavy strategy. This is not possible for most insurers because they would be told by regulators and credit-rating agencies to put most float into bonds because they are considered safer. However, bonds are not always safer, as Buffett pointed out in his 2020 letter: "bonds are not the place to be these days … Fixed-income investors worldwide – whether pension funds, insurance companies or retirees – face a bleak future. Some insurers, as well as other bond investors, may try to juice the pathetic returns now available by shifting their purchases to obligations backed by shaky borrowers. Risky loans, however, are not the answer to inadequate interest rates. Three decades ago, the once-mighty savings and loan industry destroyed itself, partly by ignoring that maxim."

6. **If you have great business with rapidly increasing intrinsic value, then paying for another company with shares can be costly unless the price is very low.** Buffett should never have given 21.8% of Berkshire for General Re.

7. **Only one well-informed decisionmaker operating with sound principles is required to invest a large fund.** General Re thought it needed 150 in its investment office, but Buffett showed them a better way.

8. **Derivatives, especially long-term ones, can become badly mispriced and cause massive losses.**

A distance travelled

By the end of 1998, Berkshire Hathaway was the largest American corporation as measured by net worth, which stood at $57.4bn. Only ten years before it had net assets less than $5bn, dwarfed by the giants of the age such as General Motors, Ford, IBM and Exxon.

Employee numbers had grown to 47,566. But all these were controlled from a "world headquarters" staffed by 12.8 people, "the .8 doesn't refer to me or Charlie: We have a new person in accounting, working four days a week."[395] This alone marked out Berkshire as being very different to its fellow corporate colossi; it was an organisation that granted extreme levels of autonomy to trusted executives at its wholly-owned or partially-owned businesses.

Buffett and Munger long ago recognised that wealthy executives and entrepreneurs within the Berkshire fold are happiest when they are left alone to run their businesses; they feel honoured by the signalling of trust when they are given so much freedom, and they reciprocate with efforts way beyond the call of duty. They like being treated with respect and being able to draw on the rationality and experience of Buffett and Munger. And they want to make Berkshire's chairman and vice-chairman proud.

Buffett and Munger's roles are to find businesses run by excellent managers of high integrity in the first place and then to assist them in any way needed; and to praise the work they did for Berkshire.

The chairman, however, does ask that all excess cash generated be sent to headquarters for him and Charlie to allocate. "By sending it to us, they don't get diverted by the various enticements that would come their way were they responsible for deploying the cash their businesses throw off. Furthermore, Charlie and I are exposed to a much wider range of possibilities for investing these funds than any of our managers could find in his or her own industry."[396]

Something else making Berkshire an outlier in 1998 was the degree of respect throughout American society afforded to Warren Buffett and Charlie Munger. Indeed, the whole world was starting to hear of the power of their ideas on the subject of investment, and the power of their example in adopting high moral principles for life and for business.

And people flocked to Omaha. Back in the early 1980s only a few dozen would turn up in Omaha for the spring annual general meeting. But in spring 1999, an auditorium – the Aksarben Coliseum no less – had to be hired to accommodate the 14,000 shareholders who hung on Buffett's and Munger's every word for the six-hour meeting. Many had bought shares solely to be able to attend, listen and join in the celebratory weekend chatting with like-minded investors. Buffett and Munger had become the world's best-known investment gurus.

Berkshire Hathaway, that firm which was only three decades before a declining hulk of a $25m textile company, now owned some fantastic businesses. As well as See's Candy, it owned GEICO, FlightSafety, R.C. Willey and many other jewels outright.

And then there was the collection of substantial stakes in stars of American corporate life, from American Express (11% of the company) and Coca-Cola (8%), to the Washington Post (17%) and Gillette (8.5%). All told, the non-controlled common-stock investment amounted to over $37bn.

The insurance float of over $22bn provided plenty more investing firepower for Buffett and Munger, as did the vast profits coming from dozens of wholly-owned businesses, from Nebraska Furniture Mart to Borsheims.

And firepower was what they needed for the next stage of their journey. They were yet to buy companies like MidAmerican Energy, Moody's, Clayton Homes, or Burlington Northern Santa Fe. These were all good reasons to tap dance on the way to work in that small Omaha office with its handful of staff in the years to come.

Notes

1. Warren Buffett, 1990 letter to Berkshire Hathaway shareholders.
2. Warren Buffett, 1990 letter to Berkshire Hathaway shareholders.
3. Warren Buffett, 1990 letter to Berkshire Hathaway shareholders.
4. Warren Buffett, 1990 letter to Berkshire Hathaway shareholders.
5. Warren Buffett, 1990 letter to Berkshire Hathaway shareholders.
6. Warren Buffett, 1997 letter to Berkshire Hathaway shareholders.
7. Warren Buffett, 1990 letter to Berkshire Hathaway shareholders.
8. Warren Buffett, 1990 letter to Berkshire Hathaway shareholders.
9. The Federal Reserve study data used for figure 1.1 is based on pretty much all US commercial banks in any given year – that is between 9,217 and 14,500 banks (the number of banks declined through time).
10. William B. English and William R. Nelson, 'Profits and balance sheet developments at U.S. commercial banks in 1997', *Federal Reserve Bulletin, Board of Governors of the Federal Reserve System (US)*, June 1998, pp391–419.
11. William B. English and William R. Nelson, 'Profits and balance sheet developments at U.S. commercial banks in 1997', *Federal Reserve Bulletin, Board of Governors of the Federal Reserve System (US)*, June 1998, pp391–419.
12. William B. English and William R. Nelson, 'Profits and balance sheet developments at U.S. commercial banks in 1997', *Federal Reserve Bulletin, Board of Governors of the Federal Reserve System (US)*, June 1998, pp391–419.
13. William B. English and William R. Nelson, 'Profits and balance sheet developments at U.S. commercial banks in 1997', *Federal Reserve Bulletin, Board of Governors of the Federal Reserve System (US)*, June 1998, pp391–419.
14. Tom Barton quoted in an article by Martha Groves, 'Wells Fargo & Co. Assumes Unusual Role: Reassurer', *Los Angeles Times*, 12 November, 1990.
15. George M. Salem quoted in an article by Martha Groves, 'Wells Fargo & Co. Assumes Unusual Role: Reassurer', *Los Angeles Times*, 12 November, 1990.

16. Richard X. Bove quoted in an article by Martha Groves, 'Wells Fargo & Co. Assumes Unusual Role: Reassurer', *Los Angeles Times*, 12 November, 1990.
17. John M. Taylor, 'A Leveraged Bet', *Forbes*, 15 April, 1991, p42.
18. G. William Tischer quoted in John M. Taylor, 'A Leveraged Bet', *Forbes,* 15 April, 1991, p42.
19. Carl Reichardt quoted in an article by Martha Groves, 'Wells Fargo & Co. Assumes Unusual Role: Reassurer', *Los Angeles Times*, 12 November, 1990.
20. Allan Sloan, 'Beauty and the Beasts: A true tale of two different investment styles'. *Washington Post,* 7 January, 1992.
21. Buffett tried to persuade him to stay. Reichardt told the *Los Angeles Times* (20 July, 1994), "He'd like to see people work forever. I told him, 'Warren, there just ain't no way.'" He remained on the board of directors until 1998.
22. Wells Fargo 1994 annual report.
23. Wells Fargo 1994 annual report.
24. Wells Fargo 1994 annual report.
25. Wells Fargo 1994 annual report.
26. Wells Fargo 1994 annual report.
27. Charlie Munger quoted in Andrew Kilpatrick, *Of Permanent Value: The Story of Warren Buffett, 2018 Condensed Edition* (2018), Andy Kilpatrick Publishing Empire (AKPE): Birmingham, Alabama.
28. Thomas Brown quoted in James F. Pelitz and David W. Myers, 'California's changing banking scene'. *Los Angeles Times,* 20 July, 1994.
29. Wells Fargo annual report 1994.
30. Reichardt quoted in Chris Kraul, 'Driving That Stagecoach: Reichardt Steers Wells Fargo to Post-Recession Expansion', *Los Angeles Times,* 6 April, 1994.
31. Reichardt quoted in Chris Kraul, 'Driving That Stagecoach: Reichardt Steers Wells Fargo to Post-Recession Expansion', *Los Angeles Times,* 6 April, 1994.
32. Wells Fargo annual report 1995.
33. Quoted in Saul Hansell, '10 Billion Hostile Bid by Wells Fargo for First Interstate', *New York Times*, 19 October, 1995.
34. Wells Fargo annual report 1996.
35. 'Why Wells Fargo Is Circling the Wagons', *Business Week,* 9 June, 1997, p92–93.
36. Wells Fargo 1998 annual report.
37. Wells Fargo 1998 annual report.
38. Wells Fargo 1998 annual report.
39. https://www.npr.org/

40. Poppy Harlow, *CNN Business*, 11 November, 2016. https://money.cnn.com/video/investing/2016/11/11/warren-buffett-wells-fargo.cnnmoney/index.html
41. Poppy Harlow, *CNN Business*, 11 November, 2016. https://money.cnn.com/video/investing/2016/11/11/warren-buffett-wells-fargo.cnnmoney/index.html
42. Poppy Harlow, *CNN Business*, 11 November, 2016. https://money.cnn.com/video/investing/2016/11/11/warren-buffett-wells-fargo.cnnmoney/index.html
43. Robert Armstrong, Eric Platt and Oliver Ralph, 'Warren Buffett urges Wells Fargo to look beyond Wall St for next chief', *Financial Times*, 7 April, 2019.
44. Charlie Munger interviewed by Katherine Chiglinsky, 'Munger says Wells Fargo CEO ought to be in San Francisco'. Bloomberg.com, 12 February, 2020.
45. Ethan Wolff-Mann, 'Munger diverges from Buffett on Wells Fargo: "Warren got disenchanted"', *Yahoo Finance*, 24 February 2021.
46. Warren Buffett, 1991 letter to Berkshire Hathaway shareholders.
47. Rasmussen, J., 'Billionaire talks Strategy with Students', *Omaha World Herald*, 2 January, 1994, p178. Quoted in Hagstrom, R. G. (1995) *The Warren Buffett Way*, John Wiley and Sons.
48. Ed Colodny quoted in Reed, T. and Reed, D. (2014) *Creating American Airways: The Converging Histories of American Airlines and US Airways*. McFarland & Co. p8.
49. Mike Flores, president of the US Airways chapter of the Association of Flight Attendants, a union, quoted in Reed, T. and Reed, D. (2014) *Creating American Airways: The Converging Histories of American Airlines and US Airways*, McFarland & Co. p12.
50. Ed Colodny quoted in Reed, T. and Reed, D. (2014) *Creating American Airways: The Converging Histories of American Airlines and US Airways*, McFarland & Co. p12.
51. Ed Colodny quoted in Reed, T. and Reed, D. (2014) *Creating American Airways: The Converging Histories of American Airlines and US Airways*, McFarland & Co. p10.
52. Ed Colodny quoted in Reed, T. and Reed, D. (2014) *Creating American Airways: The Converging Histories of American Airlines and US Airways*, McFarland & Co. p11.
53. Under federal rules for airline mergers, an acquiring airline could hold only a maximum of 10% of the target until the merger was formally approved.

54. Ed Colodny quoted in Reed, T. and Reed, D. (2014) *Creating American Airways: The Converging Histories of American Airlines and US Airways*, McFarland & Co. p14.
55. Graeme Browning, 'In an agreement with USAir, Buffett promises no surprises', *The Washington Post*, 15 August, 1989.
56. Warren Buffett, 1989 letter to Berkshire Hathaway shareholders.
57. Warren Buffett, 1989 letter to Berkshire Hathaway shareholders.
58. Warren Buffett, 1989 letter to Berkshire Hathaway shareholders.
59. Warren Buffett, 1990 letter to Berkshire Hathaway shareholders.
60. Martha M. Hamilton, 'USAir Group Flies into Turbulence', *The Washington Post*, 3 September, 1990.
61. Warren Buffett, 1990 letter to Berkshire Hathaway shareholders.
62. Warren Buffett, 1990 letter to Berkshire Hathaway shareholders.
63. Warren Buffett, 1991 letter to Berkshire Hathaway shareholders.
64. Warren Buffett, 1992 letter to Berkshire Hathaway shareholders.
65. Warren Buffett, 1992 letter to Berkshire Hathaway shareholders.
66. Warren Buffett, 1992 letter to Berkshire Hathaway shareholders.
67. Warren Buffett, 1992 letter to Berkshire Hathaway shareholders.
68. Warren Buffett, 1992 letter to Berkshire Hathaway shareholders.
69. Warren Buffett, 1992 letter to Berkshire Hathaway shareholders.
70. Warren Buffett, 1992 letter to Berkshire Hathaway shareholders.
71. 1 February, 1991 at LAX: on landing there was a collision with another plane (air-traffic-control problem) which left 34 dead. 22 March, 1992 at Cleveland: on take-off, a plane crashed just beyond the runway due to its wing not being de-iced properly; 27 killed.
72. Martha M. Hamilton, 'USAir Enters Alliance with British Air', *The Washington Post*, 22 July, 1992.
73. Warren Buffett, 1992 letter to Berkshire Hathaway shareholders.
74. Warren Buffett, 1992 letter to Berkshire Hathaway shareholders.
75. Warren Buffett, 1993 letter to Berkshire Hathaway shareholders.
76. Warren Buffett, 1994 letter to Berkshire Hathaway shareholders.
77. Colin Leinster, 'Buffett hits $200m downdraft', *Fortune*, 17 November, 1994.
78. Rasmussen, J. (1994), 'Billionnaire talks Strategy with Students', *Omaha World Herald*, 2 January, p178. Quoted in Hagstrom, R. G. (1995) *The Warren Buffett Way*, John Wiley and Sons.
79. Warren Buffett, 1994 letter to Berkshire Hathaway shareholders.
80. Warren Buffett, 1994 letter to Berkshire Hathaway shareholders.
81. Warren Buffett, 1994 letter to Berkshire Hathaway shareholders.
82. Warren Buffett, 1994 letter to Berkshire Hathaway shareholders.
83. Warren Buffett, 1994 letter to Berkshire Hathaway shareholders.

84. Don Phillips and Frank Swoboda, 'Seth Schofield retires as USAir's Chairman', *The Washington Post*, 7 September, 1995.
85. Frank Swoboba and Don Philips, 'US Airways Chairman Takes Plea to Unions', *The Washington Post*, 27 April, 1997.
86. Quoted in Frank Swoboba and Don Philips, 'US Airways Chairman Takes Plea to Unions', *The Washington Post*, 27 April, 1997.
87. Quoted in Don Phillips, 'US Airways Closing 5 Facilities', *The Washington Post*, 9 May, 1997.
88. Warren Buffett, 1997 letter to Berkshire Hathaway shareholders.
89. Warren Buffett, 1997 letter to Berkshire Hathaway shareholders.
90. Warren Buffett, 2007 letter to Berkshire Hathaway shareholders.
91. Corporate Cardmembers can use a 24/7 tollfree line to gain Amex help with emergencies, travel assistance or just information. Examples include medical assistance, dental referral, repatriation of mortal remains, assistance of an English speaking lawyer, referral to an embassy or consulate, emergency travel arrangement assistance, emergency cash, emergency hotel check in/out, translation/interpretation, and lost luggage assistance.
92. Warren Buffett quoted in 'Why Warren Buffett's betting big on American Express', written by Linda Grant and Carol J. Loomis, *Fortune*, 30 October, 1995.
93. In 1991 IDS managed, administered or owned around $70bn client assets.
94. See volume two, investment one for an account of Byrne's pulling GEICO from the abyss in the late 1970s.
95. Quoted in 'American Express: Anatomy of a coup', Brett D. Fromson, *The Washington Post*, 11 February, 1993.
96. Quoted in 'Why Amex Wooed Warren Buffett', by Leah Nathans Spiro, *Bloomberg*, 19 August, 1991.
97. The common stock was trading at $25 per share on 1 August, 1991. In the winter they sank to $13 on poor quarterly numbers.
98. Warren Buffett, 1997 letter to Berkshire Hathaway shareholders.
99. Warren Buffett, 1997 letter to Berkshire Hathaway shareholders.
100. Warren Buffett, 1997 letter to Berkshire Hathaway shareholders.
101. This assumption works with some companies, but for many others capital expenditure and working capital investment can absorb far more than the allowance made for depreciation, amortisation, etc., leaving little cash for shareholders to take away from the business without damaging its franchise, if it has one.
102. The US ten-year Treasury yielded between 5.6–8.0% in 1994, so using a 10% p.a. required return allows for additional equity risk.

103. Warren Buffett, 2011 letter to Berkshire Hathaway shareholders. The others in 2011 were Coca-Cola, Wells Fargo and IBM.
104. Warren Buffett, 2011 letter to Berkshire Hathaway shareholders.
105. Harvey Golub, reported in *AP News*, 'American Express CEO Resigns Early', 17 November, 2000.
106. '"The brand is special" Warren Buffett called on American Express' CEO to protect its reputation during the coronavirus pandemic', Theron Mohamed, *Business Insider*, 30 May, 2020.
107. Warren Buffett, 2007 letter to Berkshire Hathaway shareholders.
108. Warren Buffett, 2007 letter to Berkshire Hathaway shareholders.
109. Warren Buffett, 2007 letter to Berkshire Hathaway shareholders.
110. Warren Buffett, 2007 letter to Berkshire Hathaway shareholders.
111. Warren Buffett, 2014 letter to Berkshire Hathaway shareholders.
112. About 20% of output was conventional shoes and boots rather than work and safety boots and shoes, but its competitive advantage lay in tough USA-born products.
113. Despite the all-American image, by the 1980s H. H. Brown imported shoes and shoe components from several countries including Taiwan, Korea, China, India and Mexico.
114. Emily Steel (2015), 'Francis C. Rooney Jr. dies at 93; Turned Melville into a retail giant', *New York Times*, 26 March, 2015.
115. Warren Buffett, 1991 letter to Berkshire Hathaway shareholders.
116. Frank Rooney interviewed by Robert P. Miles for *The Warren Buffett CEO; Secrets from the Berkshire Hathaway Managers* (2002), John Wiley and Sons: New York.
117. Warren Buffett, 1991 letter to Berkshire Hathaway shareholders.
118. Frank Rooney interviewed by Robert P. Miles for *The Warren Buffett CEO; Secrets from the Berkshire Hathaway Managers* (2002), John Wiley and Sons: New York.
119. Frank Rooney interviewed by Robert P. Miles for *The Warren Buffett CEO; Secrets from the Berkshire Hathaway Managers* (2002), John Wiley and Sons: New York.
120. Warren Buffett, 1991 letter to Berkshire Hathaway shareholders.
121. Warren Buffett, 1991 letter to Berkshire Hathaway shareholders.
122. Warren Buffett, 1991 letter to Berkshire Hathaway shareholders.
123. Frank Rooney interviewed by Robert P. Miles for *The Warren Buffett CEO; Secrets from the Berkshire Hathaway Managers* (2002), John Wiley and Sons: New York.
124. Frank Rooney interviewed by Robert P. Miles for *The Warren Buffett CEO; Secrets from the Berkshire Hathaway Managers* (2002), John Wiley and Sons: New York.

125. Frank Rooney interviewed by Robert P. Miles for *The Warren Buffett CEO; Secrets from the Berkshire Hathaway Managers* (2002), John Wiley and Sons: New York.
126. Warren Buffett, 1992 letter to Berkshire Hathaway shareholders.
127. Lowell was later renamed Söfft Shoe Company.
128. Warren Buffett, 1992 letter to Berkshire Hathaway shareholders.
129. Warren Buffett, 1993 letter to Berkshire Hathaway shareholders.
130. Warren Buffett, 1993 letter to Berkshire Hathaway shareholders.
131. *Forbes*, 10 October, 1994.
132. Warren Buffett, 1993 letter to Berkshire Hathaway shareholders.
133. Warren Buffett, 1993 letter to Berkshire Hathaway shareholders.
134. A small chain of shoe stores (11 outlets) was added to the Shoe Group toward the end of 1994 for an undisclosed cost, but unlikely to be much more than $1m.
135. Berkshire Hathaway's annual report 1994.
136. Warren Buffett, 1995 letter to Berkshire Hathaway shareholders.
137. Berkshire Hathaway's annual report 1997.
138. Berkshire Hathaway's annual report 1998.
139. Warren Buffett, 1999 letter to Berkshire Hathaway shareholders.
140. Warren Buffett, 2000 letter to Berkshire Hathaway shareholders.
141. Warren Buffett, 2001 letter to Berkshire Hathaway shareholders.
142. Warren Buffett, 2007 letter to Berkshire Hathaway shareholders.
143. A tale recounted in Barnett Helzberg's 2003 book for entrepreneurs and business owners looking to build a solid company titled, *What I Learned Before I Sold to Warren Buffett: An Entrepreneurs Guide to Developing a Highly Successful Company*, John Wiley and Sons.
144. Barnett Helzberg Jr. (2003), *What I Learned Before I Sold to Warren Buffett: An Entrepreneurs Guide to Developing a Highly Successful Company*, John Wiley and Sons.
145. Warren Buffett, 1995 letter to Berkshire Hathaway shareholders.
146. Warren Buffett, 1995 letter to Berkshire Hathaway shareholders.
147. Barnett Helzberg, Jr. (2003), *What I Learned Before I Sold to Warren Buffett: An Entrepreneurs Guide to Developing a Highly Successful Company*, John Wiley and Sons.
148. Barnett Helzberg, Jr. (2003), *What I Learned Before I Sold to Warren Buffett: An Entrepreneurs Guide to Developing a Highly Successful Company*, John Wiley and Sons.
149. Warren Buffett, 1995 letter to Berkshire Hathaway shareholders.
150. Warren Buffett, 1995 letter to Berkshire Hathaway shareholders.
151. Warren Buffett, 1995 letter to Berkshire Hathaway shareholders.
152. Warren Buffett, 1995 letter to Berkshire Hathaway shareholders.

153. Barnett Helzberg, Jr. (2003), *What I Learned Before I Sold to Warren Buffett: An Entrepreneurs Guide to Developing a Highly Successful Company*, John Wiley and Sons.
154. Barnett Helzberg, Jr. (2003), *What I Learned Before I Sold to Warren Buffett: An Entrepreneurs Guide to Developing a Highly Successful Company*, John Wiley and Sons.
155. Warren Buffett, 1995 letter to Berkshire Hathaway shareholders.
156. Warren Buffett, 1995 letter to Berkshire Hathaway shareholders.
157. Barnett Helzberg, Jr. (2003) *What I Learned Before I Sold to Warren Buffett: An Entrepreneurs Guide to Developing a Highly Successful Company*, John Wiley and Sons.
158. Jeff Comment recalling the meeting in an interview with Robert P. Miles in *The Warren Buffett CEO* (2002), John Wiley and Sons: New York.
159. Barnett Helzberg, Jr. (2003) *What I Learned Before I Sold to Warren Buffett: An Entrepreneurs Guide to Developing a Highly Successful Company*, John Wiley and Sons.
160. Barnett Helzberg, Jr. (2003), *What I Learned Before I Sold to Warren Buffett: An Entrepreneurs Guide to Developing a Highly Successful Company*, John Wiley and Sons.
161. Barnett Helzberg, Jr. (2003), *What I Learned Before I Sold to Warren Buffett: An Entrepreneurs Guide to Developing a Highly Successful Company*, John Wiley and Sons.
162. Barnett Helzberg, Jr. (2003), *What I Learned Before I Sold to Warren Buffett: An Entrepreneurs Guide to Developing a Highly Successful Company*, John Wiley and Sons.
163. Barnett Helzberg, Jr. (2003), *What I Learned Before I Sold to Warren Buffett: An Entrepreneurs Guide to Developing a Highly Successful Company*, John Wiley and Sons.
164. Jeff Comment recalling the meeting in an interview with Robert P. Miles in *The Warren Buffett CEO* (2002), John Wiley and Sons: New York.
165. Barnett Helzberg quoted in Kilpatrick, A. (2006), *Of Permanent Value. The Story of Warren Buffett*, AKPE: Birmingham, Alabama.
166. Warren Buffett, 1995 letter to Berkshire Hathaway shareholders.
167. Warren Buffett, 1995 annual meeting of Berkshire Hathaway, May 1996.
168. Jeff Comment in an interview with Robert P. Miles in *The Warren Buffett CEO* (2002), John Wiley and Sons: New York.
169. Jeff Comment in an interview with Robert P. Miles in *The Warren Buffett CEO* (2002), John Wiley and Sons: New York.
170. *Kansas City Star*, 11 March, 1995.

171. Jeff Comment in an interview with Robert P. Miles in *The Warren Buffett CEO* (2002), John Wiley and Sons: New York.
172. The Borsheims story is in volume two, investment nine.
173. Warren Buffett speaking at Berkshire's 1995 annual meeting, May 1996.
174. Jeff Comment in an interview with Robert P. Miles in *The Warren Buffett CEO* (2002), John Wiley and Sons: New York.
175. Robert P. Miles, *The Warren Buffett CEO* (2002), John Wiley and Sons: New York.
176. Berkshire Hathaway news release, 6 April, 2009.
177. I'm very grateful to Bill Childs, chief architect and builder of R.C. Willey, for looking over a draft of this chapter, adding some key data and making suggestions for improvement.
178. From Benedict, Jeff (2009), *How to build a business Warren Buffett would buy: the R.C. Willey story*. Shadow Mountain.
179. Warren Buffett's foreword to Benedict, Jeff (2009), *How to build a business Warren Buffett would buy: the R.C. Willey story*. Shadow Mountain.
180. Benedict, Jeff (2009), *How to build a business Warren Buffett would buy: the R.C. Willey story*. Shadow Mountain.
181. Benedict, Jeff (2009), *How to build a business Warren Buffett would buy: the R.C. Willey story*. Shadow Mountain.
182. Benedict, Jeff (2009), *How to build a business Warren Buffett would buy: the R.C. Willey story*. Shadow Mountain.
183. Benedict, Jeff (2009), *How to build a business Warren Buffett would buy: the R.C. Willey story*. Shadow Mountain.
184. Benedict, Jeff (2009), *How to build a business Warren Buffett would buy: the R.C. Willey story*. Shadow Mountain.
185. Benedict, Jeff (2009), *How to build a business Warren Buffett would buy: the R.C. Willey story*. Shadow Mountain.
186. Benedict, Jeff (2009), *How to build a business Warren Buffett would buy: the R.C. Willey story*. Shadow Mountain.
187. Bill and Patricia have 31 grandchildren and 12 great grandchildren at the last count.
188. Bill Child quoted in Benedict, Jeff (2009), *How to build a business Warren Buffett would buy: the R.C. Willey story*. Shadow Mountain.
189. In 1996 Sheldon accepted a five year assignment in the Philippines.
190. Taken from Bill Child's Afterword in Benedict, Jeff (2009), *How to build a business Warren Buffett would buy: the R.C. Willey story*. Shadow Mountain.
191. Benedict, Jeff (2009), *How to build a business Warren Buffett would buy: the R.C. Willey story*. Shadow Mountain.

192. Benedict, Jeff (2009), *How to build a business Warren Buffett would buy: the R.C. Willey story*. Shadow Mountain.
193. Benedict, Jeff (2009), *How to build a business Warren Buffett would buy: the R.C. Willey story*. Shadow Mountain.
194. Robert P. Miles (2002) *The Warren Buffett CEO*, John Wiley and Sons: New York.
195. Benedict, Jeff (2009), *How to build a business Warren Buffett would buy: the R.C. Willey story*. Shadow Mountain.
196. Benedict, Jeff (2009), *How to build a business Warren Buffett would buy: the R.C. Willey story*. Shadow Mountain.
197. Benedict, Jeff (2009), *How to build a business Warren Buffett would buy: the R.C. Willey story*. Shadow Mountain.
198. Benedict, Jeff (2009), *How to build a business Warren Buffett would buy: the R.C. Willey story*. Shadow Mountain.
199. Robert P. Miles (2002), *The Warren Buffett CEO*, John Wiley and Sons: New York.
200. Utah Business, February 1997, reproduced in Andrew Kilpatrick (2006), *Of Permanent Value: The story of Warren Buffett*, AKPE: Birmingham, Alabama.
201. Benedict, Jeff (2009), *How to build a business Warren Buffett would buy: the R.C. Willey story*. Shadow Mountain.
202. Bill Child in Benedict, Jeff (2009), *How to build a business Warren Buffett would buy: the R.C. Willey story*. Shadow Mountain.
203. Benedict, Jeff (2009), *How to build a business Warren Buffett would buy: the R.C. Willey story*. Shadow Mountain.
204. Bill Child in Benedict, Jeff (2009), *How to build a business Warren Buffett would buy: the R.C. Willey story*. Shadow Mountain.
205. Benedict, Jeff (2009), *How to build a business Warren Buffett would buy: the R.C. Willey story*. Shadow Mountain.
206. Benedict, Jeff (2009), *How to build a business Warren Buffett would buy: the R.C. Willey story*. Shadow Mountain.
207. *Salt Lake City Tribune*, 21 October, 2001.
208. Bill Child in Robert P. Miles (2002) *The Warren Buffett CEO*, John Wiley and Sons: New York.
209. Bill Child in Robert P. Miles (2002), *The Warren Buffett CEO*, John Wiley and Sons: New York.
210. Warren Buffett, 2004 letter to Berkshire Hathaway shareholders.
211. Bill Child quoted in Greg Kratz, '50 years of furniture: Chairman builds R.C. Willey from one store to household name', *Deseret News*, 19 September, 2004.

212. Al Ueltschi speaking at The Wings Club Thirty-fourth General Harold R. Harris Sight Lecture, 21 May, 1997. https://www.flightsafety.com/html/book/tom/
213. Al Ueltschi speaking at The Wings Club Thirty-fourth General Harold R. Harris Sight Lecture, 21 May, 1997. https://www.flightsafety.com/html/book/tom/
214. Al Ueltschi speaking at The Wings Club Thirty-fourth General Harold R. Harris Sight Lecture, 21 May, 1997. https://www.flightsafety.com/html/book/tom/
215. Al Ueltschi speaking at The Wings Club Thirty-fourth General Harold R. Harris Sight Lecture, 21 May, 1997. https://www.flightsafety.com/html/book/tom/
216. Al Ueltschi speaking at The Wings Club Thirty-fourth General Harold R. Harris Sight Lecture, 21 May, 1997. https://www.flightsafety.com/html/book/tom/
217. Al Ueltschi speaking at The Wings Club Thirty-fourth General Harold R. Harris Sight Lecture, 21 May, 1997. https://www.flightsafety.com/html/book/tom/
218. Al Ueltschi speaking at The Wings Club Thirty-fourth General Harold R. Harris Sight Lecture, 21 May, 1997. https://www.flightsafety.com/html/book/tom/
219. Al Ueltschi speaking at The Wings Club Thirty-fourth General Harold R. Harris Sight Lecture, 21 May, 1997. https://www.flightsafety.com/html/book/tom/
220. Al Ueltschi speaking at The Wings Club Thirty-fourth General Harold R. Harris Sight Lecture, 21 May, 1997. https://www.flightsafety.com/html/book/tom/
221. Al Ueltschi speaking at The Wings Club Thirty-fourth General Harold R. Harris Sight Lecture, 21 May, 1997. https://www.flightsafety.com/html/book/tom/
222. Al Ueltschi speaking at The Wings Club Thirty-fourth General Harold R. Harris Sight Lecture, 21 May, 1997. https://www.flightsafety.com/html/book/tom/
223. Al Ueltschi speaking at The Wings Club Thirty-fourth General Harold R. Harris Sight Lecture, 21 May, 1997. https://www.flightsafety.com/html/book/tom/
224. Al Ueltschi speaking at The Wings Club Thirty-fourth General Harold R. Harris Sight Lecture, 21 May, 1997. https://www.flightsafety.com/html/book/tom/
225. Al Ueltschi in an interview by Robert Miles, Oct 2006. https://www.youtube.com/watch?v=Ihwtm-3MMbE

226. Available at https://www.berkshirehathaway.com/ownman.pdf
227. In Andrew Kilpatrick (2018), *Of Permanent Value: The Story of Warren Buffett*, AKPE: Birmingham, Alabama.
228. Al Ueltschi in an interview by Robert Miles Oct 2006 https://www.youtube.com/watch?v=Ihwtm-3MMbE
229. Warren Buffett, 1996 letter to Berkshire Hathaway shareholders.
230. Al Ueltschi in an interview by Robert Miles Oct 2006 https://www.youtube.com/watch?v=Ihwtm-3MMbE
231. 'Buffett Buying Pilot Training Company for $1.5 billion', *AP News*, 15 October, 1996.
232. Al Ueltschi in an interview by Robert Miles Oct 2006 https://www.youtube.com/watch?v=Ihwtm-3MMbE
233. Warren Buffett, 1996 letter to Berkshire Hathaway shareholders.
234. Warren Buffett, 1996 letter to Berkshire Hathaway shareholders.
235. Warren Buffett, 1996 letter to Berkshire Hathaway shareholders.
236. Warren Buffett, 1996 letter to Berkshire Hathaway shareholders.
237. Warren Buffett, 1996 letter to Berkshire Hathaway shareholders.
238. Warren Buffett, 1996 letter to Berkshire Hathaway shareholders.
239. Warren Buffett, 1996 letter to Berkshire Hathaway shareholders.
240. Warren Buffett, 1996 letter to Berkshire Hathaway shareholders.
241. Al Ueltschi in an interview with Robert P. Miles (2002), *The Warren Buffett CEO*, John Wiley and Sons: New York.
242. A speech on the 9 May, 2002 reported in Andrew Kilpatrick (2018), *Of Permanent value: The Story of Warren Buffett*, AKPE: Birmingham, Alabama.
243. Al Ueltschi in an interview with Robert P. Miles (2002), *The Warren Buffett CEO*, John Wiley and Sons: New York.
244. Al Ueltschi in an interview with Robert P. Miles (2002), *The Warren Buffett CEO*, John Wiley and Sons: New York.
245. Al Ueltschi in an interview with Robert P. Miles (2002), *The Warren Buffett CEO*, John Wiley and Sons: New York.
246. Al Ueltschi in an interview by Robert Miles 2006. https://www.youtube.com/watch?v=Ihwtm-3MMbE
247. Al Ueltschi in an interview with Robert P. Miles (2002), *The Warren Buffett CEO*, John Wiley and Sons: New York.
248. Warren Buffett, 2004 letter to Berkshire Hathaway shareholders.
249. Warren Buffett, 2004 letter to Berkshire Hathaway shareholders.
250. Bruce Whitman interview on *Nightly Business Report*, 3 May, 1997, reproduced in Andrew Kilpatrick (2018), *Of Permanent value: The story of Warren Buffett*, AKPE: Birmingham, Alabama.
251. Warren Buffett, 2007 letter to Berkshire Hathaway shareholders.

252. Warren Buffett, 2007 letter to Berkshire Hathaway shareholders.
253. Al Ueltschi speaking at The Wings Club Thirty-fourth General Harold R. Harris Sight Lecture, 21 May, 1997. https://www.flightsafety.com/html/book/tom/
254. Al Ueltschi speaking at The Wings Club Thirty-fourth General Harold R. Harris Sight Lecture, 21 May, 1997 https://www.flightsafety.com/html/book/tom/
255. Al Ueltschi in a speech 21 May, 1997, reported in Andrew Kilpatrick (2018), *Of Permanent value: The story of Warren Buffett*, AKPE: Birmingham, Alabama.
256. An idea developed by economist John Kay – see for example John Kay (2011) *Obliquity: why our goals are best achieved indirectly*, Profile Books: London.
257. In December 1996 another 112,655 B shares were created to give to FlightSafety shareholders in return for their shares.
258. Warren Buffett, 1996 letter to Berkshire Hathaway shareholders.
259. Warren Buffett, 1996 letter to Berkshire Hathaway shareholders.
260. Warren Buffett, 1997 letter to Berkshire Hathaway shareholders.
261. Warren Buffett, 1997 letter to Berkshire Hathaway shareholders.
262. Warren Buffett, 1997 letter to Berkshire Hathaway shareholders.
263. Warren Buffett, 1997 letter to Berkshire Hathaway shareholders.
264. Warren Buffett, 1997 letter to Berkshire Hathaway shareholders.
265. Warren Buffett, 1997 letter to Berkshire Hathaway shareholders.
266. Warren Buffett, 1997 letter to Berkshire Hathaway shareholders.
267. *Forbes,* 6 August, 1979.
268. *Forbes*, 'Look At All Those Beautiful, Scantily Clad Girls Out There!', 1 November, 1974.
269. Warren Buffett, 'You pay a very high price in the stock market for a cheery consensus', *Forbes*, 6 August, 1979.
270. Warren Buffett, 'You pay a very high price in the stock market for a cheery consensus', *Forbes*, 6 August, 1979.
271. Warren Buffett, 'You pay a very high price in the stock market for a cheery consensus', *Forbes*, 6 August, 1979.
272. Warren Buffett, 1997 letter to Berkshire Hathaway shareholders.
273. www.macrotrends.net/2577/sp-500-pe-ratio-price-to-earnings-chart
274. http://www.econ.yale.edu/~shiller/data.htm
275. *Los Angeles Times*, 'Buffett to Acquire Dairy Queen Chain for $585 Million', 22 October, 1997.
276. Buffett quoted in Kilpatrick (2018), *Of Permanent Value: The Story of Warren Buffett*, AKPE: Birmingham, Alabama.

277. Michael Assael quoted in Kilpatrick (2018), *Of Permanent Value: The Story of Warren Buffett*, AKPE: Birmingham, Alabama.
278. *QSR Magazine*, 'Dairy Queen and Franchisees Settle Dispute', 9 March, 2000, https://www.qsrmagazine.com/news/dairy-queen-and-franchisees-settle-dispute
279. Gene Rebeck, 'Dairy Queen is out to become the world's best-performing fast-food chain', 29 May, 2015. *MinnPost*, www.minnpost.com/twin-cities-business/2015/05/dairy-queen-out-become-world-s-best-performing-fast-food-chain
280. John Gainor, CEO interview at the 2016 Berkshire meeting on *Fox Business*. https://www.youtube.com/watch?v=q3z0avJcJjI
281. Warren Buffett, 1997 letter to Berkshire Hathaway shareholders.
282. Warren Buffett, 1997 letter to Berkshire Hathaway shareholders.
283. Cunningham, L. A. (2014), *Berkshire Beyond Buffett: The enduring value of values*, Columbia Business School Publishing.
284. Rich Santulli speaking to Robert P. Miles for his book, *The Warren Buffett CEO* (2002), John Wiley and Sons: New York.
285. Rich Santulli speaking to Robert P. Miles for his book, *The Warren Buffett CEO* (2002), John Wiley and Sons: New York.
286. Quoted in Warren Berger, 'Hey, You're Worth It (even now)', *Wired*, 1 June, 2001.
287. Rich Santulli speaking to Robert P. Miles for his book, *The Warren Buffett CEO* (2002), John Wiley and Sons: New York.
288. Rich Santulli speaking to Robert P. Miles for his book, *The Warren Buffett CEO* (2002), John Wiley and Sons: New York.
289. There are economies of scale here. So if 800 planes are sold to clients the core fleet need only be 80, i.e., 10%.
290. Rich Santulli speaking to Robert P. Miles for his book, *The Warren Buffett CEO* (2002), John Wiley and Sons: New York.
291. Quoted in Warren Berger, 'Hey, You're Worth It (even now)', *Wired*, 1 June, 2001.
292. From a 1996 interview with Stephen Pope, 'Santulli's Departure from NetJets', *Business Jet News*, October 2009.
293. Santulli quoted in Ron Carter, 'Executive Jet Has Big Fan: Buffett', *Columbus Dispatch*, 26 August, 1998.
294. Warren Buffett, 1998 letter to Berkshire Hathaway shareholders.
295. Quoted in Warren Berger, 'Hey, You're Worth It (even now)', *Wired*, 1 June, 2001.
296. *Forbes*, 'Flying Buffett', 20 September, 1998.
297. *Forbes*, 'Flying Buffett', 20 September, 1998.

298. Quoted in Warren Berger, 'Hey, You're Worth It (even now)', *Wired*, 1 June, 2001.
299. Santulli quoted in Ron Carter, 'Executive Jet Has Big Fan: Buffett', *Columbus Dispatch*, 26 August, 1998.
300. Robert P. Miles (2002), *The Warren Buffett CEO*, John Wiley and Sons: New York.
301. Cunningham, L. A. (2014), *Berkshire Beyond Buffett: The Enduring Value of Values*, Columbia Business School.
302. Warren Buffett, 1998 letter to Berkshire Hathaway shareholders.
303. Warren Buffett, 1998 letter to Berkshire Hathaway shareholders.
304. Dead-head, dead mileage, dead running, light running, deadheading, or empty leg costs occurs when operating without carrying passengers, such as flight time in picking up passengers away from the home base or flight time in returning to the home base or another necessary location.
305. Warren Buffett, 1998 letter to Berkshire Hathaway shareholders.
306. Warren Buffett, 1998 letter to Berkshire Hathaway shareholders.
307. Warren Buffett, 1998 letter to Berkshire Hathaway shareholders.
308. *Aviation International News*, 1 October, 1998.
309. Warren Buffett, 1999 letter to Berkshire Hathaway shareholders.
310. Warren Buffett, 1999 letter to Berkshire Hathaway shareholders.
311. Warren Buffett, 1999 letter to Berkshire Hathaway shareholders.
312. Richard Santulli speaking to Robert P. Miles (2002), *The Warren Buffett CEO*, John Wiley and Sons: New York.
313. Warren Buffett, 2001 letter to Berkshire Hathaway shareholders.
314. Warren Buffett, 2001 letter to Berkshire Hathaway shareholders.
315. Warren Buffett, 2002 letter to Berkshire Hathaway shareholders.
316. Warren Buffett, 2003 letter to Berkshire Hathaway shareholders.
317. Warren Buffett, 2004 letter to Berkshire Hathaway shareholders.
318. Warren Buffett, 2004 letter to Berkshire Hathaway shareholders.
319. Warren Buffett, 2009 letter to Berkshire Hathaway shareholders.
320. Stephen Pope, 'Santulli's departure from NetJets', *Business Jet Traveler*, October 2009.
321. Chad Trautvetter, 'Santulli resigns from NetJets; changes ahead at fractional', *Aviation International News*, 25 August, 2009.
322. Rich Santulli speaking to Robert P. Miles for his book, *The Warren Buffett CEO* (2002), John Wiley and Sons: New York.
323. Michael Riegel quoted in Matt Thurber, 'The Fractional Market', *Aviation International News*, 1 October, 2009.
324. Michael Riegel quoted in Matt Thurber, 'The Fractional Market', *Aviation International News*, 1 October, 2009.

325. Brian Foley quoted in Matt Thurber, 'The Fractional Market', *Aviation International News*, 1 October, 2009.
326. Quoted in Matt Thurber, 'The Fractional Market', *Aviation International News*, 1 October, 2009.
327. David Sokol, 'Owners, Profit Return to NetJets', *Aerospaceblog*, 2 February, 2011. https://aerospaceblog.wordpress.com/2011/02/02/owners-profits-return-to-netjets
328. Stephen Pope, 'Santulli's departure from NetJets', *Business Jet Traveler*, October, 2009.
329. Warren Buffett in a Berkshire Hathaway news release, 30 March, 2011.
330. Carol J. Loomis (2012*), Tap Dancing to Work*, Penguin Books: New York.
331. Berkshire Hathaway news release, 30 March, 2011.
332. Warren Buffett, 2010 letter to Berkshire Hathaway shareholders.
333. General Re shareholders were given the option of accepting either 0.0035 Class A shares or 0.105 Class B shares of Berkshire.
334. In 2012 Cornhusker's name was changed to Berkshire Hathaway Homestate Insurance.
335. It changed its name to Redwood Fire and Casualty Insurance in 1980.
336. Kansas Fire and Casualty is now part of Oak River Insurance, a subsidiary of Berkshire Hathaway.
337. In 1993, Goldberg was reassigned to special projects working from Berkshire's tiny Omaha HQ.
338. Warren Buffett, 1983 letter to Berkshire Hathaway shareholders.
339. Warren Buffett, 1984 letter to Berkshire Hathaway shareholders.
340. Warren Buffett, 1983 letter to Berkshire Hathaway shareholders.
341. Warren Buffett, 1984 letter to Berkshire Hathaway shareholders.
342. Warren Buffett, 1984 letter to Berkshire Hathaway shareholders.
343. Warren Buffett, 1984 letter to Berkshire Hathaway shareholders.
344. Warren Buffett, 1983 letter to Berkshire Hathaway shareholders.
345. Warren Buffett, 1983 letter to Berkshire Hathaway shareholders.
346. Warren Buffett, 1983 letter to Berkshire Hathaway shareholders.
347. Warren Buffett, 1985 letter to Berkshire Hathaway shareholders.
348. Warren Buffett, 1985 letter to Berkshire Hathaway shareholders.
349. Warren Buffett, 1985 letter to Berkshire Hathaway shareholders.
350. Ajit Jain speaking in an interview with Robert Miles (2002), *The Warren Buffett CEO*, John Wiley and Sons: New York.
351. Ajit Jain speaking in an interview with Robert Miles (2002), *The Warren Buffett CEO*, John Wiley and Sons: New York.
352. Warren Buffett, 1986 letter to Berkshire Hathaway shareholders.
353. Warren Buffett, 1986 letter to Berkshire Hathaway shareholders.

354. Warren Buffett, 1989 letter to Berkshire Hathaway shareholders.
355. Warren Buffett, 1989 letter to Berkshire Hathaway shareholders.
356. Warren Buffett, 1990 letter to Berkshire Hathaway shareholders.
357. Ajit Jain speaking in an interview with Robert Miles (2002), *The Warren Buffett CEO*, John Wiley and Sons: New York.
358. Ajit Jain speaking in an interview with Robert Miles (2002), *The Warren Buffett CEO*, John Wiley and Sons: New York.
359. Warren Buffett, 1992 letter to Berkshire Hathaway shareholders.
360. Warren Buffett, 1993 letter to Berkshire Hathaway shareholders.
361. Warren Buffett, 1998 letter to Berkshire Hathaway shareholders.
362. Berkshire Hathaway news release, 19 June, 1998.
363. Berkshire Hathaway news release, 19 June, 1998.
364. Berkshire Hathaway news release, 19 June, 1998.
365. Quoted in Andrew Kilpatrick (2006), *Of Permanent Value: The Story of Warren Buffett*, AKPE: Birmingham, Alabama.
366. Warren Buffett speaking at the Berkshire Hathaway special meeting, 16 September, 1998.
367. James P. Miller and Leslie Scism, 'Buffett's Berkshire to Buy General Re in Stock Deal Totaling $23.5 Billion', *Wall Street Journal*, 22 June, 1998.
368. James P. Miller and Leslie Scism, 'Buffett's Berkshire to Buy General Re in Stock Deal Totaling $23.5 Billion', *Wall Street Journal*, 22 June, 1998.
369. Warren Buffett, 1998 letter to Berkshire Hathaway shareholders.
370. Warren Buffett, 1998 letter to Berkshire Hathaway shareholders.
371. Warren Buffett, 1998 letter to Berkshire Hathaway shareholders.
372. Warren Buffett, 1999 letter to Berkshire Hathaway shareholders.
373. Warren Buffett, 1999 letter to Berkshire Hathaway shareholders.
374. Warren Buffett, 2000 letter to Berkshire Hathaway shareholders.
375. Warren Buffett, 2000 letter to Berkshire Hathaway shareholders.
376. Warren Buffett, 2000 letter to Berkshire Hathaway shareholders.
377. Warren Buffett, 2001 letter to Berkshire Hathaway shareholders.
378. Warren Buffett, 2001 letter to Berkshire Hathaway shareholders.
379. Warren Buffett, 2001 letter to Berkshire Hathaway shareholders.
380. Warren Buffett, 2001 letter to Berkshire Hathaway shareholders.
381. Warren Buffett, 2001 letter to Berkshire Hathaway shareholders.
382. Warren Buffett, 2002 letter to Berkshire Hathaway shareholders.
383. Warren Buffett, 2002 letter to Berkshire Hathaway shareholders.
384. Warren Buffett, 2002 letter to Berkshire Hathaway shareholders.
385. Warren Buffett, 2002 letter to Berkshire Hathaway shareholders.
386. Warren Buffett, 2002 letter to Berkshire Hathaway shareholders.
387. Warren Buffett, 2003 letter to Berkshire Hathaway shareholders.
388. Warren Buffett, 2005 letter to Berkshire Hathaway shareholders.

389. Warren Buffett, 2005 letter to Berkshire Hathaway shareholders.
390. Warren Buffett, 2005 letter to Berkshire Hathaway shareholders.
391. Warren Buffett, 2005 letter to Berkshire Hathaway shareholders.
392. Warren Buffett, 2002 letter to Berkshire Hathaway shareholders.
393. Warren Buffett, 2008 letter to Berkshire Hathaway shareholders.
394. Warren Buffett, 2016 letter to Berkshire Hathaway shareholders.
395. Warren Buffett, 1998 letter to Berkshire Hathaway shareholders.
396. Warren Buffett, 1998 letter to Berkshire Hathaway shareholders.

Index

A
ABC 7, 239, 247, 260
Accel-KKR 39
Airbus 74–6
Alfond, Harold 114–16, 122
All American Aviation 58. *See also* USAir
Allegheny Airlines 58–9. *See also* USAir
America West Airlines 65, 77
American Airlines 70, 74, 77
American Express 48, 50–1, 79–105, 128, 235, 276
  Berkshire as largest shareholder 93–6
  blunders 85–8
  Buffett's two deals 89–91
  change and continuity 102–4
  economic franchises 81–3
  emphasis on quality 84–5
  intrinsic value 96–102
  learning points 104–5
  summary of the deal 79
Andre Agassi Foundation for Education 228
Asian financial crisis 94
AT&T 87
AviationIQ 228–9
Axene, Harry 205

B
B shares 176, 188–9, 235, 260
Banc One 34
Bank of America 33
bank structures 3–5
bankruptcy 5, 65–6, 71, 73, 76–7, 139, 153
Barnes Banking Company 145
Barton, Tom 21
Baruch, Bernard 170
Beasley, H. Marvin 140
Berger, Warren 219

Berkshire Hathaway 191–4, 275–6
  and American Express 80, 82, 89–90, 93–6, 99–102, 104
  B shares 176, 188–9, 235, 260
  and Dairy Queen 190, 198, 202, 204, 207–8
  and FlightSafety International 167, 174–7, 180–1, 186–7
  and General Re 234–6, 252, 254, 257–73
  and Helzberg Diamond Shops 124–6, 128–30, 133–8, 140–1
  and insurance companies 234–47, 249–50, 252, 259–66, 269–70
  and National Indemnity 234–5
  and Nebraska Furniture Mart 156–7, 163
  and NetJets 211–12, 220–6, 228, 230–2
  and R.C. Willey 136, 144, 156–9, 161–3, 165
  and See's Candy 179
  and the Shoe Group 107, 110–13, 115–23
  and USAir 57, 62, 64, 66–7, 71–2, 76–7
  and Wells Fargo 1, 6–8, 23, 30–3, 36–7, 41–7, 50, 53, 55
Blue Chip Stamps 119
Blumkin, Irv 156–7
BNY Mellon 54
Borsheims 138–9, 157, 276
Boston Company 92
Boston Fee Party 87–8
Boston Red Sox 122
Bove, Richard X. 21
Brandon, Joe 266, 268–9, 271
British Airways 70–1, 74, 85
Brown, Henry H. 107
Brown, Thomas 30
Browning, Graeme 62
Buffalo News 129, 136
Buffett, Susan 219, 235
Buffett, Warren 275–6

Investment 1: Wells Fargo 1–56
Investment 2: USAir 57–78
Investment 3: American Express 79–105
Investment 4: The Shoe Group 106–23
Investment 5: Helzberg Diamond Shops 124–42
Investment 6: R.C. Willey 143–65
Investment 7: FlightSafety International 166–88
Investment 8: Dairy Queen 190–210
Investment 9: NetJets 211–33
Investment 10: General Re 234–74
Burke, Dan 7–8
Burlington Northern Santa Fe 276
Burr Williams, John 66
Byrne, John J. 88–9, 260

C

Capital Cities 7, 119, 247, 260
Central Fire and Casualty Company 237
Chenault, Ken 102–3
Child, Bill 143–64
Child, Patricia 152, 164
Child, Sheldon 150–1, 153, 155
Citigroup 54
Citizens Holdings Bank 22
Clayton Homes 276
Coca-Cola 39, 48, 69, 93, 103, 119, 128, 171, 179, 193, 235, 271, 276
Collins, Hugh 202
Colodny, Ed 58–62, 64, 69, 77
Cologne Re 253, 258, 262, 271
Comment, Jeff 132–4, 137–41
Commercial Credit 149
Continental Airlines 65, 70
Cornhusker Insurance 237
Coronavirus pandemic 58, 77, 103
Costco 103
cross-selling 38–9, 47–8
Cunningham, Lawrence 207, 221
CVS 109, 121
Cypress Insurance Company 238

D

Dairy Queen 190–210
 after the deal 207–9
 history of 197, 205
 income sources 197
 lead up to deal 205–6

learning points 210
quick bid 206–7
strategic positioning 198–204
summary of the deal 190
Dassault 172
Dean Witter 21
Delta Airlines 70, 85
Denham, Bob 175–6
Dexter 106–7, 114–23
discounted cash flow 67–9
Disney 69, 194
Donaldson, Lufkin & Jenrette Securities 30
dot-com crash 44
Drucker, Peter 112, 127
Dyson, James 187

E

Eastman Kodak 171
EBITDA 67
E.F. Hutton 86
Executive Jet Aviation 213–17, 220–1, 223, 225. *See also* NetJets
Exxon 275

F

Fargo, William G. 38
Fechheimer 129
Federal Reserve 65
FedEx 185
Ferguson, Ron 260–2, 264, 266
Feshbach brothers 21, 27
First Interstate Bank 22, 33–7
First National Bank of Layton 148
FlightSafety International 166–88, 235, 276
 deal with Buffett 173–80
 history of 167–73
 learning points 187–8
 summary of the deal 166
Flying Eye Hospitals 185–6
Foley, Brian 229
food prices 9–10
Ford 87, 275

G

Gainor, John 204
Gardner, Jim 75
Gates, Bill 204, 224
GEICO 51, 88, 103, 127, 235, 239–40, 247, 251–2, 259–60, 262, 265, 271–2, 276

General Electric 87
General Motors 69, 275
General Re 234–74
  deal with Buffett 260–2
  derivatives 267–8
  first five years 262–6
  key figures for 254–7
  learning points 272–4
  summary of the deal 234
  synergies 258–60
  underwriting profits 268–72
Gillespie, George 91
Gillette 103, 276
Goldberg, Mike 239–40, 244–5
Goldman Sachs 54, 110, 214–15, 218–21, 247
Golub, Harvey 90–2, 94, 99, 102
Graham, Ben 69, 196, 199, 232
Great American Bank of San Diego 22
Greene, Rob 202

H

H. H. Brown 106–13, 115–16, 118, 120–1, 123, 219
Hamburg, Marc 159
Hansell, Jordan 231
Harold Alfond Foundation 122
Hazen, Paul 7–8, 11, 18–19, 23, 27–30, 34–6, 39, 52, 55
Heffernan, Frances 109, 121
Heffernan, Ray 107–11
Helzberg, Barnett Jr. 124–6, 130–5, 137, 141
Helzberg, Barnett Sr. 130–1, 135
Helzberg, Gilbert 130–1
Helzberg, Morris 130
Helzberg, Morton 130
Helzberg Diamond Shops 124–42
  1996 shock 139–40
  and Borsheims 138–9
  history of 130–1
  Jeff Comment era 137–8
  learning points 141–2
  reasons for sale 132–4
  steady state 140–1
  summary of the deal 124
Hertz 91
Hilton Hotels 85
Hodson, Roy 150
Home and Automobile Insurance Company 238

Hotpoint 145–6, 149–50
Hymas, Scott 163

I

IBM 8, 48, 275
Icahn, Carl 60–1
Inman, Robert 202
Insurance Company of Iowa 237
International Dairy Queen Inc. *See* Dairy Queen
Issler, Jim 112, 115, 120–2

J

Jain, Ajit 244–5, 247, 249–50, 252, 266, 269, 271
JCPenney 114, 140
John Foote Shoe Company 109
Johnson, Adam 232
Jordan's Furniture 163
JPMorgan Chase 54
Justin Boots 120

K

Kansas Fire and Casualty Company 237
Kelleher, Herb 73
Kerkling Reinsurance Corporation 237
Kiphart, Dick 206
Kizer, Bill 113
Koloa Landing 163
Kovacevich, Richard M. 38–9, 44

L

Lakeland Fire and Casualty Company 237
Laplaige, Denis 35
Lehman Brothers 86, 89–90, 92
Lindbergh, Charles 167–8, 172
Lloyd's of London 251
Loan Value Group 228
Loomis, Carol 230
Loomis, John 110
Lotus, William 61
Lowell 106–7, 113, 115, 118, 123
Lubrizol 230
Lunder, Peter 114–16, 122
Lunder Foundation 122
Luther, Rudy 205–6

M

MacKay-Shields Financial Corporation 35
Mastercard 80, 85, 87, 92
McCullough, Alex 205
McCullough, John F. 205, 209
McDonald's 84, 202
McKinnon, Mike 202–3
McMurtry, Larry 202
Melville 109, 121
MidAmerican Energy 276
Midway Airlines 65
Miles, Bob 112
Milestone Aviation Group 228
Montgomery Ward 114
Montross, Tad 266, 268–9, 271
Moody's 21, 276
Mooty, John 202, 205–7
Morgan Stanley 124, 134
Munger, Charlie 73, 275–6
  and B shares 189
  and Dairy Queen 201, 207
  and FlightSafety International 175, 177, 179, 182–3
  and General Re 236, 261, 264, 267, 271–2
  and Helzberg Diamond Shops 125, 127–8, 135–7, 141
  and insurance companies 247–8
  and NetJets 223
  and the Shoe Group 116–17, 121–2
  and USAir 71–2, 76
  and Wells Fargo 3, 19–22, 27, 29–30, 50–1, 54
Munson, Frank 260
Murphy, Alma 174, 177
Murphy, Tom 7–8

N

National Dairies 171
National Fire and Marine Insurance 237
National Indemnity 119, 234–5, 237–8, 245, 251
NationsBank 34
Nebraska Furniture Mart 138, 156–7, 163, 235, 276
NetJets 211–33
  business model 212–13
  deal with Buffett 220–4
  and Great Recession 226–7
  growth of 222–6
  history of 213–19

learning points 233
recovery of 227–32
summary of the deal 211
Nicely, Tony 251
Noble, Sherb 205
Noe, Bill 232
Norrwock Shoe Company 114
Norwest 34, 38–40, 42, 47

O

O'Brien, Connie 149
oil prices 6
Olson, Frank 91
Oltz, Harry 205
Orbis International 185–6

P

Pacific Southwestern Airlines 60, 62
Pan Am 65, 169–72
Paton, David 184–5
PERCs 89–90, 93
Piedmont 60–2, 64
Pope, Stephen 219, 227, 230
Prudential-Bache Securities 21

R

Raff, Beryl 140–1
Raiguel, Kara 271
R.C. Willey 126, 136, 143–65, 276
  deal with Buffett 155–9
  diversification 151–3
  guiding principles 154–5
  history of 145–51
  Las Vegas and Boise stores 159–62
  learning points 164–5
  summary of the deal 143
Reagan, Ronald 102
recession 1, 7–8, 10, 19, 22–7, 65, 217–18, 226–7, 229
Reichardt, Carl 7–8, 11, 18–19, 21, 23, 27, 29–30, 33, 52, 55
Riegel, Michael 228–9
Robinson, James D. III 84–7, 89–91
Rooney, Frank 108–13, 115, 120–1, 123, 219
Rooney, Stephen 109
Roosevelt, Franklin D. 169
RTS Capital Services 215–16
Russell, Bertrand 10

S

Safra, Edmond 87
Salem, George M. 21
Salomon Smith Barney 54, 90, 175
Sanger, Stephen 48
Santulli, Richard 212–22, 224–8, 232
Scharf, Charlie 52, 54
Schofield, Seth 69–73
Schwarzenegger, Arnold 218
Scott Fetzer 128–9, 157, 183
Sears 87, 114
Securities and Exchange Commission 231
See's Candy 119, 128, 136, 141, 157, 179, 183–4, 193, 209, 235, 276
September 11 attacks 99, 224, 236, 265
Sercer, Richard 174–5, 177
Sessions, Lamar 145–6, 149
Shearson Loeb Rhoades 86–7, 89, 92
Shell Oil 214
Shiller, Robert 199
Shoe Group 106–23, 129
   Dexter 106–7, 114–23
   H. H. Brown 106–13, 115–16, 118, 120–1, 123, 219
   learning points 123
   Lowell 106–7, 113, 115, 118, 123
   summary of the deal 106
Siart, William 34–5
Signet 139
Simpson, Lou 251, 259
Sloan, Tim 50–1
Sokol, David 227, 229–31
Southwest Airlines 70, 73, 75
Squeri, Stephen 103
Standard and Poor's 89, 192, 199
Star Furniture 163
Steggles, John 260
Steinhardt, Michael 61
Stewart, James 213–14
Stumpf, John 48–50
Sullivan, Mike 206
Swanker, Helen 145–7, 150

T

Taylor, John 21
Tesla 69
Texas United Insurance 237
Thom McAn 109
Tibbets, Paul W. Jr. 213–15
Tischer, G. William 21
Trade Development Bank 86–7
Trans World Airlines 60–1, 65
Trautvetter, Chad 227
Trippe, Betsy 184–5
Trippe, Juan 169–72, 184
TWA 171
Tyson, Mike 251

U

Ueltschi, Al 166–77, 180–6
United Airlines 70, 74, 185
US Airways. *See* USAir
USAir 57–78, 129
   destruction of shareholder value 77
   learning points 77–8
   the Seth Schofield years 69–73
   summary of the deal 57
   the turnaround 73–5
Utah Power and Light Company 145, 149

V

value, definition of 66–9
Visa 80, 85, 87, 91–2

W

Warren, Elizabeth 48–9
Washington Post 193, 239, 247, 276
Watson, Thomas J., Sr. 8
Waugh, Jim 174–5
Weinstein, Harvey 51
Wells, Henry 38
Wells Fargo 5–56
   learning points 55–6
   mergers 22, 33–40
   performance in recession 22–7
   scandal 47–53
   shorting of 20–1
   strength in 1980s 11–20
   summary of the deal 1
Wesco 129
Whiteman, John 215
Whitman, Bruce 182–3
Willey, Helen Darline 146–7, 151
Willey, Rufus Call 143–8, 150
Williams, Ted 193
Wolf, Stephen M. 74–6
Woods, Tiger 218
World Book 129

Y

Yacktman, Stephen 201
Young, George 237

Z

Zales 139–40
Zhou Enlai 211
Zuendt, William 27–9

www.ingramcontent.com/pod-product-compliance
Ingram Content Group UK Ltd.
Pitfield, Milton Keynes, MK11 3LW, UK
UKHW021036270825
462278UK00002B/2